CARBON

CARBON

A Field Manual for Building Designers

Matti Kuittinen, Alan Organschi, and Andrew Ruff

Library of Congress Cataloging-in-Publication Data

Names: Kuittinen, Matti, author. | Organschi, Alan, author. | Ruff, Andrew, author.
Title: Carbon : a field manual for building designers / by Matti Kuittinen, Alan Organschi and Andrew Ruff.
Description: Hoboken, New Jersey : Wiley, [2022] | Includes bibliographical references and index.
Identifiers: LCCN 2021052105 (print) | LCCN 2021052106 (ebook) | ISBN 9781119720768 (hardback) | ISBN 9781119720829 (adobe pdf) | ISBN 9781119720775 (epub)
Subjects: LCSH: Carbon. | Construction industry. | Climatic changes.
Classification: LCC TA455.C3 K85 2022 (print) | LCC TA455.C3 (ebook) | DDC 620.1/93—dc23/eng/20211117
LC record available at https://lccn.loc.gov/2021052105
LC ebook record available at https://lccn.loc.gov/2021052106

Cover Design: Wiley

SKY10046999_050223

Contents

CHAPTER 4

CHAPTER 5

Preface

Late in the spring of 2020, as we worked our way through drafts of this book, human activity stumbled suddenly and then paused. Traffic came to a standstill, schools, shops, factories closed down, and people mostly stayed at home as all of us faced a new and apparently unanticipated threat to the human biome: the novel coronavirus. Since the beginning of the year, the rampage of Covid-19 has ignored national boundaries and targeted its victims indiscriminately (although the heaviest toll was levied on the most vulnerable in our society) all with generational impact: millions dead, trillions of dollars of wealth wiped out; political regimes either destabilized or consolidated in ruthless power.

Perversely, we may also have been granted—though inadvertently and with tragic implications for human health and well-being—a glimpse of nature in recovery. For those fortunate enough to have avoided the worst of its consequences, it was impossible to ignore what may have been the pandemic's only silver lining. Skies cleared over some of our most polluted cities. Ambient global noise quieted to its lowest level in decades. And though it may simply be that some of us were lucky enough to be spending a lot more time at home and out of doors and were therefore more likely to notice, the world suddenly seemed more bio-diverse, as if some new effulgence of flora and fauna had found its way onto urban balconies and into suburban backyards. In a particularly poignant, if brief and temporary, reversal of our anthropogenic global disturbance, the steady and alarming increase in atmospheric carbon concentrations slowed.

If the environmental consequences of our voracious habits of material and energy consumption had somehow remained intangible for the most obdurate among us, had its respite made them more palpable? Were we seeing, hearing, and breathing what our planet, given the opportunity to rebalance itself, might feel like? Is it possible to tease apart the seemingly inextricable relationship between global economic prosperity and growth, on the one hand, and resource consumption and ecological degradation, on the other? Or are human hardship and deprivation (such as what we've experienced in a global pandemic) necessarily correlated to the only possible means of recovering Earth's climatic and biological equilibrium?

The concerns of this book encompass the material and energy consumed in the production and operation of the built environment and the waste generated and ecological impacts incurred by these activities. As building designers and part of a global building sector responsible for those exchanges of matter, if we are to examine our own decisions in the design process, the technologies we choose and the supply chains we activate so as to ensure the systemic flow and smooth delivery of the products we call for to make our buildings, we inevitably must recognize a host of environmental consequences. These include the acidification of oceans, the eutrophication of rivers and lakes, the depletion and toxification of soils, the conversion of land from biologically diverse ecosystems into depleted and abiotic surface areas. If we were to look even more closely and honestly, we might also find human exploitation: forms of underpaid and even forced labor embedded somewhere in the product lifecycle of the tiniest of the components of the building system.

As with our initial neglect of an airborne pathogen that has now compromised our public health, stifled our economy, and destabilized our political structures, our failure to acknowledge the broad array of impacts we create through building also represents a lost opportunity to mitigate them. To that end, the subject and focus of our book are a subset of impacts that many scientists, policy-makers, and ordinary citizens now recognize as the most severe threat to the well-being and chemical stability of the planet, the atmospheric proliferation of greenhouse gases and their primary chemical element, carbon.

At a time of global crisis, whether it be environmental, political, economic, or social—or all of those sub-categories of human activity and exchange combined in a recursive cascade of causality and impact—we are often stymied in our ability to respond, unsure of how we might be most effective in our response, and unclear about our agency to make change. These questions lie at the heart of this book. Its theme is our agency—as building designers—to do everything in our professional power using the disciplinary tools at our disposal to reduce the negative environmental ramifications of our work in order to mitigate a rapidly changing climate. How the plot plays out remains to be seen.

1 CARBON?

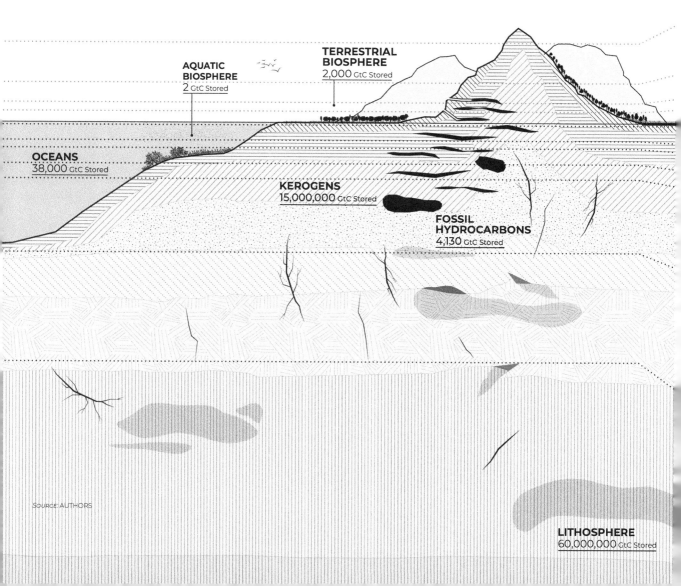

ATMOSPHERE
720 GtC Stored

AQUATIC BIOSPHERE
2 GtC Stored

TERRESTRIAL BIOSPHERE
2,000 GtC Stored

OCEANS
38,000 GtC Stored

KEROGENS
15,000,000 GtC Stored

FOSSIL HYDROCARBONS
4,130 GtC Stored

SOURCE: AUTHORS

LITHOSPHERE
60,000,000 GtC Stored

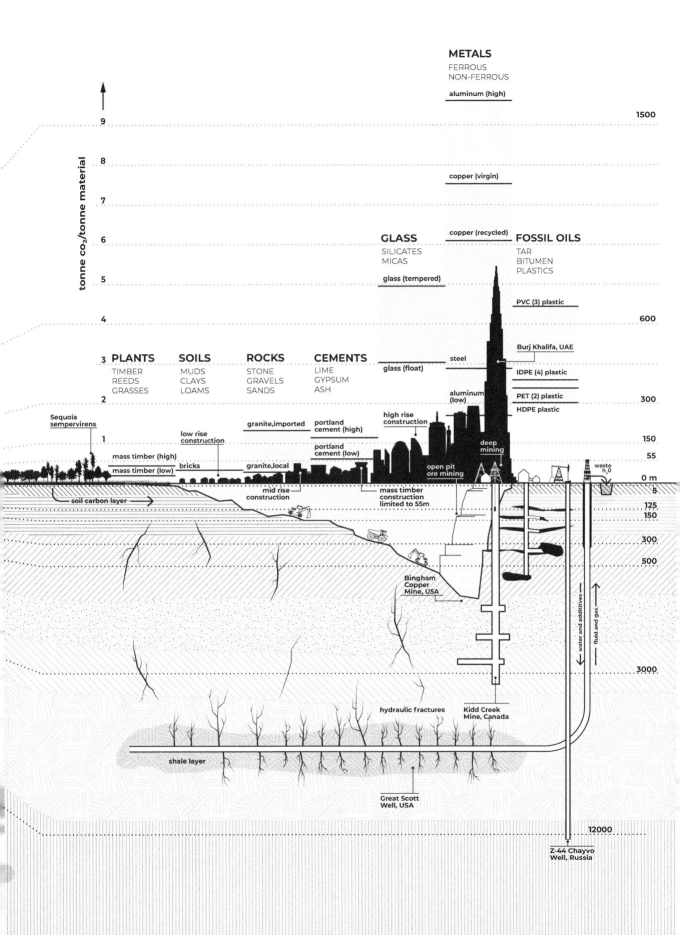

METALS
FERROUS
NON-FERROUS

aluminum (high)

1500

tonne co₂/tonne material

9

8

copper (virgin)

7

6
copper (recycled)

GLASS
SILICATES
MICAS

FOSSIL OILS
TAR
BITUMEN
PLASTICS

glass (tempered)

5

PVC (3) plastic

4
600

Burj Khalifa, UAE

3 **PLANTS**   **SOILS**   **ROCKS**   **CEMENTS**
TIMBER   MUDS   STONE   LIME
REEDS   CLAYS   GRAVELS   GYPSUM
GRASSES   LOAMS   SANDS   ASH

steel

glass (float)

IDPE (4) plastic

PET (2) plastic
300

aluminum (low)

HDPE plastic

2

Sequoia
sempervirens

high rise
construction

granite, imported   portland
cement (high)

low rise
construction

1
portland
cement (low)

deep
mining
150

mass timber (high)

mass timber (low)   bricks   granite, local

open pit
ore mining

waste
h₂0

0 m
5

soil carbon layer

mid rise
construction

mass timber
construction
limited to 55m

125
150

300

500

Bingham
Copper
Mine, USA

water and additives

fluid and gas

3000

hydraulic fractures

Kidd Creek
Mine, Canada

shale layer

Great Scott
Well, USA

12000

Z-44 Chayvo
Well, Russia

CHAPTER ONE
CARBON?

This book is designed for makers. That's not to say that our subject isn't important for consumers of all the kinds of products and services that we use in our everyday lives, but this book is directed broadly at producers and, more specifically, at those people who play a role in the conception and production of buildings. This not only includes planners, architects, and engineers but also industrial manufacturers, product suppliers, and builders, as well as policy-makers and developers—anyone who makes daily decisions about the materials and technologies we apply to the maintenance and expansion of the built environment.

Those of us responsible for the conception, design, and construction of buildings tend to think of ourselves as producers, but we're also consumers. And like all consumers of increasingly industrialized commodities—such as cars, cell phones, or ballpoint pens—we need to understand and ultimately account for the resources we call upon as well as the waste and emissions we generate. Of these many potential impacts, this book focuses on what may be the most critical one from the standpoint of climate change: the emission of carbon into the atmosphere incurred throughout the lifecycle of a building. This entails the carbon extracted from the geological seams and subterranean deposits that form the bulk of the virgin sources of construction material and energy, then released as carbon dioxide and its greenhouse gas equivalents, through all the processes we associate with manufacturing, added, in excess, to the biologically generated CO_2 and methane already emitted by weakening forest carbon sinks, from permafrost thawed by rising global temperatures, and from forest land conversion driven by suburbanization, mining, and agriculture. The accelerating rate of these bio- and geochemical reactions has upset the delicate balance of the global carbon cycle.

At this dangerous and time-critical juncture in human history, when our decisions may contribute to ongoing and potentially dangerous environmental degradation, we offer this ready-to-hand guide to help designers and builders understand and track the flows of carbon into, through, and out of the construction materials and processes through which we form our built environment.

The scientific methods for analyzing the flows of carbon may seem difficult to understand and time-consuming to use. They require a great deal of data and they demand focused attention to details, many of which are only finalized in the most advanced stages of a design's development. This leads inevitably to carbon flow assessments conducted at the end of the design process, when decisions and details have already been made, thereby limiting the utility and effectiveness of what we've gleaned from the analysis. Emerging life cycle assessment software that is integrated into building information models offers new effective means for designers to understand and to mitigate the CO_2 emissions of the buildings they design. But even these approaches can be time-consuming to use, and they are often over-simplified in order to work in a variety of design cases.

FIGURE 1.1
SOURCE: NASA'S GODDARD SPACE FLIGHT CENTER/ KATHRYN MERSMANN

For these reasons, designers need to understand the principles and assumptions that underlie different assessment methods and analytical tools. To that end, we offer the following concepts, case studies, and lessons as an aid and reference during the design process, a "field manual," of sorts, that we've developed to illuminate critical decisions and guide the instincts of design thinkers. We hope that you'll return to this manual as opportunities and challenges arise in your day-to-day encounters with the ever-changing demands and complex conditions of low-carbon and truly sustainable building design.

In one sense, this book is a guide to help account for the energy consumed in construction: in the raw material supplies and manufacturing processes needed to make building products, in their assembly into buildings, in the use, maintenance, and repair of those buildings over the course of their service lives, and—ultimately—in their disassembly and the reuse, recycling, or less sustainable means of disposal of all their constituent systems. In this book, we also discuss the impacts of the built environment on landscapes, ecological systems and specific biomes as we strive to assess our growing need for more buildings and infrastructure. But essentially, this is a story about carbon, about it its role in forming human settlements and—as has become increasingly and unfortunately apparent—in determining the future of the only habitable planet we know [1].

OUR CARBON CHALLENGE

Carbon flows through terrestrial space, matter, and time along myriad pathways—biological, chemical, geological—insinuating its particular chemistries into every process we undertake as builders. It accretes over geological epochs deep in lithospheric strata and, at notably faster rates, accumulates across continental forests. These deposits of global carbon form the ore and the fiber of building construction.

We mine and harvest that material, then transport it to factories in order to process it into building products. Throughout this sequence of events, especially during the extraction of raw material, we often irrevocably change the landscapes from which these materials are drawn. After the products are manufactured,

we transport them again to construction sites where they are assembled into buildings, which demand ongoing maintenance and repair. Finally, we choose to dismantle or demolish the building, then transport the waste from this demolition to waste management facilities, burn it for energy, or reuse and recycle the materials as much as possible.

All of these processes require a constant input of energy and rely on a vast network of physical infrastructure, which must itself be constructed, operated, maintained, and ultimately demolished. Interconnected, trans-scalar, and deeply embedded in the production of our built environment, this sequence of events represents in its essence a linear process of extraction, construction, and waste accumulation. We might think of this as an economic as well as chemical exchange of carbon, with corresponding credits and, as of the writing of this book, mostly debits.

The building sector, that portion of human activity responsible for the construction and operation of a rapidly expanding aggregation of buildings and infrastructure, has been estimated recently to account for well over half of the world's extraction and consumption of carbon-based material and hydrocarbon energy. It produces an associated share of solid waste and emits corresponding volumes of greenhouse gases [2]. As the world population growth accelerates, burgeoning populations are driven by economic and societal pressures to migrate in increasing numbers from rural settlements to urban metropolises. The building sector's demand for raw material and energy for new construction will only grow, further taxing critical, finite resources and—if our current approach remains unchecked—layering a geological stratum's worth of waste across the planet.

BUILDING ELEMENTS

The built environment is constructed from an array of materials. We tend to think of those materials as part of a familiar construction palette: reinforced concrete, steel, stone, brick and wood serve as both primary building structures and finish; glass transmits daylight through apertures in the building envelope; aluminum extrusions or milled sections of wood frame those glazed openings;

copper wires of varying diameter connect the electrical networks that power building operations; bituminous sheets protect our roofs from water and asphaltic mixtures harden the surfaces of our roads and parking lots.

Due to the logistical complexities of making even the simplest building in today's complex construction economy, we rarely gather raw materials from local sources and apply them directly to construction. For a host of reasons, we have come instead to rely on building *products*— pre-engineered and packaged windows, structural components, air handling units, toilets—to expedite the design and construction process. These commercially available building elements, fixtures, and appliances represent sophisticated systems that are composed of highly processed and often complex combinations of different materials.

However, considered at a more elemental level, our buildings contain innumerable combinations of matter: molecular configurations that make up our planet's natural resources, resources that we extract in turn from its bio-spheric landscapes and geologic strata. We reconfigure them— mechanically, chemically, and biologically—to serve specific technical and aesthetic programs.

A prominent industrial ecologist has remarked that the smartphone, perhaps the most ubiquitous of contemporary consumer products, is composed of nearly all the elements in the chemical periodic table (with the exception of radioactive isotopes). By extension then, a similarly sophisticated nexus of chemical elements—on a dramatically larger scale and with significantly greater impact—forms the constructed landscapes we inhabit.

KING CARBON

For the purposes of this book, the specific ingredient of building on which we'll focus is carbon, the sixth element of the periodic table, the fifteenth most abundant in Earth's crust, and the fourth most abundant in the universe. Its allotropes, various chemical configurations comprised solely of carbon atoms, range from the soft and opaque (graphite) to the dense, hard, and transparent (diamond). Carbon is the defining element of organic chemistry and thereby a chemical constituent of life itself. This "King of the Elements," so called for its ubiquity and its chemical capacity to form myriad monomers that polymerize readily at terrestrial pressures and temperatures, insinuates itself into every aspect of building. It is a critical element of the fuels we use to produce and operate our buildings, the materials with which we form them, and the waste we leave behind.

At a planetary scale, carbon is stored in a range of terrestrial pools or sinks: the Earth's atmosphere, its forests, its oceans, its soils, and its rocky crust. Bonded with two oxygen atoms, carbon forms a major gaseous component of the Earth's atmosphere, carbon dioxide. CO_2 is an essential reagent in the reciprocal biochemical reactions of photosynthesis and respiration that together create the global carbon cycle. Atmospherically speaking, the delicate balance of carbon absorbed photosynthetically by plants and CO_2 emitted through decomposition of organic matter, animal and, to a lesser degree, plant respiration and the combustion of hydrocarbons for fuel, is critical to maintaining habitable conditions on our planet. It is the geologically recent anthropogenic disruption in the balance of those carbon pools that has emerged as a primary concern of climate scientists, environmental policy-makers, and an informed citizenry.

The Anthropocene, our current geological age, is so named for the extent that human activity has indelibly etched itself into the Earth's climatic and environmental record [3]. By layering the planet's surfaces with industrially processed material, by altering our air, water, and soil, and by driving countless species to extinction, the human species has fundamentally altered the Earth's geological, chemical, and biological composition. Of all the anthropogenic impacts associated with construction and industrial processes and their reliance on fossil hydrocarbons, the accelerating emissions of carbon dioxide may prove to be the most totalizing in their implication for our global future [4].

A significant by-product of our activities as builders and consumers, carbon dioxide belongs to the class of infrared energy-absorbing and energy-radiating

chemicals known as greenhouse gases. Although transparent, tasteless and odorless, less voluminous than water vapor and less aggressive in trapping heat than methane or chlorofluorocarbons, CO_2 is more prevalent and more durable than other greenhouse gases. Its rapidly increasing atmospheric concentration and its relatively long half-life plays a primary role in causing long-term global warming. The carbon dioxide we emit today compounds past emissions, overwhelming the Earth's capacity to reabsorb excess CO_2 photosynthetically, with lasting, cumulative impacts. The concentration of CO_2 in the atmosphere has today reached levels higher than at any time in over 800,000 years [5] and its so-called "climate forcing" is perhaps without precedent in the last 420 million years [6]. Climate change and its host of correlated impacts present a new existential threat [7], setting our planet on a course toward "hothouse Earth" conditions [8]. Depending on how we choose to view it—and how we choose to act to reduce the volume that we emit—carbon is either the stuff of life on Earth or the means to end it.

A GLOBAL CARBON BUDGET

Through our species' recent activities as voracious consumers of global resources and excessive producers of terrestrial waste, we have created a dire planetary crisis. In order to understand the scale of this crisis and the current global environmental challenge, it may help to trace its origins along a historical timescale and to anticipate its potential outcomes if we fail to act. Finally, it's important that we recognize our agency and unique opportunity in answering those challenges. Put another way, as responsible consumers of global resources, we need to understand our carbon expenditures and our remaining carbon budget.

For millennia, the concentration of carbon dioxide in the Earth's atmosphere remained fairly stable at roughly 280 parts per million. There were relatively subtle changes of atmospheric CO_2 during that period of stability and these were due to anomalous climatic events or more regular seasonal swings in photosynthetic activity [9]. It was not until

the mid-nineteenth century and the birth of the industrial revolution that the world began to see a dramatic increase in the amount of carbon dioxide in the atmosphere. By the late decades of the twentieth century, the atmospheric carbon pool had absorbed more carbon dioxide than the biosphere could re-absorb photosynthetically, surpassing what scientists have identified as a sustainable atmospheric limit and the trajectory of rising anthropogenic greenhouse gas emissions continues to steepen. At the current pace and despite the best intentions that underlie current national and regional policy pledges, the gap between our emissions targets and the relatively unabated level of carbon emitting activity continues, and the gap to required emission reductions is widening to over 30 gigatonnes within a decade [10]. Without radical action, our window to prevent anthropogenic global warming in excess of 1.5 degrees Celsius will close.

A correlated historic growth in global human population—and the associated demand for resources, industrial activity, and greenhouse gas emissions—suggest that unless we are able to decouple population growth from carbon emissions, we will be unable to arrest this atmospheric chemical trend as global demand for food, consumer goods, energy, housing, and infrastructure inevitably rises.

Considered as an economic calculation, with CO_2 serving as our currency, we might say that we are in danger of exceeding our allotted atmospheric budget. Over the past century and a half, since the birth of the industrial revolution when we began to dump excess carbon into the atmosphere, scientists have estimated that we could add as much as 1 trillion metric tons (one *teraton*) of CO_2 to that carbon pool before we created irreversible damage to terrestrial habitats [11]. This amount of atmospheric carbon emitted would correlate roughly to a 1.5 degrees Celsius increase in global temperatures.

As of this writing, we are only few decades short of emitting the trillionth tonne, and have witnessed a corresponding rise in the world's temperatures and associated anthropogenic disturbances in nearly

FIGURE 1.2
Source: Brian Patrick Tagalog
(Unsplash)

every physical, chemical, and biological system on Earth [12]. Of all the sectors of human industry and consumption that have created this dangerous situation, our activities as builders and building inhabitants may play the most significant role in determining whether we will ultimately arrest or exacerbate climate change. If we take into account the impacts associated with both the production and operational stages of the building life cycle, the building sector is responsible for over a third of all anthropogenic emissions of carbon dioxide and its greenhouse gas equivalents. This may not be so surprising if we consider the extent of material and energy consumption required to extract, process, transport construction materials, assemble them in factories and on building sites into structurally sound, functional buildings, to operate and maintain those buildings over the course of their lifetimes and finally to demolish or dismantle them and dispose of the resulting waste material.

Every year, the building sector consumes over half the steel produced globally, half of its harvested timber and drives demand for nearly three-quarters of global cement production [13]. In addition, the production and operation of the built environment consume close to half of global energy and produce a third of waste [2]. Now that we understand the disproportionate share of global atmospheric impact associated with constructing and maintaining buildings, we'll look next at the carbon cycle as an ideally balanced or "homeostatic" system essential to the existence of life on our planet and consider the anthropogenic distortions that threaten it.

THE CARBON CYCLE IN BUILDING HISTORY

The global carbon cycle is a life-giving, synergistic chemical exchange of atmospheric carbon dioxide and oxygen that takes place between plants and animals. In the chemical reaction of photosynthesis, plants absorb atmospheric CO_2 in the presence of light-energy and water to synthesize two chemical compounds that provide critical ecosystem services:

the first by-product of the reaction, cellulose, is a complex carbohydrate that gives structure to the walls of plant cells. As the constituent building block of woods and grasses, cellulose has been used historically as an important building material. It is also a critical source of energy, both as food and as fuel. The second by-product is oxygen, the air we breathe.

In the complementary process of respiration, animals consume the oxygen and carbohydrates produced by plants through a process of cellular combustion which translates those chemical ingredients into the metabolic energy that fuels animal activity and life. A by-product of this biochemical reaction is carbon dioxide. At a macroscopic scale, plant cellulose and oxygen can combine in a form of combustion that provides industrial energy capable of powering manufacturing processes as well as the continuing operation of the built environment. The formation and consumption of carbohydrates in the presence of CO_2 and oxygen are described as the fast domain of carbon storage and release.

Plant cellulose that is not consumed by aerobic species for metabolic energy—bacteria, fungi, larger herbivores, and human beings—slowly accumulates in the Earth's soils, itself an important terrestrial carbon pool. Over hundreds of millions of years, that accumulation of soil-based carbon has transformed from plant carbohydrates into complex molecular formations in a slow-moving physio-chemical transformation catalyzed by eons of geological pressure and temperatures. These so-called fossil hydrocarbons were locked in the seams of the Earth's crust as deposits of coal and reservoirs of oil and natural gas. The formation of these geological carbon pools is described as the slow domain of carbon storage and release.

In the centuries leading to the industrial revolution, human builders used indigenous plants of different species, along with surface rocks and soils, to give their buildings material form. As our species became more technologically advanced, we excavated and bored ever-deeper through a succession of

FIGURE 1.3
SOURCE: MARK ANGOR
(SHUTTERSTOCK.COM)

geologic substrata, extracting minerals and ore for various building applications—iron, cements, glass, metal alloys, plastics, and bitumen—then processing these with manufacturing technologies of increasing sophistication. We learned to employ dense hydrocarbon energy sources to power sophisticated industrial processes, inventing more advanced technological and physical infrastructure that would enable us to release those fuels from deep geologic seams and pools before refining them for their ultimate use. Finally, by creating the buildings and infrastructure of human settlement itself, we covered over and destroyed forests, grasslands, wetlands, and coastlines—thereby transforming biologically productive soils and photosynthetic landscapes into inert, impervious surfaces that further reduce the capacity of the Earth's surfaces to process the CO_2 we emit. With this accounting, we can begin to visualize the role of the entire building sector as a consumer of global resources and as a significant source of carbon emissions, both of which make it a powerful driver of climate change.

From a broader perspective, we can survey a geologic history of the carbon cycle, one that spans from the carboniferous period hundreds of millions of years ago to our own more recent and relatively short Anthropocene era. What began 350 million years ago with the rapid photosynthesis of woody matter formed in lush swampy forests of ferns and fern-like trees, progressing with the slow accumulation and fossilization of that plant matter to form deep lithospheric carbon reserves, has culminated today in the dramatic and comparatively instantaneous release of that embedded carbon back into the atmosphere.

In the next section, we'll consider more precisely the role of the building sector in creating that atmospheric carbon imbalance, the flow of carbon through the building life cycle, and the methods we might consider as designers and builders to arrest those flows and radically reduce the environmental impacts that they cause.

CARBON FLOWS IN BUILDING

As we've seen, carbon is a constituent element of all buildings and flows through the life cycle of the built environment in two forms: as material and energy. By dint of the law of the conservation of mass, which states that matter never disappears but simply changes state, carbon will inevitably be a component of all the waste that emanates from the built environment. When that waste is gaseous or prone to decomposition, the carbon within it is added to our atmospheric carbon pool. If we examine the building life cycle, we recognize the origins of carbon in buildings as well as the sinks (or storage repositories) into which we may ultimately direct it.

The geologic accretion of terrestrial carbon and the more rapid biologic cycle of photosynthetic carbon uptake form the lithospheric hydrocarbons and land-based biomass that are the initial sources of the material and energy we consume of the building life cycle. With increasing intensity and at an accelerating rate, we have extracted those raw materials and associated carbon in order to meet the demands of a growing global population. Inevitably, that carbon will be released back into the atmosphere as a greenhouse gas. The ultimate atmospheric impact of our building activities depends heavily on which sources of material we choose to exploit and the means and methods (tools and fuels) by which they are extracted and processed. Of course, the range of those materials as well as the sources and technologies employed in their extraction are enormous, varying widely across industries, economies, and geographies. From the cutting of grasses with a scythe to the mining of fossil oils deep in the Earth's crusts, materials are inextricably bound to the means by which they must be extracted.

We process and refine those materials—mechanically, chemically, and occasionally biologically—into products that form a palette of products for construction and the fuels that power our

construction activities, as well as the buildings those processes produce. The technological sophistication and industrial intensiveness of those manufacturing processes—from the most basic to the most complex and energy-demanding—will contribute varied shares of building life cycle emissions.

Contemporary construction materials and methods often rely on a robust global economic exchange, so it is frequently the case that source landscapes, processing sites, and manufacturing facilities—mills, refineries, factories—are geographically remote and distant from the locations in which we build. This entails the use of extensive systems of transport —marine, rail, highway, air—and the consumption of fuels required to operate those critical networks also contributes greenhouse gas emissions. The amount of CO_2 and its equivalents that we emit in moving building material along the supply chain is subject to a number of conditions that include the type and efficiency of the mode of transport, the distance traveled and even the topography of the route. And we should expand the framework of our consideration to include the emissions embodied in these varied systems of transport and their infrastructure: the gravel, sand, concrete, steel, asphalt, and fuel required to build the roadways, bridges, railbeds, ports, and pipelines. All are essential to the conveyance of material and energy used in construction, and therefore contribute to the greenhouse gas emissions of the building sector.

It goes without saying that we use raw and processed materials to construct our buildings, but we also use a host of tools, machinery, and services as well, each with their own embodied emissions. We consume energy throughout the construction process and produce material waste that may decompose in landfills, be burned for fuel, or be directed for reuse or recycling. To varying degrees, each of these outcomes produces its own emissions that we must attribute to the construction process. We might even go so far as to include the emissions created in the daily transport of personnel to and from the construction site. All this opens up a complex network of interdependent actions that account for the total carbon emissions we attribute to the construction sector and the built environment.

Over the course of a building's operational life, energy will be consumed (and carbon emitted) in the heating, cooling, and illumination of its spaces. As the building ages, it is subjected to normal environmental stresses and everyday use as well as eventual changes to its programmatic requirements and shifts in its occupancies. Inevitably, materials will be replaced and more energy will be consumed in the building's maintenance, repair, and refurbishment. These processes will produce additional emissions that compound over the building's lifetime

Finally, the building will reach the end of its life when it is no longer useful, when its mechanical systems are obsolete or its envelope is beyond repair. At that point, the demolition and removal of all of the material that gave the building its original form, structure, and functionality will compound its life cycle emissions. We can assume that the waste generated in this final phase of the building's life, regardless of whether it is deposited in landfills, incinerated for energy, recycled, or even reused, will introduce even more greenhouse gas to an already encumbered atmosphere.

STAUNCHING THE FLOW

No building is a closed system. Whether viewed from a cultural, social, economic, or thermodynamic perspective, any building exists because of a set of conditions external to its enclosure or the boundaries of its site. In the same way, we can understand and appreciate that the flow of carbon in building and buildings is part of an extended, trans-scalar system of material consumption and energy use and waste expenditure.

We can identify, assess, and prioritize the different sources of energy available to us that make the construction and operation of any given building possible. Each energy source has its particular ramifications for the flows of carbon through the building life cycle and there are two main options for mitigating these energy-related carbon flows. First, we can enhance the energy-efficiency of both building process and the buildings themselves. This may take place during the stages of energy production, energy delivery, energy use, energy storage,

and energy recovery. Second, we can seek to generate renewable energy on the building site, reducing our need to acquire and transmit or transport energy from other sources.

We can consider the physical properties and trace the biological, chemical, or geological origins of the building materials we specify and can thereby predict their potential carbon impacts, based on a range of factors: weight, processing intensity, transport distance, anticipated durability, and associated cycles of replacement. The carbon embodied in a building material originates in the technological complexity and associated energy intensity of the processes by which the raw material is extracted. In our contemporary construction economy, the transport and manufacture of building products tend to demand fuels with high-energy density. Fossil hydrocarbons, such as coal, gas, or oil, are by far the most widely used in the manufacture of building materials and account for significant emissions in the production stage of the building life cycle.

Many materials contain carbon at the molecular level but the implications of that carbon content for a building's carbon footprint vary. Wood, for example, is formed largely from atmospheric carbon fixed in its cellular structure during photosynthesis. As a result, half of the dry weight of wood is carbon that has been removed from the atmosphere [14]. As long as that material is protected in well-detailed and durable buildings, its carbon will remain fixed, making the building a carbon storage site. Other materials, such as plastics, are made of hydrocarbon chains of mostly fossil origin. Although originally sequestered from the atmosphere millions of years ago, that carbon must be extracted from fossil deposits in the Earth's crust and industrially reformulated so that we can apply it to a range of consumer products, including building components.

Finally, we can attempt to predict the many sources and forms of waste that our buildings will inevitably generate over their lifetimes. Those plastics synthesized from fossil hydrocarbons will either end up as insoluble waste matter adrift in oceans and scattered across landscapes or, through our circular economic ingenuity, redirected into new manufacturing processes as new "raw" material.

In later chapters of this book, we'll describe some tools and techniques that building designers can use to assess and quantify the carbon flows of the buildings they design and their cumulative life cycle impacts. Based on what we can already discern about that life cycle—the biological, chemical, and geological formation of raw material and energy, the stages of their refinement and application in construction, their uses throughout the service life of a building, and finally how they are disposed of at the end of that lifespan—we can begin to change our design approach. No longer a narrow technical or aesthetic exercise, the design process embraces and accounts for an expanded system of concerns and decisions, each with significant environmental implications. Even without the aid of detailed and time-consuming quantitative analysis, and instead based on clear principles and informed intuitions, we can begin to identify and subsequently seek to avoid those materials and energy sources with the most deleterious environmental effects. We can specify materials of local or regional origins to reduce transport emissions. We can create construction details that promote the dismantling of building assemblies and the reuse of building materials, thereby avoiding the destructive effects of indiscriminate demolition and non-diverted waste streams.

In a sense, we have begun to conceptualize a decarbonized design process, one that systematically tracks and manages the consumption of material and energy and the generation of waste in an attempt to arrest or at least limit the quantity of carbon that flows through the building life cycle. Rather than a conventional linear "take, make, and dump" process of construction, we can envision a circular economic approach to design and construction, one that anticipates the highest and best use of material and energy in the beginning, throughout the duration, and at the end of the useful life of a building. This is a design approach that prioritizes life cycle and environmental systems thinking, embraces renewable energy sources, deploys materials drawn from industrial and consumer waste streams or from biologic landscapes that absorb and store carbon. This approach seeks to anticipate and promote through careful design, a second, third, and even fourth life of the materials we employ to make our buildings; long after their first application is obsolete, in a looping manufacturing cycle of innovative reuse. Waste, the physical vestiges of each building material's life cycle, is endowed with greater value, as a repurposed consumer or building product or as a raw material ready for remanufacture.

TIME MANAGEMENT IN CARBON MITIGATION

A note about time and the management of carbon flows in the built environment. We've seen that carbon is emitted at every stage of the building life cycle. We've also taken stock of the disproportionate share of anthropogenic greenhouse gas emitted by building sector activities. The alarming and correlated trends of global population growth and an increase in atmospheric concentrations of carbon have created a consensus within the world's scientific community that only a narrow window of opportunity remains —at the time of writing of this book around a decade [10] —to change course and take effective climate action. This will entail a worldwide reduction of emissions across all sectors of human activity, effectively restructuring our global economy and many of our social, political, and cultural institutions. And it raises a fundamental question for building designers seeking to employ the tools and techniques of sustainability in building. What, for this critical decade (and perhaps beyond), is the most effective means to reduce building sector emissions and their associated impacts?

Later in this book we'll introduce a standardized system of categorization used to describe the four phases of the building life cycle. At a more generalized level, we typically divide those life cycle impacts into two distinct categories: (1) *operational impacts* incurred through the consumption of energy and water associated with the occupation and use of the building; and (2) *embodied impacts* which include all those that accrue through the consumption of material and energy associated with the industrial and construction activities required to produce, maintain, repair, dismantle the building and then, finally, redistribute or dispose of its residues.

Recent efforts in the design of sustainable buildings have tended to focus on the operational efficiency of environmental control systems, the renewability of energy sources, and the thermal insulation and airtightness of building envelopes. These were legitimate concerns and necessary steps in our collective efforts to reduce energy consumption and, to a degree, greenhouse gas emissions. During this era of sustainable design, *embodied emissions* were largely discounted as insignificant contributors to the overall carbon footprint of building.

Today, as new buildings have become increasingly energy-efficient, we've come to recognize and acknowledge that the huge amount of material and energy consumed by the processes of material extraction, manufacture, transport, assembly that we undertake to *produce* our built environment contributes significantly to its carbon footprint. Exactly when those emissions occur during the building lifecycle becomes a critical factor as we consider ways to manage and mitigate them most effectively in the face of a rapidly changing climate.

If, over a set period of time, we compare the emissions profile of an existing building with average energy efficiency to a brand-new, high-performance building, we begin to see the challenges we face. A new operationally efficient building demands a large share of its life cycle greenhouse gas emissions at the very beginning of the life cycle, as the raw material that will ultimately form the building is gathered, processed, transported, and assembled [15]. Then, due to its modest energy consumption, the high-performance building slowly recovers from the initial "carbon spike" of the production stage, usually over three to five decades of efficient operation. That it will take decades for the putatively "sustainable" building to outperform the lower performing building in its total life cycle emissions must be a critical consideration for the contemporary building sector in its response to climate change. It is a dangerous irony that the ostensibly high-performance sustainable building has emitted the largest share of its life cycle carbon only to recover it after that critical window for climate action has closed.

This shows us that we should first do everything we can to reuse and adapt existing buildings to new programs of occupancy and use. It also gives us critical insight into how we might best respond as building designers to the alarming increase in global building sector emissions and the associated global warming which will change the biological face of our planet. We must radically reduce building emissions across all phases of the building life cycle, but we must focus our attention on flattening the initial carbon spike of the production phase. Through circular economic material reuse and carbon sequestration in bio-based building assemblies, we will begin to mitigate building sector carbon impacts at the precise time we most need them: right now.

RE-BALANCING THE PLANET: AGENCY AND OPPORTUNITY

We live in momentous times, with intricately interconnected global challenges that can seem insurmountable for the individual designer seeking to mitigate the environmental impacts of her or his work. It's important to recognize, however, that those of us who make everyday decisions about the consumption of material and energy—consumption that takes place on the spatial scale of buildings and on the temporal scale of the building life cycle— have an outsized share of agency and opportunity in the fight against climate change. In the following pages, we aim to expose those design opportunities and deepen our technical and environmental agency. As participants in such a significant sector of economic activity, those profound and daunting environmental and economic challenges constitute our field of action.

In less than two decades, our planet will experience an unprecedented construction boom [16]. As global populations and the cities that house them continue to grow, the demand for buildings and infrastructure, along with the material and energy required to produce and maintain them, will increase dramatically. The effects of climate change on our inhabited landscapes will accelerate those demographic trends. As global warming increases and ice cover melts, sea levels rise, and weather patterns shift, formerly hospitable regions may no longer prove habitable. We may choose to physically barricade ourselves against those climate-driven events—coastal and inland flooding, drought, forest fires—or we may flee from them and relocate our homes elsewhere, but in either case, we will inevitably try to have to build our way out of the climatological challenges we face.

Whether driven by population growth or migration, this anticipated construction will entail a global investment over the next several decades that is estimated to reach $90 trillion [17]. To put that into perspective, this volume of construction will surpass the current value of the Earth's existing built environment. In the next century, we will add another planet's worth of building to the Earth's surface. On the bright side, as spending on construction grows, trends show that investments in more sustainable construction methods are increasing with it. At current rates, the value of that transition to low-carbon materials, systems and building techniques is expected to reach $25 trillion by 2030, a significant incentive for the building industry to assess its habits of consumption and its protection of the environment [18].

So, it is critical that we carefully consider how to direct that investment and rebalance the planet. If we continue along our current path of linear consumption and CO_2 emission, that $90 trillion investment in buildings along with energy and transport infrastructure will consume at least one-third of our remaining carbon quota. Our task as builders—as it should be in all other sectors—is to limit anthropogenic CO_2 emissions to levels that would restrict the planet's warming to levels well below 2 degrees Celsius and to build in a way that doesn't exceed our share of allowable carbon impacts. These are the building and energy targets that we need to hit in order to mitigate potentially catastrophic climate change.

To rebalance the planet's metabolism so that it can absorb, healthily and sustainably, the stress and strain of a growing population seems to be an overwhelming challenge. It will require economic and behavioral shifts as well as political and environmental strategies that are comprehensive and systemic. But of all the sectors of human activity which must participate in this fundamental shift, our sector—encompassing the production and maintenance of the built environment—may offer the greatest means with which to respond. Which other industry holds so many cards in its hand, comprising half of the annual raw material consumption, a third of waste and 80% of national wealth [19]? As UN Secretary-General António Guterres put it at the World Mayors summit in 2019, "Cities are where the climate battle will largely be won or lost." If this is true, then it could be said that the greatest potential for balancing planetary material and energy flows lies in the construction of those cities. Reduction of raw material consumption, energy use, and waste is fundamental. In conjunction with these efforts, we must also ask some serious questions about sufficiency: what is enough, how will we measure it, and how fairly are we able to share the finite resources of our planet?

Because of the urgent need to mitigate anthropogenic climate change, and because of the huge share of greenhouse gas the building sector emits, it is critical that building designers take a leading role in controlling the flows of carbon through the built environment. The ways in which our buildings consume and generate energy and the manner in which they're made and maintained lie largely in the hands of the design team. From this point forward, building designers will need to assert their agency in shifting construction economies from their currently linear flows of carbon—starting with raw material extraction and ending in waste disposal—into healthier, circular flows that minimize carbon emissions and reabsorb carbon through the building process. The enhancement of the circular economy in the building sector is a dire necessity from an environmental standpoint. We should also consider it a source of real and meaningful economic and creative opportunity. Put another way, the scientific understanding and technological ingenuity that have been instrumental in magnifying our human environmental footprint—if deployed with carbon-consciousness and ecological efficacy—may prove essential in our efforts to shrink it.

ABOUT THIS BOOK: AN OVERVIEW

As building designers, we can work—both individually and in concert within our discipline and beyond its professional boundaries—to dramatically reduce our carbon footprint and effectively contribute the weight of our ingenuity and technical knowledge to achieve a new balance in the planet's eco-systemic function. This demands, however, that we reorganize our toolbox, adding new tools, sharpening existing ones, and applying them to the specific objective of decarbonizing building. This book neither attempts nor claims to offer solutions, but instead seeks to describe that toolbox and the means by which we might apply the specific tools it contains.

This chapter has attempted to outline, in broad form, the challenges we face and the special responsibility and opportunity they offer. The next chapters are intentionally more granular. They provide the approaches—both conceptual and methodological, quantitative and qualitative—that we will need to adopt and refine in response to the dynamics set in play by our first moves in this complex and existential game.

In Chapter 2, we'll examine ways to quantify a building's carbon footprint using the principles, terminology, information sources, tools, and methodologies of material flow analysis and life cycle assessment. These form the methodological platform we'll need to optimize the many objectives entailed in any given building project, so it results in a rebalanced flow of material and energy and associated reduction in carbon-related impact. The quick methodological explanation offered here is not intended to replace more detailed lifecycle assessment guidelines and standards, but rather to exemplify how carbon accounting can fit into the building design process. We'll also consider the conceptual limitations of the building life cycle as an analytical framework and will posit an expanded set of spatial and temporal boundaries that we believe to be critical to thinking broadly and systemically about the impacts of our work as designers and builders.

Chapter 3 offers two carbon case studies, examples of recently completed buildings that sought to reduce their overall carbon footprint through a variety of means and using different strategies. These examples illustrate the lifecycle assessment techniques we describe in Chapter 2 and expose where impacts were embedded in the design process. We'll consider how the design teams approached the problem of decarbonization and will assess the life cycle carbon flows that resulted in each building within its geographic, political, and economic context.

Chapter 4 focuses on the decarbonized design process. It considers our agency generally and within the different phases of the design process to draw down the greenhouse gas emissions of the buildings we create. It addresses the way in which we might best apply the information we glean from our quantitative assessments and posits a set of principles intended to fortify our instincts as low-carbon thinkers and makers.

Finally, in Chapter 5, we'll look at a set of broader objectives for the building sector and consider the prospect of a circular economic and ecologically regenerative approach to building design. These objectives aim to minimize the consumption of material and energy, to reframe waste as a potentially valuable resource for newly reconfigured industrial processes and building practice, and to integrate the production and operation of the built environment into a healthy metabolism for the planet.

Visualizing Carbon Flows

The intangibility of carbon, unlike much of the waste we generate through our activities as builders, represents a significant challenge in its accounting. It has no tangible weight or palpable dimension, offers no immediate feedback; the consequences of its emissions are far-reaching but remain remote from our daily work.

In our design process, however, we regularly employ tools of graphic visualization that are abstract in their representation—no one can actually *see* the plan of a building—and elastic in their scalar shifts.

But they form the essential means of iterative study and assessment in the design process. Even as we refine the technical details of a building assembly, we use orthographic drawing conventions and physical and digital modeling techniques at scales far smaller than the actual building we're proposing to build. In the earliest phases of design, we're accustomed to communicating ideas through what are essentially crude representations of the physical object and its position on its site. For the uninitiated, these visualizations with which we're so fluent and familiar, would be meaningless without some introduction and explanation.

In order to give visual weight to the otherwise intangible process of carbon accounting we've brought those same tools of abstraction to bear on our discussion: orthographic section cuts and paraline mapping serve to describe, albeit in diagrammatic form, the flow of carbon through building and buildings, its emission, and its potential storage. That flow is measured against a continuous line that reappears throughout the pages of this book. Above that line we measure carbon dioxide and associated greenhouse gases emitted through a particular building activity. Below the line we tally carbon sequestered and stored in bio-based building components. The line serves as our carbon transect.

A transect is an analytical tool used by scientists to survey quantities and their distribution. Repeated survey and measurement along a given transect over time can describe the change or flux in a quantity of any given substance or population within a bounded area. Our line is intended to serve as a reference within the boundaries of the building life cycle, a consistent datum along which we can measure the ebbs and flows of molecular carbon, absorbed and emitted over cycles of geologic formation, plant growth, or construction. We vary the degree of precision and the scale of our measurement—molecular, anthropometric, territorial, or global—but we always measure from that datum in order to reckon with the atmospheric impacts of human settlement: individual buildings or the massive aggregations of constructed habitation we call cities.

For our purposes this so-called *carbon transect* is a conceptual tool that we deploy to aid our visualization. A related, metaphorical line runs through our built environment, across waste landfills and brownfields, bisecting buildings abandoned and in disrepair, functional and fully used, or as yet under construction. Its longitude tracks back along transportation corridors, across landscapes of industrial residue and production, over sites of mineral excavation and extraction, and through natural global biomes—all by now altered at least to some degree by anthropogenic activity—but where biogenic material is still steadily accruing mass.

The line has no precise geographic or historical location although we can attribute to it both spatial and temporal dimension. Its origin lies at a point in time and somewhere on the surface of the Earth (or within its upper geological strata) at which a geo-chemical or biochemical reaction was initiated to form physical matter or, more specifically, any of the variety of materials we use to produce and operate our buildings. Its endpoint falls in some projected human and global future, a future of our planning and making.

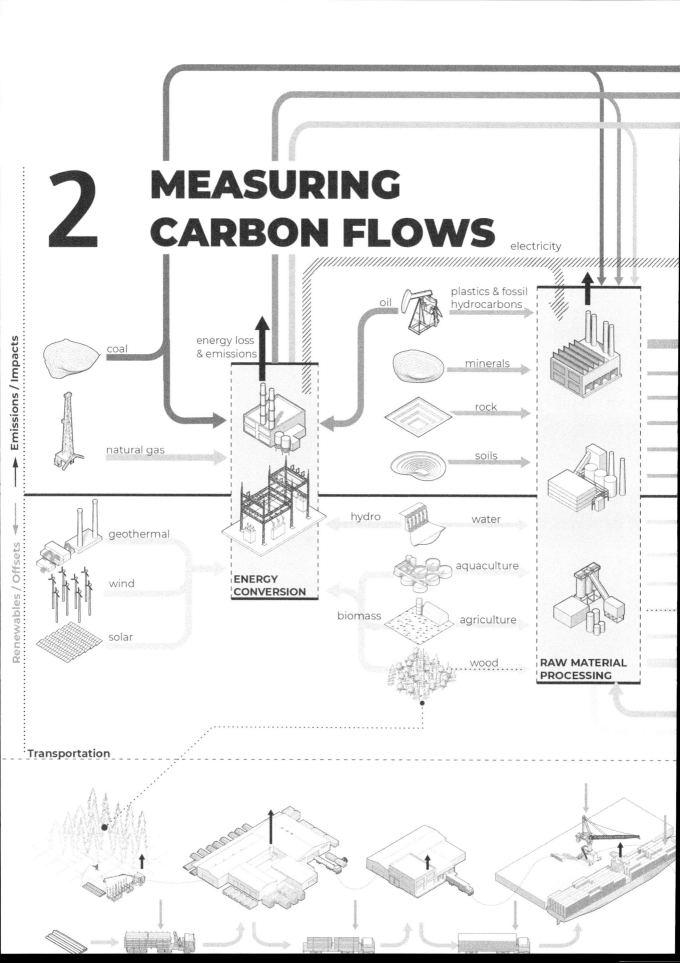

2 MEASURING CARBON FLOWS

Emissions / Impacts →

Renewables / Offsets ←

coal

natural gas

geothermal

wind

solar

energy loss & emissions

ENERGY CONVERSION

oil

plastics & fossil hydrocarbons

minerals

rock

soils

electricity

hydro   water

aquaculture

biomass   agriculture

wood

RAW MATERIAL PROCESSING

Transportation

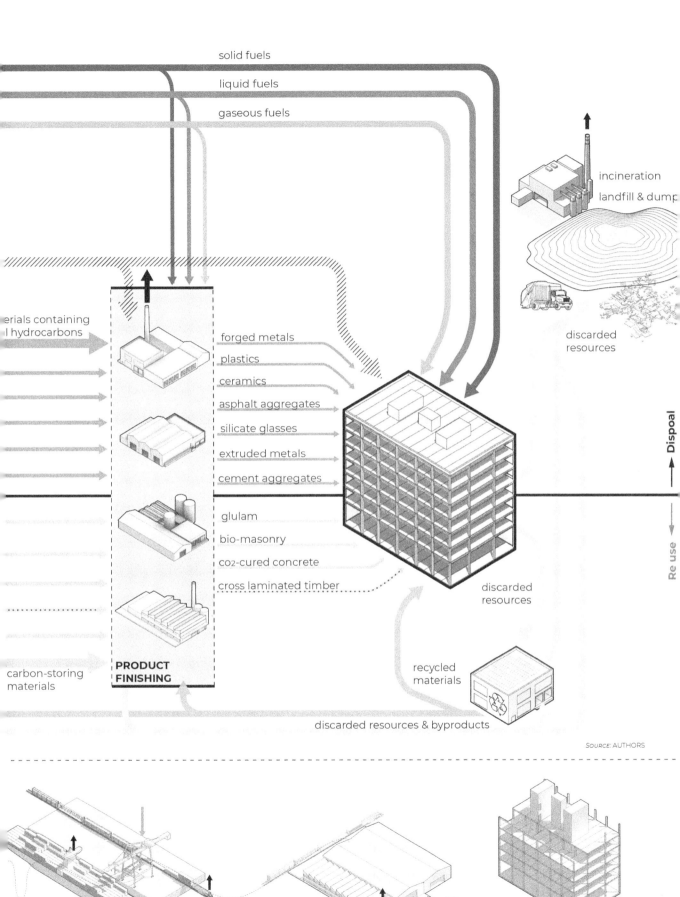

solid fuels

liquid fuels

gaseous fuels

incineration

landfill & dump

discarded
resources

...erials containing
...l hydrocarbons

forged metals

plastics

ceramics

asphalt aggregates

silicate glasses

extruded metals

cement aggregates

glulam

bio-masonry

co2-cured concrete

cross laminated timber

discarded
resources

Dispoal

Re use

PRODUCT
FINISHING

carbon-storing
materials

recycled
materials

discarded resources & byproducts

SOURCE: AUTHORS

CHAPTER TWO
MEASURING CARBON FLOWS

"If you can't measure it, you can't manage it," an adage attributed to the organizational management expert Peter Drucker, is often quoted as a managerial truth and, in an area of data-driven decision-making, equally derided as a dehumanizing, technically deterministic nostrum. How do we appropriately weigh the competing criteria for building design—utility and functionality, strength and durability, technical feasibility and potential cost, aesthetics and cultural considerations, the social and individual experience of architectural space and form—with their overarching impact on the Earth's biological, chemical, and physical systems? And with respect to the flow of carbon through the building process and its role in creating our current atmospheric imbalance of carbon dioxide, how does merely measuring the embodied and operational greenhouse gas emissions of a given building offer designers a meaningful and responsible course of action, given the sprawling scope of the political economic forces and human behaviors that so often determine the extent of our global carbon footprint? And conversely, how can we make informed decisions in the design process without a true measure of their potential environmental impact?

In this chapter, we offer a simplified means to quantify the carbon footprint generated by our design solutions and we identify strategies for designers to incorporate these quantitative assessments into their design process. We'll have a look at life cycle assessment (LCA) from four viewpoints: First, we'll discuss its relevance and importance for building designers. Then, we'll present its fundamental principles, terms, and concepts and discuss the life cycle stages, their assessment methods and related standards. After

that, we'll have a tour through the process of assessing the different life cycle stages of a building. Finally, we'll take a look at the way in which digital tools can ease the work required with a practical LCA. We'll accompany all these stages with illustrations and example calculations.

LIFE CYCLE ASSESSMENT: WHAT'S IN IT FOR BUILDING DESIGNERS?

An Opportunity

As discussed in Chapter 1, building designers have a unique capacity to shape both the built and the natural environment. By understanding the life cycle of the products and systems we employ in the design of buildings and their infrastructure, we can more judiciously manage our raw material consumption, our energy demands, and the implications of these systems on the flow of carbon through the processes we invoke. A decarbonized design process entails our careful consideration of all the potentially harmful carbon impacts that might arise through a building's production, use, and disposal. Critically, this practice relies on a scrupulous assessment—using standardized processes for quantifying their impacts—of alternative materials and methods that might contribute to or, alternatively, ameliorate the forces that drive climate change. This combination of overview and assessment, framed by the entire life cycle of the building as a complex system, represents a life cycle approach to design.

The earliest stages of the design process, when most decisions about the specific siting, massing, material assembly, and operational systems of a building still lie ahead, is precisely the point at which an overview of the building life cycle offers the building designer some of the most significant opportunities to anticipate, communicate, and avoid potential life cycle carbon impacts. A command of the terminology and its definition—as well as the concepts and systems of assessment—is a first critical step in limiting impact.

The process of LCA can certainly be outsourced to specialists well-versed in its method or computed through software plug-ins to building information models (BIM) that can dramatically accelerate the process of data collection and processing. Various sustainability certification programs internalize its principles and conceptual frameworks, with varying scope and degrees of effectiveness. In an era of increasingly complex building systems and assemblies, complicated supply chains and intensive modes of manufacture and transport, it may seem challenging to constantly reassess, in real time and through the naturally iterative and trans-scalar process of building design, the impact of a particular decision or building scenario. A carbon footprint calculation based on a design iteration developed at the start of a week may no longer be relevant by that week's end. However, the downside of relying on specialized software or sustainability checklists is twofold: (1) the underlying data may be contested and potentially inaccurate, obscured by the black box of technological product development; and (2) the assignment of quantitative values to a given material, process or strategy may be heavily inflected by any number of factors ranging from obsolete information to political or economic motivations. For these reasons, even an elementary understanding of life cycle assessment has become essential knowledge for architects and builders concerned about the impacts of their work and seeking to optimize the environmental benefits of their decision-making process.

Carbon Measurement for Carbon Management

Despite their complexity, the flows of carbon belong to those aspects of sustainable design that can be quantified with a satisfying level of accuracy. In the built environment, we can estimate the emissions that arise from processes that we invoke as designers, either by intention or neglect: the production, construction, use,

demolition, and recycling of buildings. In doing so, we can make better choices with respect to those processes and their carbon impacts.

The potential environmental loads or, alternatively, benefits of construction are always case-specific. Depending on a building's location and orientation in its site—and its intended use—there are alternative pathways for the management and mitigation of the harmful impacts of construction. However, only a few of these impacts may apply to a given project. Even energy efficiency, the primary focus of the past several decades of sustainable building, is not a universal indicator of impact, as it may have very little to do with buildings, such as parking garages, warehouses, or the majority of physical infrastructure elements, such as bridges, roads, or parks.

Though it may not be possible to apply general rules of thumb to mitigate the harmful impacts of every construction project, we can apply similar assessment methods to every project. The essential ingredient for our efforts to mitigate impact is rooted in tracking the flows of material and energy, which directly correlate to the intensity and volume of harmful impacts.

Depending on which sorts of energy or material are used in a given construction project, the resulting environmental, social, or economic burdens differ. An energy-consuming building has different environmental impacts if its energy is produced from either fossil or renewable sources. Likewise, the production of the material we use for a given building may yield significantly different impacts, depending on what we select to construct functionally and technically similar components or assemblies. Furthermore, our selection of materials can significantly affect the durability and technical service life of the building and can make their potential reuse or recycling more feasible and therefore more likely.

When applying life cycle assessment methods during the design process, we should always keep in mind that an LCA can provide only an estimation of anticipated carbon flows. We cannot precisely predict, for example, the duration or intensity of the building's use phase, nor can we accurately anticipate when or how the building will be demolished, or how much of its materials and components might be reused or recycled. Although we can apply *sensitivity analyses* (discussed later in this chapter) to determine how much of an effect those variables may have on a given outcome and begin to address those lingering uncertainties, we should simply seek to be as thorough and realistic as possible in our estimations of potential demands or stresses on a building and remain cognizant of their ramifications and alert to opportunities that arise through an integrated design and assessment process.

THE FUNDAMENTAL CONCEPTS

The Approach

Between the cradle and grave of a building, huge amounts of energy and material are consumed for the purpose of providing space, comfort, and services for the users and ensuring the building's functionality. This consumption, however, leads to a myriad of interlinked resource flows and ultimately to waste and emissions that end up in our land, water, or air. These, in turn, cause direct and indirect impacts to human and environmental health, all with long-term implications for our economy and society.

In a life cycle approach, our aim is to consider everything that happens between the beginning and end of a building's life. We can estimate the impacts that arise from the production of construction materials with sufficient accuracy, and the same applies to most of the processes of manufacturing, transport, and construction. But the further we project our analysis into the future, the more uncertain we inevitably become about the outcomes we seek to predict and the many possible alternative futures we may seek to ascribe to our building's life cycle. The need to replace components of the building assembly, for example, depends not only on the materials themselves, but to a great extent the cycles of wear and tear the building experiences over its lifespan. Any attempt to estimate different future outcomes requires that we develop scenarios. Despite their potential inaccuracies and hypotheses, these scenarios become an inseparable part of the life cycle approach and these predictions, as well as the range of outcomes they imagine, help us make better-informed decisions and, as a result, design more

resilient buildings with longer service lives. Our simple observation of the way in which buildings around us age—along with a significant amount of statistical information—makes our scenarios relatively reliable predictions rather than mere guesswork. Later in this chapter, we'll describe the subdivision of the building life cycle into modules that can significantly ease the analytical work and clarify our communication of its results.

The lenses through which we examine the potential impacts incurred over the building life cycle incorporate various metrics of environmental, social and economic sustainability. Acidification, eutrophication, ozone depletion, particulate emissions, and (for the purposes of this book) carbon emissions and their global warming potential are categories of environmental impact. Life cycle costing, on the other hand, can provide quantitative information on costs, investments, incomes, fees, or taxes that potentially take place over the years in a given use scenario. These sorts of economic estimates assessments have a long track record and we can therefore rely on their accuracy. Less common and potentially more complex than economic or environmental assessment would be the study of the social impacts that accrue over the life cycle of a building, in order to understand its sustainability in a broader sense: the safety of working conditions, the health and well-being of workers and, later, of building users. We might even assess the impacts of the buildings on human rights and potential sources of human exploitation hidden in the building product supply chain. In principle, a life cycle approach represents our best means of anticipating impact and avoiding the harmful consequences of our activities as makers and builders. Although our focus in this book and in the LCA process will be carbon emissions, we can use the same steps and apply nearly any impact criteria to the prediction of our building's impacts on the Earth's air, water, and land, and to its extraordinary array of species, including our own.

Life Cycle Boundaries, Scales, and Periods

The life cycle of a product or a building conventionally refers to a linear and finite process bounded at the beginning of its life by the extraction of the raw material needed to produce it and, at the end of its useful life, by its demolition or disassembly and the dispersal of its materials and systems. The stages that lie between and include those two temporal and spatial boundaries entail all the processes we associate with the design of buildings: component manufacture and transport, construction, occupation and operation, maintenance and repair, and demolition and disposal. All stages include a set of measurable inputs of material and energy and outflows of waste (solid debris, liquid effluents, and gaseous emissions). The processes of consumption and waste represent the building's life cycle impacts. An analysis of those impacts so bounded would be described as a "cradle-to-grave" LCA.

If we choose to narrow that assessment (in order to reduce the analytical uncertainty of how a product or material might be used by its consumer or perform during that use phase, for example), we might stop our analysis at the moment the product is ready for distribution from the factory. This particular way of framing the process would be described as a "cradle-to-gate" LCA.

We'll discuss in subsequent sections of this chapter the methodological importance of establishing clear boundaries for our analysis along with the intermediate phases that comprise it. But for our immediate purposes, it is critical that we recognize that the inclusion or exclusion of certain stages of a building or product life cycle—how we choose to bracket our analysis—represents a critical decision which, whether by intention or through a lack of critical awareness, will define both the specific value (or usefulness) and broader values (philosophy and ethos) of the assessment. The "cradle-to-grave" metaphor, despite its apparent comprehensiveness, must ignore significant factors that contribute to the overall impact of a building in the same way that a newspaper obituary of a beloved relative will most likely omit mention of the genetic material that gave life to that individual or describe the process of decomposition of the body after burial or during cremation. In that sense, it's important to consider, as part of the terrestrial system in which we operate, how we might expand the concept of a building life cycle to better understand the

timeframes and physical forces associated with the formation of the natural resources we draw into that building, and to acknowledge the implications of the waste that flows out of it. This revised framework of a building life cycle might serve to better account for the finite nature of some resources and the renewability of others, and for the overarching political structures or embedded economic externalities that play such a critical role in setting the terms of what is available, affordable, or sustainable in a particular context.

A broader, more holistic way of describing the manifold processes and impacts of the building life cycle might be the "cradle-to-cradle" metaphor, popularized within the building sector by William McDonough and Michael Braungart [1]. The concept is rooted in a systemic, regenerative approach to design that supports permaculture and biodiversity, while promoting circular economic practices that aim to extend the value of an extracted and processed material through continued cycles of reuse and remanufacture. Another valuable analogy in thinking about the carbon embodied in the buildings we make is "emergy," a concept rooted in ecosystem science that seeks to describe the comprehensive flow of energy through the geological, chemical, and biological systems that form the raw material we use in building [2]. If a building can be described as not only consuming energy but as having an "energy memory," it might also be understood to have a carbon memory. Together, the metaphors of emergy and cradle-to-cradle life cycles help us establish a significantly broader conceptual framework, one that projects backward into some deep biochemical and geochemical past that formed the raw materials of building and forward to looping cycles of reuse and recycling through an expanded time horizon of repeated implementation and use. Economically speaking, we might describe this as a means to amortize the environmental debt we incur in the initial extraction and subsequent processing of a raw material.

In the specific case of carbon, these broader philosophical frameworks help us understand the deeper implications of our actions as builders:

how we're essentially tapping into existing carbon sinks and, at some stage in the building life cycle, releasing that carbon in the form of gases that escape into the atmosphere, or alternatively, trapping and storing that carbon in the assemblies of the most durable consumer product our society produces: the built environment. In effect, the latent capacity for the built environment to durably store carbon transforms buildings into potential carbon storages instead of emitters and, when they are no longer functionally useful or technically sound, turns them into a valuable source of raw material for future construction projects or other industrial uses. Such an approach has significant implications for the building design process and it starts with the goals we set at the start of any project.

It is important to recognize that different products, materials, and buildings operate within a wide range of life cycle timelines. For example, a building product, such as a window, has a typical life cycle of a few decades. After being deemed unfit for continued use in the original building, the same window might be reused in another building, assuming that it still fulfills adequate functional or normative requirements. Once it no longer meets basic performance standards or simply ceases to function properly, its raw materials—wood, glass, and metals—can be recycled into other products. Wood may be reused to make engineered boards and panels; glass, for the manufacture of glass wool; and metals melted down and cast into new products. Technically speaking, materials in their elemental form are practically eternal: we can break them into smaller and smaller increments, down to even a molecular level, but we never entirely eliminate them through industrial or waste management processes. We must understand this as a fundamental value. Material is a durable asset.

Some of the materials in a building can be directly *reused* (though building material reuse remains uncommon and inadequate). Reuse lengthens the effective lifespan of a material and optimizes its initial manufacturing inputs. We should understand these inputs to include the energy, human labor, and capital required to source, produce, and transport the original product. Compared to many of the individual components that comprise them, we usually expect buildings to have longer lifespans—depending on structural type, location, and program—that range from several decades to centuries in duration. In many cases, a well-considered architectural design—paired with robust engineering, responsible construction, and regular maintenance and repair—can extend the lifespan of buildings indefinitely. This way, a building acts as a framework within which shorter life cycles of building products and mechanical installations occur in regular and repeating periods. We can manage those sub-cycles of material and component exchange if we design with them in mind.

Cities typically have life cycles that outlast the buildings that make up their fabric, enduring for centuries or—in some cases—several millennia. Over the course of a city's lifespan, numerous buildings are built, demolished, and built again, often on the same site but usually with different uses and in varying forms. Material and carbon flows through cities, unlike individual buildings, include not only construction material, energy, and capital, but also encompass the basic necessities of human life such as food, commodities, and transportation. In its scale and complexity, the metabolism of a city resembles a natural ecosystem more so than any other human construction.

Despite their different timeframes, the life cycles of building products, buildings, and cities are profoundly interconnected. The quality, use, and maintenance of products influence the life cycle of a building. The design, functionality, and flexibility of individual buildings contribute to the vibrancy and health of the city. So, it is important that designers optimize the carbon life cycle at each and every scale if we are serious about creating robust, efficient, and sustainable built environments. How and what we choose to specifically quantify of the manifold ways in which carbon flows though all scales of the designed and built environment are the subject of this chapter.

Operational and Embodied Impacts

The environmental impacts that accrue through the life cycle of a building fall into two categories. *Operational* impacts are those associated with the period of a building's use by its occupants, attributed primarily to the consumption of energy and water but, for the specific purposes of our discussion, the emission of greenhouse gases that arise almost entirely from that energy use. *Embodied* impacts are those generated by processes that contribute to the *making* of the building— the extraction and processing of raw materials into building components, their transport and assembly on site during construction as well as those same processes associated with the building's maintenance, repair, and refurbishment over the course of its functional lifespan. Embodied impacts are also generated during a building's *unmaking*, all the processes required to demolish or dismantle its structural assemblies and its mechanical, electrical, and plumbing systems along with the waste management network engaged to reuse, recycle, and redistribute or otherwise dispose of the building's constituent materials.

It is critical to distinguish between these two categories of impact for a variety of reasons. Until recently, efforts to make buildings more sustainable have focused on the reduction of operational impacts, achieved through the continuing refinement of building efficiencies: improved mechanical, electrical, plumbing, and lighting systems, fixtures, and appliances, better insulated and more airtight building envelopes, increased daylighting for reduced electrical loads, and on-site energy generation to offset non-renewable energy consumption. However, as buildings have become increasingly energy-efficient and their operational stage impacts have been reduced as a relative share of overall life cycle impacts, the raw material and energy consumed and waste generated during the production and destruction of a building have come into necessarily sharp relief [3–6]. The use of a polyurethane foam panel may increase the insulative value of a wall assembly and thereby serve to reduce a building's operational emissions, but the impacts created in the formation of that hydrocarbon-based plastic and, at the end of a

building's life, its addition to the waste stream, may offset any operational benefits we gain. That the less visible environmental ramifications of the building life cycle may play an increasingly dominant role in our understanding of the relative impacts of our activities as builders, represents a paradigmatic shift in our approach to sustainability in the building sector.

From a political economic perspective, as Kiel Moe has keenly observed in his study of the development and construction of the Empire State Building, the economies of land use and building development will inflect how material and energy are directed to buildings and aggregate emissions [7]. In dense urban areas, where land values are high, corresponding demands for financial returns on initial investment favor operational efficiency and cost reduction over the less-easily quantified impacts that arise through the technical cycles of the broader industrial economy. Whereas operational emissions arise largely from the consumption of water and energy, which are readily metered and measured, embodied impacts are closely correlated to the more distributed material processes of building production, with environmental ramifications that tend to be externalized by economic analyses that typically focus on short-term costs and returns.

Our ability to measure and control these externalities, however, will have significant temporal implications for our ability to combat climate change. As noted in Chapter 1, embodied emissions accrue mostly in the first year of the building life cycle, whereas operational efficiencies offer emissions reductions that accrue over the multi-decade lifespan of a building. The international scientific community, along with the United Nations and the Intergovernmental Panel on Climate Change, has identified 2030 as a critical milestone for the reduction of global greenhouse gas emissions, so at this particular moment in our climate history, our continued pursuit of operational refinements will provide little relief for a rapidly changing climate if we neglect the embodied emissions we incur in the process. As the energy networks that serve our buildings and the buildings themselves become increasingly efficient in their operation and more sustainable in their energy generation, the sourcing, processing, and recycling or reuse of building materials will be the next frontier in the reduction of the built environment's carbon footprint and the creation of a circular construction economy.

The Stages of the Building Life Cycle

As we've seen, understanding at which point during the building life cycle and through which processes emissions are generated and other environmental, economic, and social impacts incurred is critical in our efforts to minimize our carbon footprint. To facilitate measurement and to clarify the communication of our results, we seek to categorize critical processes within the lifespan of a building. According to internationally adopted standards of life cycle assessment, the life cycle of a building (or a building product) is divided into four stages. These are its production, construction, use, and end of life. Each of these stages is further divided into sub-categories: codified divisions that ease the understanding and communication of the critical impacts and benefits that may occur during the projected life cycle of a product, building, or city.

The *production stage* spans all of the processes involved in transforming a raw material into a commercial material product. According to the protocols of assessment, this initial life cycle stage is partitioned into three primary sub-stages: (1) a raw material stage which addresses the processes of its extraction; (2) a transportation stage; and (3) a manufacturing stage that typically consists of several consecutive phases of material processing. The production of a cross-laminated timber panel, for example, includes the process in several steps of turning saw-logs into dimensional lumber—sawing, drying, planing—which is then combined with adhesives in a hydraulic press to form large structural sheets, cut to size and finally packaged for delivery. This is the point in which the production stage ends: the manufactured billet of cross-laminated timber (CLT) is a commercial product, prepared for further processing and elaboration based on whatever building applications are specified.

The *construction stage* includes all activities that are initiated after a more generic building material begins to be shaped into a specific building component or introduced into system or assembly, as when the billet of CLT, a faucet, a piece of door hardware, or a coil of plastic piping, or a bundle of steel reinforcing bar leaves the factory. The construction stage continues until all building activity on site is complete and the building is ready for use. Depending on the distances between factories, warehouses, and the construction site, the share of emissions from transport may be either marginal or significant. In most construction projects, however, the emissions from the construction stage are relatively low. However, for infrastructure or landscape projects with a large quantity, volume, and weight of building products, the role of transport may prove more significant in the overall life cycle of building material-energy consumption.

The *use stage* is usually the longest in a building's life cycle. This stage includes several sub-stages that represent the building systems' consumption of all the energy required to provide and process services like water and electricity through the operation of its systems of fixtures, appliances, and mechanical equipment. We consume energy and material in the building's periodic maintenance, repair, or refurbishment and these processes may play a measurable role in the building's carbon emissions during the use stage. The longer the building is able to serve its users, the more emissions are likely to be incurred in the replacement of the products most prone to wear and tear. It's important to remember, then, that when our aim is to reduce overall impacts, we should select durable materials and make them easy to maintain, access, and replace as an overall strategy that improves the feasibility of repair and potentially lengthens the service life of the building.

A building's *end-of-life stage* includes all of the emissions that arise from the energy expended during demolition, the transportation of materials away from the building site, and the sorting, reuse, recycling, or landfilling of the accumulated waste. Since buildings contain a significant volume of material—including structural components,

32

CRADLE TO GATE

CRADLE TO GATE
WITH OPTIONS

CRADLE TO END-OF-USE

CRADLE TO HANDOVER

CRADLE TO SITE

CRADLE TO GATE

A1–A3 PRODUCTION	A4–A5 CONSTRUCTION	C USE		C END-OF-LIFE
A1 raw material supply	**A4** transport to site	**B1** use	**B5** refurbishment	**C1** deconstruction
	A5 construction work	**B2** maintenance	**B6** operational energy use	**C2** transport
A2 transport to factory		**B3** repair	**B7** operational water use	**C3** waste processing
A3 manufacturing		**B4** replacement		**C4** disposal

benefits and loads beyond
the system boundary

insulation, interior finishes, roofing substrates, and even foundations and fills—the amount of these waste materials flows can be significant, with high energy demands or destructive land use impacts which in turn diminish the processes of biogenic CO_2 reabsorption that would otherwise naturally occur in those landscapes.

When we analyze the sum total of greenhouse gases emitted during the life cycle of a single building, we see that the use of energy and the production of materials account for most of the emissions. In contrast, the construction and end-of-life stages are significantly less critical to the building's overall carbon life cycle [8].

However, if we consider the flow of material into and back out of that building throughout its life cycle, the production phase clearly dominates the construction, use, and end-of-life phases. During the use phase, materials are naturally replaced or repaired, but are rarely reintroduced in larger quantities than were initially utilized during the building's construction phase. What is most important to remember is that well before materials arrive on a site and far in advance of the building going into operation, architects and engineers design the building, specify materials and products, elaborate components and systems, and work closely with the client and builder to project and refine construction costs. Therefore, it is obvious that in the design phase of a building, there is the greatest potential for avoiding up-front emissions, reducing material consumption, and adopting circular economic practices. We'll address this more specifically in Chapter 4.

If we focus on the outflow of material of the building at the end of its life cycle, we see significant carbon benefits in the recycling or, even better in terms of reduced energy and raw material demands, the *reuse* of building products. If portions of the building are reusable—and especially if they can substitute for more harmful industrial products—those reused materials offer us the very real potential to avoid emissions in future product manufacture. Correspondingly, if products contain harmful materials, they may require dramatically

more energy- and cost-intensive waste management processes to prevent collateral environmental damage. It is crucial then, from the viewpoint of a circular construction economy, that we anticipate how materials might be feasibly and realistically reused after their initial life in a first building incarnation.

As we'll see, both the general operational and embodied impacts—and, more specifically, the potential carbon emissions—of a building life cycle can be estimated during the design phase. A broad range of factors, however, will inevitably determine the relative dominance of different life cycle stages. A building's program of use and occupancy, for example, may create different space requirements, mechanical systems, utilities, or energy and water demands. Different building sites may require varying amounts of tree-clearing and soil disturbance or provide different opportunities for on-site energy generation. The soil conditions of a specific site may require pilings, deep excavation, or stabilization, which would entail using large quantities of cement, steel, or technically intensive equipment. The assemblies of a more heavily insulated building envelope might shift impacts from the use phase back onto the production phase. The mix of energy sources available in a particular location or the existence of a certain material supply chain may significantly alter the balance of carbon emissions. The sophisticated waste management systems necessary for the sorting, processing, and redistribution and reuse of construction waste during both the construction and end-of-life phases may exist in one region and not in others. Even regulatory requirements may shift the dominance of embodied and operational impacts and their sub-phases. For example, a zoning ordinance that limits building height might drive a less efficient massing or one that requires a certain architectural form that demands more material per occupiable floor area. A building code might restrict the use of a particular structural material despite its significantly smaller carbon footprint in the production phase and its greater amenability to reuse at the end of a building's life. Recognizing and identifying these myriad externalities and variables during the design process—and accounting for their

FIGURE 2.2 LIFE CYCLE STAGES AND TEMPORAL SYSTEM BOUNDARIES OF A BUILDING. *SOURCE:* AUTHORS

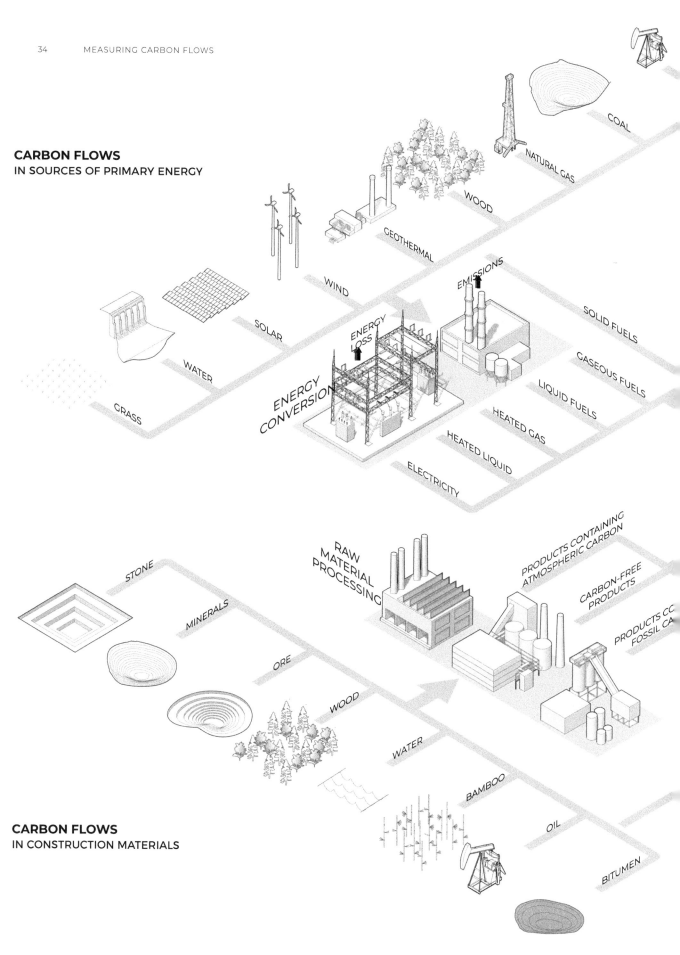

CARBON FLOWS
IN SOURCES OF PRIMARY ENERGY

COAL

NATURAL GAS

WOOD

GEOTHERMAL

WIND

SOLAR

WATER

GRASS

EMISSIONS

ENERGY
LOSS

ENERGY
CONVERSION

SOLID FUELS

GASEOUS FUELS

LIQUID FUELS

HEATED GAS

HEATED LIQUID

ELECTRICITY

RAW
MATERIAL
PROCESSING

STONE

MINERALS

ORE

WOOD

WATER

BAMBOO

OIL

BITUMEN

PRODUCTS CONTAINING
ATMOSPHERIC CARBON

CARBON-FREE
PRODUCTS

PRODUCTS CC
FOSSIL CA

CARBON FLOWS
IN CONSTRUCTION MATERIALS

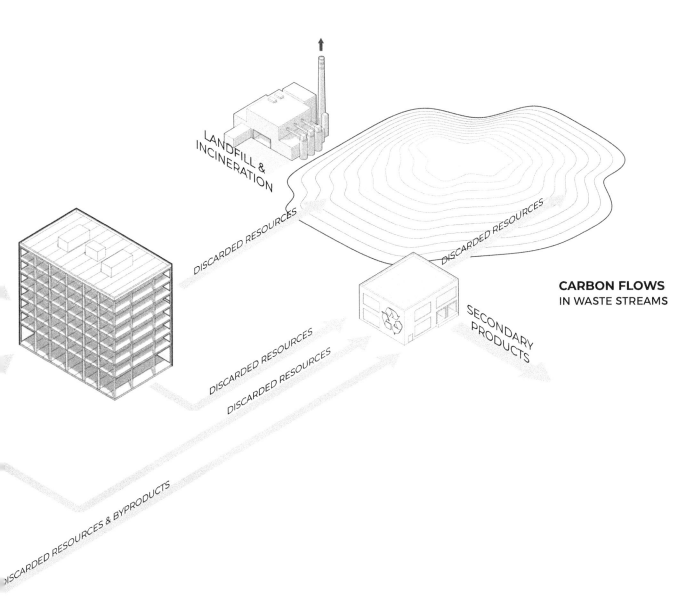

LANDFILL &
INCINERATION

DISCARDED RESOURCES

DISCARDED RESOURCES

DISCARDED RESOURCES

SECONDARY
PRODUCTS

CARBON FLOWS
IN WASTE STREAMS

DISCARDED RESOURCES

DISCARDED RESOURCES

DISCARDED RESOURCES & BYPRODUCTS

FIGURE 2.3
CARBON FLOWS IN THE BUILT
ENVIRONMENT.
SOURCE: AUTHORS

potential impacts on carbon emissions—enrich the architectural design process, dramatically expanding its conventional system boundaries.

A life cycle approach to building design demands that we consider all the potential consequences of the decision-making process and seek to be guided by the quantitative feedback we can gather from our assessments. Some of those consequences of our design choices, such as the end-of-life impacts of an intended material disassembly strategy, are remote from us in time and will have inevitably higher degrees of uncertainty than the choices with respect to the production and construction phases. Just as we seek to anticipate building energy consumption over the timespan of its occupation and use, we can form different assessment scenarios for the redeployment of material in its end-of-life stage, leading to a building assembly better calibrated for reuse and to an end-user better informed about low carbon options for the building's disposal or dispersal.

Assessment Methods

In order to meaningfully use assessment strategies throughout the design process, design professionals have a number of tools, strategies, and protocols at

their disposal. Conceptually, there are two primary and complementary methods to track the flows of embodied carbon and to calculate the carbon footprint of a building: (1) material flow analysis (MFA); and (2) life cycle assessment (LCA). Both MFA and LCA are valuable analytical tools that share many principles and techniques but the latter is more commonly applied to evaluate the environmental ramifications of the design decisions we make.

MFA is a method for systematically assessing the flows and stocks of material within a system and usually focuses on a single substance. In contrast, LCA is a tool for the "compilation and evaluation of the inputs, outputs and potential environmental impacts of a product system throughout its life cycle" [9]. As a more expansive analysis, an LCA usually examines the flows of several substances within or through the defined system. The common denominator for both the MFA and the LCA is a careful inventory of all the materials we apply to a building over a defined temporal duration. From the standpoint of establishing an order of operations, MFA can be understood as a method for establishing the full material inventory required for an LCA.

Info box 2.1

Alternative Routes to LCA

The benefits of LCA lie in the holistic nature of its environmental assessment, its consideration of wide range of potential impacts, and its assertion that we can and should expose and quantify every stage of a product´s or building´s life cycle. As the name implies, the LCA process tracks environmental impacts throughout a given product's life cycle which—in the case of a building—is modularized to ease and clarify the communication of its results. The most condensed form of LCA addresses the first module, or the production stage (A1–3) and is called "cradle-to-gate" assessment.

There are multiple paths through the process of an LCA. The main alternative methods are attributional LCA (aLCA) and consequential LCA (cLCA). The main difference between the aLCA and the cLCA methods lies in their scope. While aLCA aims to assess the direct emissions of a process or product's life cycle, cLCA looks at the changes in total emissions that result from several marginal changes in the production, consumption, and disposal chains associated with the subject of the assessment. It's important to recognize that aLCA and cLCA cannot be removed because they are complementary. In a sense, we can say that cLCA is better suited to exposing wider, systemic changes, whereas aLCA is more streamlined for repetitive routine assessments. The latter approach, attributional LCA, will be the tool we'll cover in this book.

LCA calculations can be conducted at different scales and with different focuses, for example, in some cases a specific structural assembly or a subcomponent of the building's architectural organization can be treated as a product. As we'll see in the case studies in Chapter 3, for example, the production of a typical standardized prefabricated module used as a temporary structure or deployed within the repetitive organization of a residential building might be the subject of an LCA. The results of the unit LCA would then simply be multiplied by the number of units deployed into the built environment, effectively converting a complex architectural object into a scalable, single-attribute bounded component.

The process of LCA entails four steps: (1) the definition of the goals and scope of the assessment; (2) an inventory analysis; (3) an impact assessment; and (4) the interpretation of the results. As we'll see in the following sections, these steps are conducted iteratively throughout the design process. It's important to note that because the definition of goals and scope, the quality of data, and the structuring of system boundaries used in the calculations may differ among LCAs of the same product or building, they may not produce comparable results. This makes the communication of the premises and assumptions of an LCA to its intended users a critical aspect of the life cycle approach to design.

Standards

Varying international and regional standards seek to make LCAs easier to compare and to encourage the establishment of more normative carbon limits for building across jurisdictions. These standards are technical documents developed jointly by industrial, governmental, and user organizations that set out clear processes in order to ensure the quality and utility of the results. They can be used in the calculation of a carbon footprint or to establish a range of other environmental, social or economic impacts.

A uniform LCA process is delineated in ISO 14040 [9], an international standard created to address quantitative methods for the overarching assessment of the environmental impacts of a product or service through all four phases of LCA: this is the system of categorization as the standard we will refer to throughout this chapter.

THE PROCESS OF LIFE CYCLE ASSESSMENT

Defining the Goal and Scope of Assessment

Tracking the flows of carbon starts with an objective. Defining exactly why the assessment is needed may help to establish a scope and, ultimately, to communicate the results. Different goals will entail different analytical boundaries, different data sets, and inevitably guide the focus of the assessment. One objective might be to compare alternative building sites or different positions of a building on a site. Another might be to test alternative massing strategies for a building or to assess a range of material options for the structure or exterior siding. Yet another might be to understand the temporal implications of a design specification; for example, to determine, over the intended lifespan of a building, whether it's more environmentally beneficial to specify double- or triple-glazed windows. An LCA is applicable to all of these questions and its utility is optimized when the designer understands how and with what degree of specificity to deploy it.

It's often the case during the design phase of a building that cost optimization is a priority. LCA and life cycle cost analysis (LCCA) can be used to weigh up the implications of a particular cost-cutting measure for the building life cycle's environmental efficacy. The results of that clearly defined cross-comparison can then be articulated and evaluated by the members of the design team and their client. Establishing a clear goal of an assessment—whether it is architectural, social, economic, ecological—enables the LCA results to simultaneously inform and optimize the design, meet specific project goals, and potentially reduce the building's long-term environmental impacts.

The purpose of an assessment may be to meet regulatory requirements. The agencies responsible for the formulation and enforcement of building regulations in several countries are introducing mandatory LCA or carbon footprint assessments for new buildings and significant renovation projects. In such cases, those agencies with jurisdictional authority will establish both the goals and the criteria for the assessment. But these frameworks may provide only the normative minimum requirements, and a design team, the client, or the project stakeholders may choose to employ LCA for additional reasons and, potentially, to meet more stringent performance standards.

Scope Definition: What to Assess?
The scope for an LCA study should inevitably support its goals. In defining its scope, we make fundamental choices that will have a profound impact on the results as well as their usefulness as a decision-making guide and as a basis of comparing alternative scenarios.

One of the first aspects to be defined is the *object of the assessment*. This is a question of scale and scope but seeks to establish the dimensional boundaries and, to a degree, the focus and level of specificity of our analysis. A city block, one of its buildings, one of its structural bays, or even a single structural member are all legitimate objects of an assessment.

Based on this selection, we can set the *study period* for the assessment, which can range from a few decades to centuries, depending again on the goal and scope of the assessment. Most often, the study periods in building LCA range from 50 to 100 years, as the degree of uncertainty increases steeply as a function of time. We also define the LCA's *functional unit* needs which allows us to ascertain the "quantified performance of a product system for use as a reference unit" [10]. Typically, we base the functional units in a building LCA on the unit measurement of a building floor area (in square meters or feet) over a chosen study period, which produces the common functional unit for energy assessments ($kgCO_2e/m^2$). But rather than the area of an entire building, the critical measurement might be the linear dimension of a structural member over its technical service life if the structural frame of a building is the object of the assessment. A consistent functional unit is critical for the results of an assessment to comparable.

Setting the System Boundaries: What to Include?
An essential part of establishing the scope of an assessment is drawing its boundary lines and deciding what to include and what to leave out.

A building consists of thousands of components, some of which may be replaced several times during the service life of the building. Water and energy are consumed daily, in parallel to the daily generation of operational waste. Various appliances or equipment installed within the building are microcosms of the built environment, each with its own respective consumption and circulation of material and energy. The site around the building may contain other physical structures, but also vegetation, soil and water, biomes, and systems with their own behaviors, life cycles, and material flows. And no building is an island: its thermal envelope cannot define a thermodynamic system, just as the metes and bounds of a building lot cannot enclose an ecosystem. Buildings rely on a much wider flow of material and energy supply, whether from the climate and environment or, more directly, through municipal utilities and their potable water, energy, or sewage treatment infrastructure. Beyond the physical infrastructure connecting individual buildings into an interwoven built environment, buildings also host a range vectors affecting the consumption of material and energy: its occupants arrive and depart using various modes of transport, goods are delivered with different types of vehicles and handled with a range of equipment, and its waste heat—generated via urban heat island effect or directly exhausted from the building envelope—increases energy demands in surrounding buildings and infrastructure. All these forces and flows act on a building as a function of time and on a site that may witness the construction and demolition of many consecutive structures. This results in a complex network of life cycle factors and impacts that are, to varying degrees, interdependent.

We establish an analytical *system boundary* to bring conceptual order and hierarchy to these interdependencies in order to determine what is critical to include for meeting the goals of our assessment and establishing what data is extraneous. We draw these boundaries based on any number of factors—the objectives of the assessment that were either agreed upon or required, the availability of reliable information, time or funds—and we define them as a matter of convention using three frameworks: a temporal, physical, or process-related boundary.

Temporal System Boundaries

A temporal boundary defines a stage or sequence of stages of a given building or product life cycle that we choose to include in the assessment. Here, we will describe the standardized life cycle stages of a building and the temporal system boundaries that might be drawn when developing the analytical framework.

According to our international standard, the most limited carbon footprint calculation for building products includes only the production stage. As discussed earlier in the chapter, an analysis bounded in this way is usually referred to as *cradle-to-gate*, meaning that it describes the impacts associated with the product from the extraction or collection of raw material until it leaves the factory. This temporal frame established the minimum requirement for the compilation of environmental product declarations (EPDs) for building products. It's important, however, to keep in mind that, by focusing only on the production stage of a building material or product, we may miss critical aspects of its potential environmental impact that may be postponed until later stages of the life cycle. For example, a product that lacks durability may need to be replaced during the use phase of the building life cycle; alternatively, a particular material that may not be amenable to reuse at the end of a building's life will likely enter the waste stream. These later stage impacts may be "baked into" a product during the production stage but would not be exposed by a cradle-to-gate assessment.

If we add to our cradle-to-gate assessment the impacts incurred in the transport of a product from the factory to the construction site, we describe the expanded temporal system boundary as a *cradle-to-site* estimation. If we also include the construction stage, the assessment is referred to as a *cradle-to-handover* assessment. As both transportation and construction activities are to take place in temporal proximity to the processes of the production stage, we can make relatively reliable estimates of their correlated impacts and ensure any uncertainty factors remain at a moderate level.

Although it's important to understand how these different temporal system boundaries are delineated, it would be a serious oversight to neglect the primary source of carbon emissions impacts that take place during the use stage of the building life cycle: the consumption of energy during the use of the building. At a minimum, we would seek to add projected energy use to a system boundary that is described as a *cradle-to-gate with options* assessment. This boundary expands the production and construction stage assessment to include only those emissions associated with building energy consumption while avoiding other carbon-emitting activities typically considered in the use stage. This is not to suggest that the impacts from other activities that take place during the operational life of the building (sub-modules of the use-stage)—such as estimations of material and equipment-related emissions of repair work or building component replacement—should not be included, but rather that their inclusion would depend on the goals of the assessment established at the outset.

We can further extend the temporal boundaries to include all the *use stage* impacts along with all those from the production and construction phase in a *cradle-to-end-of-use* assessment. The most comprehensive quantitative boundary we can draw around the building life cycle is described as a *cradle-to-grave* assessment. This adds the final *end-of-life stage* to our analysis and provides perhaps the best estimation of overall impact, and the most systemic understanding of the relative dominance of impacts over the course of a building's life. To estimate the potential impacts based on activities and processes likely to take place decades in the future, we create scenarios that aim to address the uncertainty associated with potential shifts in building economics and construction practice and their ramifications for our building's carbon footprint. For example, uncertainty associated with changes in energy technology and its carbon intensity, the promise of new and better replacement materials, and the hope that the waste management infrastructure may become more effective in the reuse and recycling of material all represent scenarios that we should account for as we consider the potential outcomes of our design decisions.

As noted earlier, the further our temporal system boundary expands into the future, the more potentially inaccurate our predictions of the activities, their energy and material demands, and their correlated impacts become.

Physical System Boundaries

A physical system boundary defines the parts of a building and portion of its site that we wish to account for in an assessment. With a temporally defined analysis, we draw our system boundary around a particular timeframe or a sequence of processes within the building life cycle. A physical boundary, on the other hand, can be measured more readily in spatial terms, with a line that circumscribes a material component or building assembly, a piece of equipment or system, a series of site accessories, or the building property line. What we choose to include in our assessment relies heavily on robust sets of data on the elements we seek to analyze. This has a significant impact on the need for data and thus the resources needed for the assessment effort.

A typical physical system boundary (based on standard EN 15978 [11]) includes all the material and energy inputs and outputs that move across the limits of the building site, even including such temporary installations as scaffolding or construction job trailers or dumpsters. This is still a broad definition, however, so we often to confine our assessment to only the structural or mechanical elements of the building and site installations.

In theory, a physical system boundary allows us to assess potential impacts to a high degree of specificity. We could feasibly list all the bolts in all the connections in a building. Or we could anticipate the number of coats of paint required on any given surface, quantify the volume of grout used to seal a bathroom tile floor, or count the number of individual door hinges on cabinet doors or the quantity of electrical outlets. The deeper we dive into these details, the more time we would need to spend completing the assessment. But not all of this analysis is relevant for an LCA for two primary reasons. First, the increase in precision may not necessarily change in any significant way the overall results of an LCA study. Second, achieving this level of detail inevitably leads to the postponement of the LCA process until the end of the project when we expect to have all that information but when it can have no bearing on design decisions. A relevant level of detail, then, is set by an assessment of those things we can select or affect through our design choices, and that mostly reside in the design phases in which the largest material decisions are made, decisions that accrue the greatest material quantities and that have the greatest weight (physical and conceptual). These impactful decisions typically include site work, the building's structural system and enclosure, and its primary mechanical, electrical, and plumbing systems.

In many cases, however, the goal of our physically bounded calculation may be to isolate and compare embodied environmental impacts of design alternatives. If we wish to compare the potential benefits or impacts of the massing and orientation of a building, and its position on the site is to remain the same, then we exclude the site from our analysis. If we seek to understand the relative impacts of different structural framing systems and can assume that the interior surfaces and exterior cladding would be the same in either case, than we isolate the structure from all other elements. If we seek to fulfill the requirements of a regulation or funding source, then we would observe the system boundaries established in those requirements.

System Boundaries Defined by Activity or Process

The sequence of operations we attribute to the building life cycle—material extraction or harvest, manufacture, transport, construction, maintenance, repair, renovation, demolition, waste processing, and recycling—represent a set of activities or processes which inevitably branch out to correlated sequences with potential implications for assessment. The construction process requires that workers travel to the building site, a necessary condition which incurs impacts associated with their various means of transport. In theory, each worker may shower each morning before work, brew a cup of coffee or read the morning paper. We could in principle link these activities to a chain of life cycle impacts: the construction of potable water infrastructure, the agricultural operations of the commercial coffee industry, the processing of pulp and inks for printing. But each has an increasingly tenuous connection to the impacts we can justifiably ascribe to our building. And each has little significance for our calculations. Even the design process has nested within it a set of material and energy inputs and human behaviors that entail consumption and impact and, more specifically, produce a carbon footprint. Process-based system boundaries help to define which of these numerous and diverging branches of activity we need to account for in our assessment. The most typical system boundary includes only those activities and processes that unfold within the building life cycle. We'll return to process-based system boundaries later in this chapter as we examine successive production, use, and end-of-life stages, consider which of those potential offshoots of activity and process may prove inconsequential and which may have critical implications for our assessment.

Whichever system boundary we choose to draw, it's fundamental that it reflects the goal of our analysis and that we clearly define, describe, and justify it. Our failure to do so may lead us to unreliable and even biased conclusions.

Life Cycle Scenarios

Setting Scenarios

As noted previously, setting scenarios is a fundamental component of the assessment process because the nature of an LCA requires that we estimate potential resource flows and their associated impacts that will take place in the near or distant future. All scenarios are inherently uncertain, we accept that uncertainty while seeking to address it so that we may make design choices today that foster better building performance with fewer environmental impacts tomorrow.

We create scenarios to posit alternative conditions, events, and outcomes that may occur within the system boundary we have established and guide the way we calculate their potential impacts. We may derive those scenarios in response to the requirements of governing regulations, a client's brief, or existing practice standards (such as EN 15978 [11]). We should avoid overly optimistic or excessively conservative predictions for the performance of any of the components, systems, or processes that we have chosen to analyze and instead represent what we understand to be their status at the time of the assessment. If we propose to advance a new material or process that is not accounted for in the datasets we employ, then it is our responsibility to model them, as thoroughly and with as much transparency as possible, so that the analytical scenarios we set are comparable. As with all our estimates, we should clearly communicate the premises and assumptions that underlie our scenarios so that they may be understood by all those who review and seek to make decisions based on the results of our analysis.

Although our scenarios may fail to predict what actually unfolds in the future, they still serve two principal functions. First, the scenario we choose offers the building's end-user a baseline to plan maintenance strategies and optimize its actual performance. Second, establishing scenarios helps us to identify and consider the relative ramifications and attributes of alternative solutions. This might include the comparative service life of a

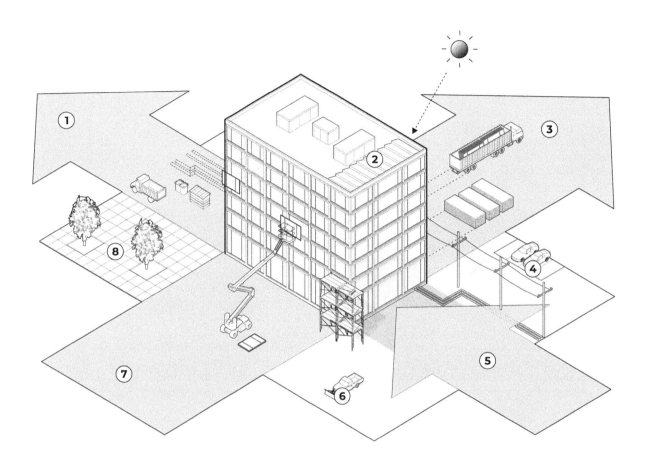

(1) MUNICIPAL WASTE

REUSE OF BUILDING PRODUCTS
AND RECYCLING OF MATERIALS
MAY ALSO AVOID EMISSIONS
FROM WASTE MANAGEMENT
AND FROM NEXT BUILDING´S
LIFE CYCLE.

(2) ON SITE ENERGY

RENEWABLE ENERGY
GENERATED ON SITE
SUBSTITUTES GRID ENERGY
AND AVOIDS EMISSIONS.

**(3) CONSTRUCTION AND
DEMOLITION WASTE**

WASTE TREATMENT CAUSES
EMISSIONS. THE REUSE OR
RECYCLING OF PRODUCTS
MAY AVOID EMISSIONS.

(4) NOT INCLUDED

TRANSPORTATION OF BUILDING
INHABITANTS TO AND FROM THE
BUILDING IS NOT INCLUDED IN
STANDARD LCA.

(5) ENERGY FROM GRID

PRODUCTION OF ENERGY,
FUELS AND CLEAN WATER, AS
WELL AS THE MAINTENANCE
OF GRID INFRASTRUCTURE, IN
MOST CASES GENERATE CO_2
EMISSIONS OFF SITE.

(6) MAINTENANCE

ENERGY AND MATERIALS
USED FOR BUILDING
MAINTENANCE CAUSE
EMISSIONS.

**(7) REPAIR AND
REPLACEMENT**

PRODUCTION AND ASSEMBLY
OF REPLACED CONSTRUCTION
MATERIALS CAUSE EMISSIONS.
BIO-BASED MATERIALS STORE
CARBON. MOST MACHINES
AND VEHICLES USED FOR
REPAIRS GENERATE EMISSIONS.

(8) SEQUESTERED CARBON

TREES, VEGETATION, SOIL,
AND CEMENT-BASED
SURFACES ABSORB CARBON
FROM THE ATMOSPHERE.

material assembly, the cycles and complexity of its replacement or refurbishment, the feasibility of its disassembly and reuse of its components, and the associated environmental costs of its life cycle. It may seem challenging to develop scenarios for the actual fate of those components, especially considering the near impossibility of accurately predicting the normative, economic, or technological constraints that might apply at the end of its service life and that factor heavily in the ultimate outcome. Although we cannot validate the accuracy of our scenarios during the assessment phase, our informed predictions of potential consequences should play a role in the choices we make and the justifications we provide for them.

The scenarios we set help to either expose or determine *life cycle dominance*, the stage of the building life cycle in which a building will incur the predominant share of its environmental impacts. We may choose to establish the relative dominance of distinct stages as a goal of the design process. We might aim, for example, to reduce impacts during the *use stage* by increasing the thermal performance of the building envelope through the selection of materials and assemblies with higher *production stage* emissions and more potential at generating waste at the end of the life cycle. The concept of life cycle dominance is often used as a metric for cost-planning across the building's service life (its LCCA) in which the expenses incurred are balanced against the predicted ebbs and flows of revenue. As discussed earlier, the relative dominance of life cycle stages will play a critical role as we develop strategies to combat climate change within a narrowing time-frame for effective action.

To establish benchmarks and performance standards across the building lifespan—and to understand their implications for its overall carbon footprint—we need to set scenarios that acknowledge the potential shifts in the predominance of carbon emissions at each stage. It is considerably easier to predict and manage emissions that will occur in the more immediate future and we do so most effectively through our careful selection of low-impact construction materials and a building site with the least ecological sensitivity, one that requires the least amount of disturbance and is best suited to the programmatic demands of the project. If we focus our efforts on making meaningful reductions in our building's operational emissions, we can only assume the behavior of its end users and their compliance with our specified operations and maintenance plan. As the operational stage is so dependent on changes in the uses, occupancies, or ownership of a building, we have little control over the potential cycles of renovation and none over the management of the building's demolition or disassembly. But design choices that make that operational management more clearly legible, logistically simpler, and economically efficient may significantly improve the likelihood that building materials and components will be reused in future buildings or recycled as a new raw material for future manufactured products. In considering our agency as designers to affect specific outcomes of the building life cycle, it is clear that the more temporally remote the environmental benefits are from the planning process, the greater the uncertainty that those benefits will—or can—be achieved.

Uncertainties

Potential uncertainties bear heavily on the way we should develop and weigh up assessment scenarios with implications for a high degree of variability in our analytical results.

For example, if we assume that the consumption of energy will remain consistent throughout the use phase of the building and that the sources of that energy will also remain unchanged, then we might also assume that operational energy use will dominate life cycle greenhouse gas emissions. In response to that assessment, we might very well focus our design efforts on reducing that stage of energy consumption through the specification of robust building insulation systems and demanding airtightness standards. However, through both

FIGURE 2.4 A BUILDING'S ENERGY AND MATERIAL FLOWS. *SOURCE:* AUTHORS

the natural evolution of the renewable energy industry and the devolution of its fossil fuel counterpart, or through the national and regional regulatory restrictions that encourage or mandate decarbonization of their energy infrastructure, those assumptions—and the scenarios that arise from them—may become obsolete within the operational life of a building. More importantly, the side effects of having implemented more energy- or emission-intensive material systems may never achieve their intended benefits, given their contributions to a significantly increased carbon emissions spike at the beginning of the building life cycle.

As a part of international agreements that seek to mitigate anthropogenic climate change, several countries have developed alternative scenarios that account for potential future changes to national energy policy. These policy scenarios (that may affect—but should not be confused with—the LCA scenarios we've previously described) are typically divided into two classes: "*With Existing Measures*" (WEM) and "*With Additional Measures*" (WAM). The former predicts how emissions will evolve, based on the policies that have already been implemented and the latter shows the need for new policies that are necessary for meeting international climate agreements—and, at the moment, the policies in place do not go far enough to achieve the goal of keeping global warming below a 2-degree Celsius increase [12]. Similarly, we should recognize the potential implications of the implementation of those policies on the LCA scenarios we consider and their respective attribution of dominance to different life cycle phases.

Sensitivity Analysis

Like the uncertainty inherent in the process of prediction, the sensitivity of a building's cumulative carbon footprint to the scenarios we develop and the system boundaries we draw are critical considerations in the assessment process. Each has significant implications for the depth and intensity of analysis and resources (data, time, and money) needed to carry them out.

Sensitivity analysis is the process by which we consider the parameters of a calculation and their relative significance for our results. This type of analysis is important, especially in cradle-to-grave calculations, due to the high degree of uncertainty of the assumptions we are forced to make.

For example, a scenario that describes the recycling of timber reclaimed from a building may be sensitive to the transportation distance of timber from the demolition site to the recycling location. Key factors that may define the feasibility of recycling as a low carbon strategy include the distance from the demolition site to the recycling location, the carbon intensity of fuel consumed in transport, the moisture content of the reclaimed timber, or the energy used at the recycling location. A sensitivity analysis would require that we identify these different processes and activities that may be factors and ascertain their relative magnitude and determine whether changing those parameters would change the results significantly.

It is valuable to report the results of any sensitivity analysis we conduct along with the findings of the study. They may contain dispositive information for a client or a builder as they consider different material sources, means and methods of construction, maintenance, and repair.

Cut-Off Rules

To ease the compilation of data and reduce the intensity of our LCA, we can use cut-off rules to eliminate certain marginal parts of a process or activity or a potential branch of a bounded system from our required calculations. Such rules are sometimes referred to as *truncation criteria*. The production stage emissions of a piece of door hardware or a volume of paint left unused during the recoating of a ceiling or the recycling energy required to recycle the nails used to frame a floor structure, are all candidates for elimination from our assessment. In theory, we could zoom into many details of the building, but gain only marginally relevant information for the purpose of the LCA.

FIGURE 2.5 STAGES OF THE PRODUCTION PROCESS OF DIFFERENT BUILDING PRODUCTS. *SOURCE:* AUTHORS

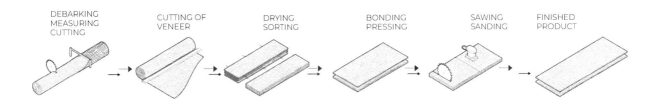

DEBARKING MEASURING CUTTING → CUTTING OF VENEER → DRYING SORTING → BONDING PRESSING → SAWING SANDING → FINISHED PRODUCT

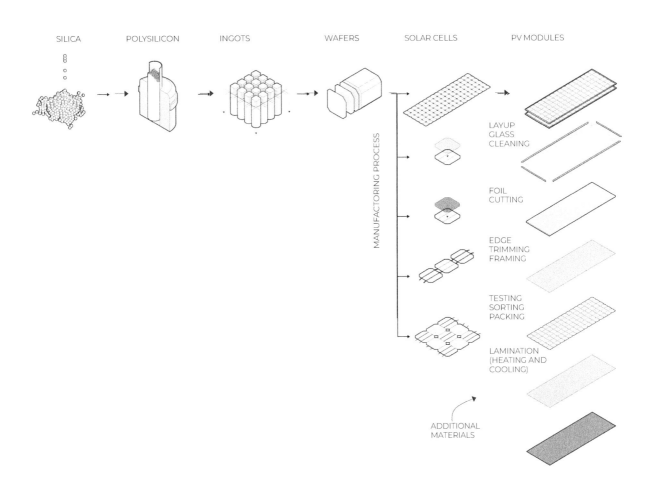

SILICA → POLYSILICON → INGOTS → WAFERS → SOLAR CELLS → PV MODULES

MANUFACTORING PROCESS

LAYUP GLASS CLEANING

FOIL CUTTING

EDGE TRIMMING FRAMING

TESTING SORTING PACKING

LAMINATION (HEATING AND COOLING)

ADDITIONAL MATERIALS

Although LCA standards often define the cut-off threshold of a given impact as a percentage of the overall impact calculation (standard EN 15804 allows for a cut-off of an input or output that accounts for less than 1% of the overall mass or primary energy usage), in practice, it's difficult to eliminate items from the analysis based on their relative significance without first calculating it. We need therefore to rely, at least to some degree, on our intuition, our experience, and based on case-by-case considerations. In a small building, the fasteners may not inflect our calculation but in a larger building with a more complex structural system that demands more intensive and frequent connections, the measurement of impacts associated with the forging of metal fasteners may prove significant. As with all the assumptions and precepts of our assessment, our cut-off criteria should be included in the description of the goal, scope, and methodology of the assessment.

THE PRODUCTION STAGE

Materials Make a Difference

The production stage of the building life cycle includes all the material, energy, and processes entailed in the manufacture of a building product, such as a length of steel W-section, a coil of insulated copper wire, or a sheet of plywood. The extraction of the necessary raw materials and their handling and transport to a manufacturing facility and all the processes encompassed in the product manufacture belong to this phase. These processes mostly result in carbon emissions except, in the case of a biogenic building material like wood, we must also consider the capacity of material to store, rather than emit carbon. We'll discuss this prospect in later sections of this chapter and book.

For example, the production of wooden siding entails a specific set of processes that include all of those associated with logging, the transport of logs to a sawmill where they're sawn into rough boards,

dried (most often in a kiln), planed, and milled into their final profile, and, then, packaged and stored until purchased by a builder. Throughout that sequence, there are energy inputs and waste residues that result from each step. For other material products the process can be much more complicated and energy-intensive. For instance, the production phase of a solar panel includes the extraction of several raw materials that serve as ingredients for the manufacture of semi-conductors (e.g. ore, silicon, oil, chemicals, and rubber), and the sintering of a photovoltaic cell onto a substrate (e.g. glass, material) and finally the assembling of the final merchantable product, the solar panel, which is then carefully wrapped in protective layers of plastic and cardboard packaging, for delivery to distributor's warehouse or construction site. In such a cascading production process, there are also interim steps that resemble microcosmic versions of the entire production stage, entailing the transport, handling, packaging, and storage of each subset of materials. All of these contribute to the overall emissions profile and carbon footprint of a given product.

Because building products are manufactured in often distinct locations, each drawing on a mix of energy types and sources with different efficiencies, the resulting carbon emissions embodied in the manufacturing process will also differ, even among products of equivalent properties of shape, dimension, weight, and performance. Therefore, we need to understand where potential differences in production stage emissions may arise and how we might best mitigate impacts through the design process: the selection, specification, and procurement of all the products we propose to use.

In examining the individual flows of material and their attendant flows of carbon through the course of a building life cycle, we see that the production stage introduces the majority of all those materials that will be applied, maintained, repaired, replaced, or removed in all other stages of the that life

FIGURE 2.6 COMPONENTS AND MATERIALS OF A BUILDING. *SOURCE:* AUTHORS

BUILDING

COMPONENT

MATERIAL

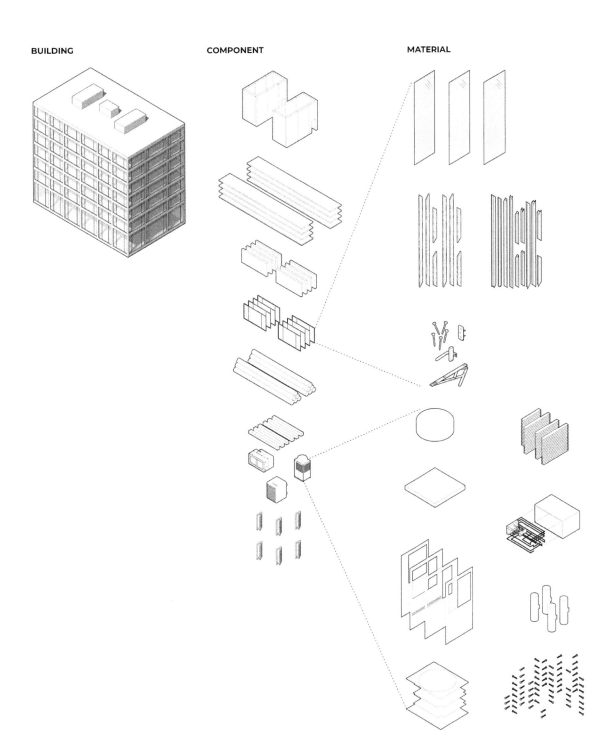

cycle. That initial stage can be said, then, to bring material to the "system" of a building in a process that itself consumes energy and generates emissions and waste. Of course, at the end of their service life, when we remove them from the building system for the purpose of replacement or demolition, those materials do not disappear. And though their utility and quality are most likely degraded, their environmental significance may actually increase. Their obsolescence, in the framework of our current linear construction economy and according to the conventions of conventional life cycle assessment, assigns them the status of "waste" with its own set of environmental impacts. How we choose to reconsider and seek to endow that so-called waste material with new-found value will have critical implications for our transition to a circular economy—we'll discuss this further in subsequent chapters of this book. What is significant for our discussion of the production stage, is that the likelihood that that material will be reused or recycled rather than landfilled at the end of its service life, is often "baked into" the earliest processes of its manufacture. This form of "systems thinking" gives real agency to the design team, allowing them to select not only materials with the lowest embodied emissions but also ones that are optimized at the outset for a succession of useful life cycles.

Calculating the Carbon Flows in the Production Phase

The calculation of carbon flows in the production of building material is mathematically quite simple. To estimate their emissions, we list all building materials that comprise our building and we multiply them by the CO_2e emission factor assigned to the unit of measure of each material. These units may be given in weight, area, length, volume, or number, depending on the product.

If we seek to estimate the carbon that is *stored* in a bio-based material, we simply multiply the dry weight of the material with their corresponding biogenic carbon factor, which describes as a percentage of that weight the amount of carbon that exists in that material. Obviously, a material's capacity to store carbon has significant implications for the reduction of a building's carbon footprint and may serve as an important counterweight in the mitigation of climate change caused by anthropogenic greenhouse gas emissions, a topic we'll discuss in subsequent chapters. But for the sake of the clarity of our assessment, it's important that we separate the emissions and storages in order to distinguish the debits and credits in our carbon account.

We can quantify those materials we assign during each successive stage of the design process with increasing accuracy as detail develops. It's possible to retrieve the information from basic orthographic or paraline drawings, but those take-offs, especially as design detail develops, can be time-consuming. As designs become more refined, building information models (BIM) can be extremely helpful, accompanied as they typically are by quite agile software plug-ins that support an iterative LCA process. If a BIM is not available, another option is to use the same quantity take-offs required for building cost estimates. We can also record and sum up the results of the calculations we've described using a spreadsheet, which maximizes the transparency the LCA and its supporting detail and various scenarios. Regardless of the means we choose to measure and organize this information, we need to first meet certain simple preconditions so that we can begin to effectively calculate all material-related carbon emissions. These preconditions include the assembly of an inventory of materials and the collection of data that quantify the associated emissions and storages or potential sinks of carbon.

Inventory of Materials

Bill of Quantities

Although the calculations we've described are not complicated, the exhaustiveness of the task lies in the number of individual materials found in even a relatively simple building. Compiling a list of building products, known as a bill of quantities (BoQ), is one of the prerequisites for a carbon footprint calculation and it can amount to thousands of lines in a spreadsheet. As the products are further broken down into their respective bills of materials (BoM), the number of entries increases. Furthermore, the task of identifying the emission factors that correctly correspond to each of the specified materials can be an additional time sink requiring a notable attention to detail. And the fact that the results gleaned from carbon calculations would be most valuable if we were to apply them in real time to the alternative schemes we consider in the earliest phases of design and again, repeatedly, throughout what is typically an iterative process with increasingly nested layers of information and detail, makes such calculations for even a few design alternatives feel like an almost unbearable burden within the normal scope and pace of professional building design practice.

The compilation of a BoQ is not an unfamiliar step in design, just one that is typically taken during the cost estimation phase after many of the decisions that most affect a building's carbon footprint have already been made, cemented in layers of technical detail and documented in extensive drawings and specifications. At this point, the substitution, for example, of a structural system with lower embodied emissions would prove extremely challenging and time-consuming. The methodological benefits of access to a tool like BIM are therefore obvious, providing the necessary data and relevant levels of quantification for iterative carbon footprinting throughout the design process. But in the earliest phases, when a design is still nascent and unformed, it's possible to get a rough sense of a building's potential carbon footprint using design intuition that is reinforced by our familiarity with the stages of the building life cycle, its necessary inputs and inevitable sources of emissions and waste. With the help of statistical data drawn from buildings of similar type and size, and collected by some pioneering companies and forward-thinking governments, it's possible to set benchmarks for our building's material impacts, and during the process of its design development to verify that we've met those goals.

For the purpose of calculation, we need to specify the quantity of each building material that comprises the building system. A glance at a conventional BoQ or BoM will show some materials listed by weight, some by volume or area and others by varying units of measure. These units need to be paired with corresponding values that describe their carbon emissions and carbon storages. Such values may be given per weight, length, area, volume or simply number of products, depending on how the producer or data provider has chosen to present it. If no other reference values are given, then the dry weight of each material is the foundation for all LCA calculations.

In order to translate those non-weight-based units into the exact weight of the material, or to determine the weight of a material not listed in the conventional inventory, we need to check the technical specifications of its producer or consult tables of material weights and measures provided by manufacturers' organizations. Many LCA tools and BIM applications already include the weights of products, but if a number of materials comprise a commercial assembly or piece of equipment, quantifying the weight of each material component may be time intensive, if at all necessary.

Accuracy of Estimations in the Early Design Phases

In most cases, the initial sketches of a building may only imply materiality or mechanical function. Prior to the design's evolution and subsequent to that, the consultation of a structural or environmental systems engineer, an architect's conception of a building remains in the realm of the experiential, of massing, volume, and spatial configuration. At this early stage, a design team tracks the potential emission of carbon by availing themselves of average area or volume-based values retrieved from statistical databases or precedent calculations of similar projects. As the design develops materiality in its structure and surfaces, correspondingly detailed and relevant material quantifications become more available.

Ideally, if there were a set of emissions factors for a range of primary building types, spatial definitions, and structural systems, we might apply those factors and adapt them to the size and initial material prescriptions of our building in its earliest phases of conception and design. Drawn from existing as-built calculations and reverse-engineered to fill the inevitable gaps in accurate information, these factors would shed light on the way in which emissions would potentially accumulate in alternative design scenarios and aid in the establishment of performance benchmarks and targets. As we write these words, numerous software developers and their regional and national sponsors are already in the process of gathering the base information and engineering its applicability to the preliminary designs of buildings ranging in type, system and assembly configuration, and size.

Data for Material-Related Emissions

Emission and Storage Factors for Materials

From the standpoint of climate change, there are several harmful greenhouse gases other than CO_2 with the capacity, in high concentrations, to warm the atmosphere. Methane (CH_4), chlorofluorocarbons, and nitrous oxide (N_2O) are much stronger though less atmospherically durable greenhouse gases than CO_2. To facilitate impact calculation, existing protocols assess the global warming potential (GWP) of various greenhouse gases and translate their impacts into the equivalent impacts of CO_2. The resulting emissions factor is described as a carbon dioxide equivalent (CO_2e) and consolidates the warming potential of the greenhouse gases that are the constituents of emissions arising from the production of a given material.

We can retrieve general data on the sources and storages of CO_2e emissions from two alternative sources: general databases or product-specific environmental product declarations (EPDs).

Material-related data should be as recent as possible and should "reflect the physical reality" (as EN 15978 [11] puts it) of the product or product group we intend to implement in our building. We should utilize the information provided by databases or standardized EPDs that are no older than five years. Although this requirement may seem strict and challenging given the current availability of EPDs, the outlook is increasingly bright with respect to product information: the practice of providing EPDs is taking hold within the manufacturing sector.

Databases

Existing and emerging databases make life cycle assessment more practical and easier to implement. They consist of general environmental emission factors of hundreds of building materials and, in some cases, generic products. We can find these emission factors from any number of individual product LCAs or base them on EPDs.

There are several commercial and a few open-source databases available. Unfortunately, due to varying compilation methods and the geographical specificity with which their background studies were conducted, the emission and storage factors in different databases may vary. As a result, estimates of carbon flows we generate from those different sources for the same quantity of building material will inevitably vary as well. It is critical therefore to recognize that the databases we choose to use and the quality of their data will be significant criteria when comparing LCAs. This is especially the case when we use BIM-integrated assessment tools, so we should make sure that the datasets pertain to the region in which our building will be located. Some software also offers correction factors based on the mix of energy sources for a given region so that general data from the USA or the EU is adjusted appropriately for an assessment of a project, if appropriate local data are not available.

Databases describe the average emissions of a typical product. The actual emissions of a product may differ from product-specific environmental information. It is good practice to use databases in the early phases of design, but as we begin to identify the individual products that comprise an assembly or system, it is also important that we check our initial assumptions and the resulting calculations against the more precise information that producers may provide.

Environmental Product Declarations

Product-specific environmental information compiled by a manufacturer (and verified through a process of third-party review) is called an environmental product declaration (EPD). The compilation process is governed typically by international standard ISO 14025 [13] or regional standards (e.g. EN 15804 in the EU [14]). There are two main types of EPD: an average EPD for a product group or a specific EPD for an individual product.

We would typically use a product-group EPD to understand the average environmental impacts of a product that is customized for a specific application, such as a window configuration, door lay-up, or stair assembly windows, due to the impracticality of issuing an EPD for every project-specific configuration of a product. Group EPDs are also often issued jointly by a group of manufacturers who each lack the resources or capacity to make their own individual EPDs. Typically, a manufacturer considering the use of EPDs or a consortium of smaller manufacturers that produce similar products, such as log homes, for example, will take part in issuing a group EPD. Product-specific EPDs are more typical for highly standardized and mass-produced building components, such as brick, glulam beams, or insulation material.

Although an EPD is much more accurate in its information than what a database can provide, it still can only describe the emissions of an average product in an average production year. Annual variations inevitably affect the actual environmental impacts of the production stage. These variations might be driven by marginal changes in the energy mix that a factory uses, for instance, by purchasing a larger share of electricity with different emissions per kWh from a neighboring country during winter months. Another variable might be a change in transport distances traveled, due to the reduced availability of certain ingredients required in the manufacturing process or changes to the make-up of those ingredients, such as the glue used to laminate CLT panels or the additives for cement of a concrete panel. These adjustments may occasionally prove significant, so an EPD is usually valid for a period of only five years. After that, it's considered out of date and needs to be revised to reflect the changes to its process of production.

Reducing the Carbon Footprint in the Production Stage

We can most assuredly minimize emissions associated with the production stage through the materials we specify and the efficiency with which we deploy them. Our material selection has critical ramifications for the carbon footprint of our building. As we consider alternatives for the building's primary structure or its cladding, we face a series of options, all of which may fulfill the same functional requirements but each with different production stage impacts and possibly necessitating different material quantities. (It is also important to keep in mind that those material selections will have consequential impacts in later life cycle stages, such as their durability with respect to potential replacement requirements during the use stage, or their amenability to reuse or recycling at the end of a building's service life.) After we've selected the material system we want to use, we should compare the relative carbon footprint of comparative products within the same product group. Two similar façade bricks, for example, may incorporate raw materials from different source sites with differing extraction impacts, may have been manufactured in different factories that utilize different energy mixes, or may entail different transport distances and their correlated impacts.

Info box 2.2

Calculating Material-Related Impacts

Practical Examples

Let´s assume that our material list looks something like this:

- 728 tonnes of ready-mix concrete
- 693 tonnes of gravel
- 267 tonnes of cross-laminated timber
- 109 tonnes of gypsum boards

To calculate the emissions, we simply log the quantity of each item into our LCA tool, and it performs calculation based on material- or product-specific emission factors:

Material	Weight (kg)	Emission factor (kgCO$_2$e/kg)	Emissions (kgCO$_2$e)
Ready-mix concrete C30/37	728,000	0.0932	67,849
Gravel	693, 000	0.0065	4,504
Cross-laminated timber	267, 000	0.2	53,400
Gypsum boards	109, 000	0.25	27,250

(Note that the numbers and factors in this example are only for demonstration purposes.)

Most tools include conversion factors between typically used units, so regardless of whether we fill in the data by weight or volume or even area for some products, the calculation is the same.

Bio-based products also have carbon stored in them. The calculation of this amount of stored carbon follows similar principles:

Material	Volume (m^3)	Carbon content per unit (kgCO$_2$e/m^3)	Carbon storage (kgCO$_2$e)
Cross-laminated timber	580	687.0	398,460

Typically included in production phase LCA:

- Raw material extraction
- Transportation to factory
- Production process
- Packaging
- Processing of production waste

Typically excluded from production phase LCA:

- Manufacturing of machines for the production
- Transportation of labor to the factories
- Value chains of secondary products from the production
- Cultivation processes for vegetation planted on the site

We develop material efficiencies at a number of scales in our building. At the building or room scale, we can optimize material using basic surface area-to-volume calculations or comparing the relative area of a material used to the program area to which we apply it. We can solve for identically programmed rooms or spaces with different spatial geometries, but one solution may consume more or less material than another.

At the product scale, we can optimize our material consumption by calibrating our space dimensions to the unit dimensions of the selected material (a sheet of plywood, a cement masonry block, the geometry of a glazing panel), so that we minimize waste. The architectural form of our building is directly linked to the type and quantity of material we consume and thus to their corresponding manufacturing emissions.

The specification and deployment of building material give the designer the most agency in limiting the accumulation of GHG emissions during the production stage. In the early design phases, when we choose the class of material—wood, metal, cement, ceramic, plastic—and the geometries of the building's architecture, our decisions have significant ramifications for the size of its carbon footprint. As the design proceeds to more developed technical phases, our choice of the lowest carbon option within a product or material class represents another significant point of inflection. In the early phases of design, databases are practical sources of information; in the later phases, environmental product declarations offer more precise and reliable bases for comparison and may provide us the greatest opportunity to curtail our production stage emissions.

THE CONSTRUCTION STAGE

From Material Components and Products to the Building System

The calculation of construction phase emissions includes all those associated with the transport of materials from the factory to the building site and all the operations, along with the energy that fuels them, that take place on site during construction. The contribution of the construction stage to a building's carbon footprint is almost entirely comprised of emissions as there are practically no opportunities to store additional carbon though the construction process.

As with the ingredients entailed in product manufacture during the production stage, the material a designer selects may be sourced during construction from different suppliers in different locations, each with varying transport impacts. Since the specific selection of materials, means, and methods is often outside the remit of the building designer, it is important that low carbon objectives of the project are articulated to the members of the construction team responsible for material procurement. Longer transport distances consume more fuel but the construction and material trades do not yet account typically for such externalities as environmental impact. However, those impacts may very well be reflected in the cost of a material or product and that can become a synergistic criterion in the ultimate selection of a product by a builder.

During the construction process, we use fuels and ancillary products (such as scaffolding and formwork, water and electricity, packaging and protective barriers) to transform material products into a building. Depending on its degree of prefabrication, that process may be affected by weather conditions, site access, and the availability of sufficient working space. If we hope to realize the circular economic priorities of reducing waste and extending the useful lifespan of a material for as long as possible, then the care in the execution of the construction process and all the factors that bear on it must be critical considerations for the technical development of the design and especially for the planning of the means and methods of construction. The environmental benefits of even the most carefully manufactured materials with the lowest embodied emissions may be offset by a poorly managed construction process and their technical service life shortened with improper handling and installation. Again, these processes

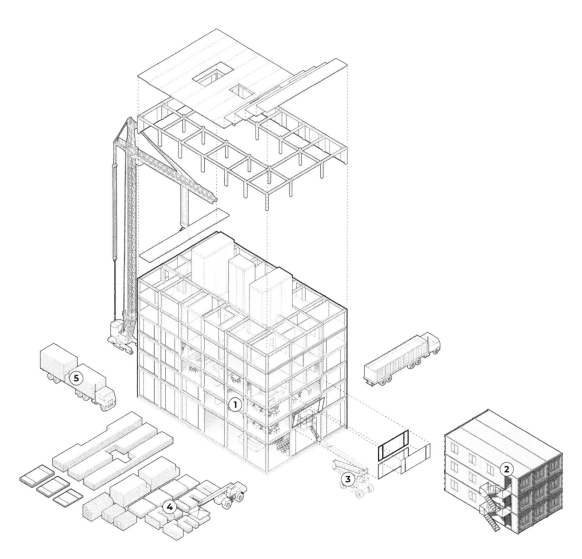

1 ENERGY FOR THE CONSTRUCTION SITE

Heating, drying, lighting, and ventilation require energy. This depends on technology, degree of prefabrication and construction season.

2 TEMPORARY FACILITIES

On-site spaces installed to support construction consume energy and electricity. Furthermore, their transportation to and from the site consumes fuel.

3 MACHINERY

Equipment and machinery consume energy, but also oils, coolants, and other ancillary products. This consumption depends on the construction technology and degree of prefabrication.

4 MATERIAL EFFICIENCY

The building site accumulates left-over materials, construction waste and packaging waste. Sorting these potential waste streams is essential for maintaining their reuse or recycling potential.

5 TRANSPORTATION

The movement of building materials, waste, and machinery to the site requires separate estimation (see modules A4 and C2).

may lie beyond the scope of the design process, but we should certainly consider the logistics and schedule of construction and component assembly or the capacity and accessibility of a site when weighing up many of the design decisions we are required to make. Ultimately, the calculation of carbon flows during product transport and handling and all the activities that take place during the construction stage can only help to shed light on the number and range of individual processes required, and help us recognize impacts that we may incur in construction and seek to mitigate them wherever we can.

Transport

Estimating Distances

If we are able to ascertain the specific products that we'll use in the construction of our building, we can determine the exact transport distances they will travel and use them in our assessment calculations. It's usually the case, however, that such information is only available for a few specific products. For all others, we resort to using average distances in our impact estimates. Because emissions from the transport of building materials or equipment represent a relatively small percentage of the impacts incurred during the building life cycle, the standard assumptions for travel distance and modes of transport embedded in most assessment software are practical means to quantify those impacts.

An easy way to estimate the distance traveled by a given material or product is to locate the facility in which it was manufactured and use an average distance in the calculation. We should remember to calculate the emissions associated with travel to and from the factory. In reality, the transport of material from the factory to the site unfolds in several stages and along the way a product may be stored in a warehouse before it is distributed to the building site. If we were to be absolutely precise in capturing all the potential emissions associated with material transport, we would, in theory, allocate all the energy used in that warehouse for lighting, heating or cooling to that transport phase. In practice, however, such estimates are difficult to attribute to a given volume of material with any certainty and may be subject to the cut-off rules we discussed earlier in this chapter.

Selecting the Modes of Transport

We use different modes of transport to move building materials from the factory to the site, each employing different vehicle types that use different fuels with potentially different emissions. If the building site is located in proximity to a railroad or a harbor, then we might legitimately assume that some significant portion of the transport will be by rail or marine vessel. That assumption of a particular transport mode should be based on representative examples from practice.

The means of transport and in some cases the specific route taken will significantly affect the emissions we incur. Transport by truck, train, ship, or plane will consume considerably different quantities of fuel in transporting the identical cargo and their relative emissions result from the type and rate of consumption of fuel per weight of the material to be transported. Each mode of transport has an established average rate of fuel consumption which we can retrieve from national datasets or from the transport contractor's average data for their vehicles or vessels.

In addition, especially in the case of transport by road and highway by truck, the profile of the route will also influence transport emissions. The same distance covered with the same load over either flat or hilly terrain will entail different amounts of fuel consumption and carbon emissions. If we seek to source materials locally, it is incumbent upon us to differentiate, for example, between the 500 miles of transport travel across the Rocky Mountains and the same distance covered across the Great Plains and to acknowledge those differences in our estimates and subsequent material choices. The percentage of a transport vehicle's load will also affect the

FIGURE 2.7 THE CONSTRUCTION STAGE. *SOURCE:* AUTHORS

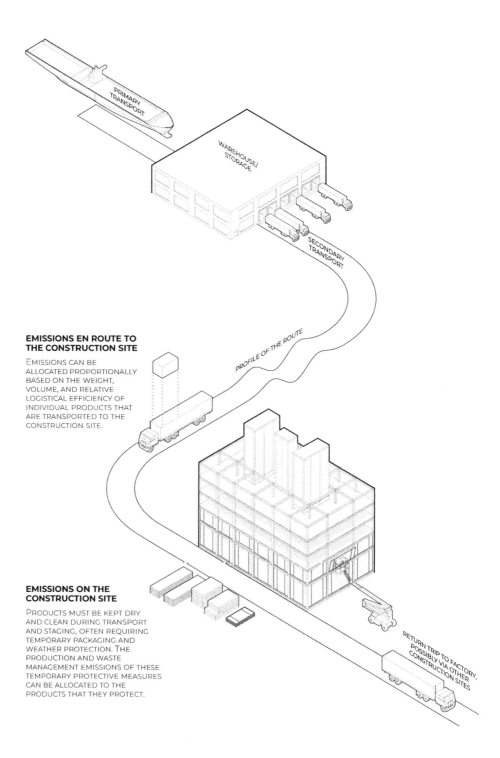

PRIMARY TRANSPORT

WAREHOUSE/ STORAGE

SECONDARY TRANSPORT

PROFILE OF THE ROUTE

EMISSIONS EN ROUTE TO THE CONSTRUCTION SITE

EMISSIONS CAN BE ALLOCATED PROPORTIONALLY BASED ON THE WEIGHT, VOLUME, AND RELATIVE LOGISTICAL EFFICIENCY OF INDIVIDUAL PRODUCTS THAT ARE TRANSPORTED TO THE CONSTRUCTION SITE.

EMISSIONS ON THE CONSTRUCTION SITE

PRODUCTS MUST BE KEPT DRY AND CLEAN DURING TRANSPORT AND STAGING, OFTEN REQUIRING TEMPORARY PACKAGING AND WEATHER PROTECTION. THE PRODUCTION AND WASTE MANAGEMENT EMISSIONS OF THESE TEMPORARY PROTECTIVE MEASURES CAN BE ALLOCATED TO THE PRODUCTS THAT THEY PROTECT.

RETURN TRIP TO FACTORY, POSSIBLY VIA OTHER CONSTRUCTION SITES

emissions and we would attribute those influences to the transport process. Because of the potential complexity of these factors, it is typical in the calculation process to use general distance- and load- based fuel consumption data. It's fairly certain what types of fuel will be used by different transport modes for at least the proximate future in our building life cycle.

Info box 2.3

Calculating the Impacts of Transportation

In practice, the assessment of transport is often done in an LCA tool at the same time when we log in the material data. We can either rely on the preset values for transport-related emissions or replace them with more exact values as follows:

1. **Identify the heaviest materials** based on the inventory of materials and manually update their transport data in the LCA tool. For example:
   - 728 tonnes of concrete
   - 693 tonnes of gravel
   - 267 tonnes of cross-laminated timber
   - 109 tonnes of gypsum boards

2. **Locate the factories that produce them.** Check distances between the site and the factory from a map application. For example: ready-mix concrete can be purchased from three locations near the site. Distances for these are 52,121, and 325 km, from which the average is 166 km. We will replace the default distance value of the LCA tool with this more accurate number.

3. **Select the vehicle type.** Most LCA tools include a list of typical vehicles. For ready-mix concrete, a concrete mixer truck could be used. If you want to be very precise, you can also include the fill rate of the truck, if the load is very small and would not take the full capacity. For CLT, the typical vehicle could be a trailer combi, and again we can adjust the fill rate of the load. Since it is often difficult to know the fill dates in advance, we can make a conservative assumption that the entire transport is for our project only and calculate the emissions accordingly.

4. **Log in the data into the LCA tool**

As a result, the calculation for the transport in the LCA could follow this example:

Material	Weight (tn)	Distance (km)	Emissions
Cross-laminated timber	267	166	267 tn * 166 km = 44,322 tkm 44,322 tkm * 1,207 g/tkm = 53,496 kgCO$_2$e

Typically included in transport in building LCA:
- Transport of products and materials from a factory to warehouses and building site
- Fuel consumption and associated emissions

Typically excluded from transport in building LCA:
- Production of vehicles
- Maintenance, lubricants, oils, and spare parts for vehicles
- Construction and maintenance of road and other transport infrastructure

FIGURE 2.8 TRANSPORTATION IMPACTS.
Source: AUTHORS

Construction Method

In an orthodox interpretation of international LCA standards, we would consider prefabrication to be part of the production stage. This makes sense when considering the historical evolution of window construction. What might have taken place a century ago, when a carpenter assembled an operable window on site from different sash and muntin profiles, glass sheet, and putty, is now entirely premanufactured by a product supplier and shipped to the site for installation. In the same way, as large component and even whole building prefabrication techniques gain sophistication and broader application, the extent and degree of prefabrication may become increasingly comprehensive and significant and fairly attributed to the construction stage of the building life cycle. In this way, if we seek to compare an on-site construction alternative to a prefabricated modular (volumetric) process or flat-packed system of manufacture and assembly, it's appropriate and relevant that system manufacture be compared as part of the construction stage.

Emissions from prefabrication arise mostly from the energy consumed at the module or component manufacturing facility, which includes all the energy used in the operation of the equipment and in the lighting, heating, and/or cooling of the facility itself. We should include all of these associated carbon emissions in our calculations, and we can calculate those emissions based on the amount and of type energy used and its associated greenhouse gas emission factor.

We can make a fair estimate of the sum of energy consumed in the manufacture of a prefabricated module or building component by simply by dividing a manufacturing facility's monthly energy consumption by the number of premanufactured units produced within the same timeframe. If that information is not available, then we can roughly allocate an amount of energy consumed per weight of manufactured component during our set timeframe. Such a simplification comes, of course, with embedded uncertainty, and we should report the method of calculation and that associated uncertainty along the findings of the study.

On-site Work and Assembly

The main source of construction site emissions is found in the energy consumed there during the building process. These emissions are usually relatively low (less than 10%) of the emissions incurred over the life of a building. Obtaining accurate information on the rates of energy consumption and the types of fuel used on the building site constitutes a labor-intensive and therefore challenging task. For this reason, as a short cut, we often calculate the emissions from construction activities using typical values based, for example, on the floor area of the building. In theory, the disturbance of existing soils during the excavations may create emissions, as the process may affect the decomposition rate of the organic carbon stored in site soils. But such contributions to a building's carbon footprint, while critical to acknowledge and understand from a conceptual standpoint, are not typically considered in building LCAs.

Energy is consumed on the building site for the operation of power tools, equipment, and machinery, for the lighting and heating of semi-finished workspaces, and for temporary facilities such as construction trailers, and their estimates inevitably depend on the size of the project and its workforce. It's typical that a builder or a client will monitor the amount of electricity used on site over a period that spans from construction ground-breaking to building handover. The consumption of electricity during this period is usually metered and therefore easily quantified and we can readily calculate the greenhouse gas emissions associated with that consumption or predict it based on similar precedents. We can retrieve values for the production emissions associated with electrical energy supply from the local electrical utility.

Fuel consumption on site, associated with the operation of heavy machinery, such as bulldozers, loaders, backhoes, cranes, as well as generators, space heaters, and dewatering pumps, is a significant source of greenhouse gas emissions. We can try to predict these emissions by collecting data on the kinds of machinery to be used during different phases of construction. We then estimate

FIGURE 2.9 CALCULATING EMISSIONS FROM CONSTRUCTION ACTIVITIES. *SOURCE:* AUTHORS

CALCULATE THE EMISSIONS FROM TRANSPORTATION (MODULE A4)

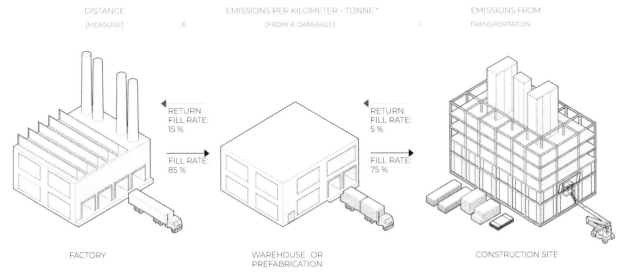

DISTANCE   X   EMISSIONS PER KILOMETER - TONNE *   =   EMISSIONS FROM

(MEASURE)   (FROM A DATABASE)   TRANSPORTATION

RETURN FILL RATE: 15 %

FILL RATE: 85 %

RETURN FILL RATE: 5 %

FILL RATE: 75 %

FACTORY   WAREHOUSE OR PREFABRICATION   CONSTRUCTION SITE

*A KILOMETER - TONNE:
ONE TON OF CARGO, TRANSPORTED WITH A GIVEN TRANSPORTATION MODE FOR A DISTANCE OF 1 KILOMETER

CALCULATE THE EMISSIONS FROM CONSTRUCTION WORK (MODULE A5)

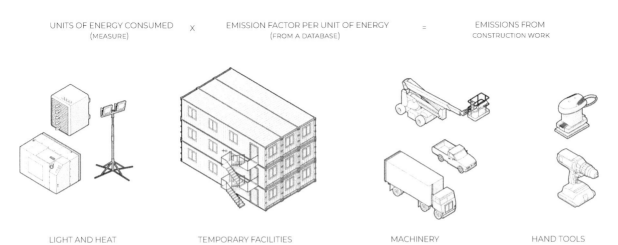

UNITS OF ENERGY CONSUMED   X   EMISSION FACTOR PER UNIT OF ENERGY   =   EMISSIONS FROM
(MEASURE)   (FROM A DATABASE)   CONSTRUCTION WORK

LIGHT AND HEAT   TEMPORARY FACILITIES   MACHINERY   HAND TOOLS

Info box 2.4

Calculating the Impacts of Construction Activities

Usually, LCA tools have an option for using preset average values for construction works. If we wish to calculate them manually, we could focus on the most polluting machinery, which in most cases is the heavy equipment.

Let´s assume that our construction site requires the use of the following heavy equipment:

- 2 excavators for 5 weeks
- 3 bulldozers for 10 days
- 3 loaders for 15 days
- 1 tower crane for 20 days

Based on the hourly fuel consumption, we can calculate the overall fuel consumption for the excavators as an example:

- 2 excavators x 5 days = 10 days = 80 hours (a round figure for our example)
- Fuel consumption per hour varies between 6 and 12 liters = 9 liters on average (this information is available from machine and vehicle databases or from manufacturer)
- 9 liters of fuel x 80 hours = 720 liters

Next, we can either look for a typical CO_2e value for a liter of fuel for the chosen machine from a database. Alternatively, we can calculate the CO_2e emissions for fuel type used in our excavator. In our example, we will use ultra-low sulfur diesel fuel (ULSD), which can have a carbon footprint of 101.05 gCO_2e/MJ. By using a conversion factor for diesel fuels (36 MJ/liter), this equals to 2.81 $gCO_2e/liter$.

Finally, we will calculate the total emissions for the excavators:

720 liters x 2.81 $gCO_2e/liter$ = 2,021 gCO_2e = 2.02 $kgCO_2e$

The same routine applies for other machines, too. If we would like to reduce the emissions from these machines, there could be several options starting from the efficiency of the engine to the fuel used. From a project management perspective, one option could be to require in the bidding round machinery that operates either on electricity or low-emissions fuels.

Typically included in construction (A5):

- Construction work onsite
- Energy and materials for temporary facilities
- Transport and processing of construction waste

Typically excluded from construction (A5):

- Commuting of construction workers to and from the building site
- Prefabrication of building elements or volumetric units (part of production phase A1–A3)
- Production of construction tools and machines
- Lubricants and oils for tools and machines
- Materials for scaffolding (although required by EN 15978)
- Changes in the biogenic carbon content of the soil and its vegetation (removal of soil, trees, etc.)
- Benefits or loads from the use of recycled construction waste

the number of hours of use for each machine, checking their average fuel consumption rates and then multiplying the resulting total volume of fuel with their respective GHG emission factors for the types of fuels they use. Although this may seem to lie far outside of the scope of design consideration and be difficult information to obtain, it is important to remember that these calculations are all part of the cost estimating process and that builders typically keep good records of the machine hours logged and the fuel consumed. These records from past similar projects can serve as data sources. Barring their availability, information on machinery requirements for a given job, the fuel efficiency of a given piece of machinery, and the types of fuel it consumes are difficult to ascertain during design phase assessments. In those cases, we make rough estimates from statistical data or industry literature sources.

It is also possible to harvest energy on-site during the construction phase. A small photovoltaic array can charge batteries for hand-powered tools. Although negligible, the use of renewable solar energy can offset some of the emissions we attribute to the construction process.

Heating semi-finished buildings can be very energy-intensive and expensive and may seem to be an unnecessary expenditure of money and avoidable source of emissions. But we need to recognize that maintaining moderate temperatures and levels of humidity in critical locations on construction sites will inevitably prevent material and system damage or loss due to freezing or moisture absorption and may avoid unsafe or unhealthy working conditions. All of these may affect not only the immediate condition of the material but also the quality of their handling and installation, all of which may bode poorly for their durability and performance. And these failures will have inevitable impacts on the environment.

THE USE STAGE

Embodied and Operational Impacts

The environmental impacts incurred during the use phase of the building life cycle provide good examples of both operational and embodied emissions. The sources of operational emissions that accrue in the use phase typically arise from the day-to-day consumption of energy and water. Embodied emissions sources during this life cycle stage are somewhat more episodic, associated as they are with the processes of maintenance, repair, and refurbishment, required for the safe, comfortable occupancy and functionality of the building. Even within the service life of a relatively short-lived building, there is still plenty of time—usually decades—for both operational and embodied impacts to accumulate during the building's use stage.

As this phase greatly depends on how the building is used and its systems are maintained, the behavior of its occupants, and the environmental stresses it must endure, such as severe weather and other climatic forces, it is challenging to estimate the operational impacts during this long stage of the building's functional life. During this extended time period, patterns and programs of use may change significantly and environmental factors associated with climate change may intensify demands on building systems. This is why the *scenarios* we described earlier in this chapter play such an important role in the assessment of impacts during the use stage. To incorporate alternative eventualities affecting energy and water consumption, we consider and set as realistic scenarios as possible, and we use sensitivity analyses to determine which parameters of the building's use may create the largest uncertainties with the most potentially dispositive impacts. These concepts and their associate methods make it possible for a designer to future-proof a building and make design decisions that may improve its long-term utility, resiliency, and durability.

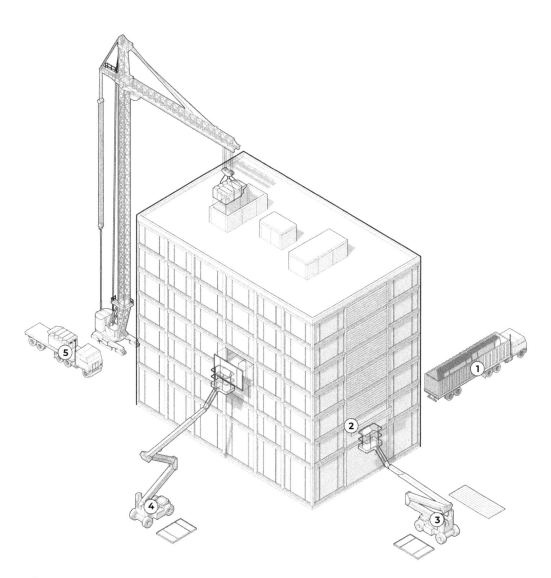

1 BUILDING MANAGEMENT

• Transportation of waste to reuse/recycling, energy recovery, or landfilling
• Cleaning and maintenance of facilities
• Related process emissions

2 PRODUCTION OF NEW BUILDING MATERIALS

• Replaced building components and materials
• Ancillary materials for the refurbishment site

3 CONSTRUCTION AND DEMOLITION WASTE

• Waste generated during the installation of new building materials
• Packaging waste
• Construction and demolition waste from refurbishment

4 MACHINERY

• Use of energy
• Use of oils and coolants

5 TRANSPORTATION

• Delivery of building materials and machinery to site
• Construction waste from site

A realistically conceived schedule of maintenance and repair, implemented with regular attention and care, will contribute significantly to the realization of the circular economic principles that are so fundamental to the conduct of a low-carbon construction economy. We'll consider other means by which we can reduce embodied emissions in the use stage of the building life cycle in Chapter 4, but the prerequisite for employing those strategies is the calculation of carbon flows throughout this stage, a topic we will address here.

Emissions from the Use of Energy and Water

Energy Consumption

We use energy modeling to simulate use-stage energy consumption. Available modeling software offers typical use profiles and energy mixes. For this reason, we'll focus in this section on critical points of inflection at which the building designer can potentially reduce the area of a building's overall carbon footprint that is associated with operational energy consumption.

The key factors that affect operational energy consumption and GHG emissions include the following:

- the total amount of energy consumed in the operation of the building;
- the carbon footprint of each unit of energy consumed;
- the patterns of use of the building;
- realistic scenarios for the future decarbonization of the energy supply;
- future energy-related upgrades to the building;
- types of energy supply.

The building designer has the greatest possibility to influence the energy consumption of the building through the following considerations:

- the location and micro climate of the building;
- the shape of the building and its form factor;
- the thermal conductivity and air-tightness of the building envelope and the elimination of thermal bridging throughout;

- the thermal mass of the building (which may have either a beneficial or harmful impact);
- the size and orientation of glazed apertures and their solar shading (also including vegetation);
- the use of passive heating and cooling techniques and their associated geometries and details.

Building Form Factor

There are three main options by which we assess the geometry of a building from the standpoint of its energy efficiency: (1) area to volume (A/V) ratio; (2) area to program area (A/A) ratio; and (3) weighted area to program area (A/Aweighted) ratio. These are helpful tools that allow us to quickly compare alternative approaches to building massing and program distribution and their respective energy efficiency. As noted earlier in this chapter, these ratios reflect material efficiency as well.

We can assess the geometric efficiency of our building by calculating its area-to-volume (A/V) ratio. We divide the area of the building's envelope by the conditioned (heated or cooled) volume of the building. A high area to volume ratio means the building geometry is more likely to have a high level of efficacy with respect to use-stage emissions.

An A/V ratio may not be the optimum means for assessing the efficiency of a design alternative as it does not show its efficiency with respect to its intended use. To ascertain its effectiveness as a solution, we instead apply an area to program area (A/A). This describes the ratio of the surface area of its envelope to its usable floor area.

A weighted A/A ratio, as suggested by passive house specialist Kimmo Lylykangas [15], offers an even more nuanced assessment of the geometric efficacy of our building design by accounting for the thermal conductivity of the building's envelope. In this approach, we multiply the areas of exterior walls, roofs, floors, windows, and doors by their thermal conductivity value (U-value). This approach takes into account the specific energy performance of the particular building components that comprise the enclosure system and offers us the most comprehensive understanding of the relative efficiency of different building geometries.

FIGURE 2.10 BUILDING MAINTENANCE AND REFURBISHMENT. *Source:* AUTHORS

Info box 2.5

Calculating Operational Energy-Related Emissions
The amount of purchased energy is usually used for the calculation of operational energy-related emissions. This figure is available directly from energy declarations (in regions where they are mandatory), but it can also be calculated with the help of an energy simulation. That is a specific process of its own, for which there are many manuals available and therefore it is not described here.

We´ll assume that the amount of purchased energy is 98 kWh per m² annually. And from the energy declaration or from simulation data we will also learn that this is a sum of 51 kWh of district heating and 47 kWh of electricity. Based on these figures, our LCA tool can do the following calculation:

Annual amount of consumed district heating	Emission factor for district heating	Emissions from district heating (per year and per m²)	Annual amount of consumed electricity (kWh)	Emission factor for electricity	Emissions from electricity (per year and per m²)	Total emissions (per year and per m²)
51 kWh	0.154 kgCO$_2$e/kWh	51 x 0.154 = 7.85 kgCO$_2$e	47 kWh	0.141 kgCO$_2$e/kWh	57 x 0.141 = 6.63 kgCO$_2$e	7.85 + 6.63 = 14.48 kgCO$_2$e

Now we have the annual amount of emissions per each square meter of the building. Next, we need to extend the calculation over the chosen *reference study period*. In this example, we can use 50 years. The important things to consider here are the *decarbonization scenarios* for all forms of energy that the building consumes. Such scenarios should only be applied, if there are reliable sources for them, and should by no means be estimated case-by-case.

In our case, we can refer to a decarbonization scenario from local normative LCA guidance (in this example, in Finland [16]), and learn that emissions for district heating and electricity are expected to decrease as follows:

Decade	District heating (kgCO$_2$e/kWh)	Electricity (kgCO$_2$e/kWh)
2010–2020	0.154	0.141
2020–2030	0.130	0.121
2030–2040	0.093	0.057
2040–2050	0.063	0.030
2050–2060	0.037	0.018

If our LCA tool does not support the calculation of decarbonizing energy, we can also do the math in a spreadsheet tool. This is done by multiplying the emission factor for each decade with the amount of energy consumed in that decade. If there is no other guidance available, we can assume that the emissions decrease step by step and not linearly.

Typically included in the consumption of energy (B6) and water (B7):

- Production of energy and resulting emissions
- Transfer of energy and transfer losses
- Consumption of electricity for building-related use (heating/cooling, building service machines)
- Production of renewable energy on-site
- Processing of water and resulting emissions
- Transfer of water to the building

Typically excluded from the consumption of energy (B6) and water (B7):

- Construction and use of infrastructure required for the production and transfer of energy and water
- Emissions from the life cycles of the energy- and water-related machines (included in other parts of the life cycle, e.g., production, replacement and end-of-life phases)

**Energy Types and Potential Changes
Through the Building Life Cycle**

During the building design stage, the development and design team will make a decision which may have the greatest single life cycle impact: the choice of an energy system. Alternative energy sources carry the potential to dramatically reduce a building's carbon footprint and the various means of on-site energy generation has become a standard approach in sustainable building design. In most cases the decision to employ renewable energy systems in a building represents an effective, if reflexive, emissions-reduction strategy. Depending on the regional and political economic context in which it is used, it may even prove to be cost effective within a relatively short time-frame.

There are some factors, however, that we should not neglect when we consider implementing on-site renewable energy systems as a means to reduce our carbon footprint. One factor is the source of energy supplied to district energy systems or regional electrical grids. The second is the emissions embodied in the manufacture and installation of the services and structures required to generate renewable energy.

The carbon footprint of district energy systems or grid electricity varies greatly depending on a region's or utility provider's energy mix. It goes without saying that energy supplied to district heating or cooling systems or electrical grids that is produced through the combustion of fossil fuels will probably add significantly to use-stage building emissions. In this case, the decision to specify on-site renewable energy generation makes a good deal of sense. If, on the other hand, regional energy is generated with hydro, wind, or solar power—as is the case in most Nordic countries and increasingly in some regions or states in the US—the overall potential emissions benefits captured with on-site renewable energy generation may prove negligible.

Many countries and regions have outlined ambitious plans for lowering the carbon footprint of their energy supply. Some have compiled and committed to strategies that would entail significant reductions in global warming potential. Typically, in a life cycle assessment that seeks to make conservative assumptions, we would discount the potential benefits associated with such decarbonization schemes. Including these impacts as part of our sensitivity analysis, however, will shed light on the potential benefits of low carbon energy policy and may offer future potential to further reduce carbon emissions that arise from operational energy consumption.

The embodied emissions entailed in the production of the components of renewable energy systems are also a serious consideration. The manufacture of solar photovoltaic panels, for example, may demand considerable energy expenditure and emit an associated share of greenhouse gases. If we think of those manufacturing emissions as a kind of environmental debt, then it may take a considerable amount of time before the efficiencies gained through renewable energy generation effectively *amortize* that initial carbon debt. The term of that amortization depends, of course, on the type of semi-conductor, the way in which it is applied to a substrate, and the type of energy used to produce the panel. Some studies have indicated that the period required to offset those emissions recovery can extend longer than 20 years [17], about the same timeframe as the effective service life of the PV panels themselves. In order to avoid such unintended consequences of our best—if unconfirmed—low carbon intentions, we need to gather reliable data on production stage emissions and weigh the benefits against potential environmental costs.

The on-site generation of energy, however, may have benefits other than direct CO_2 savings and we should take them into account. Depending on the system, on-site energy systems improve the resilience of the building, making it less vulnerable to intermittent or more serious failure of the grid, creating potential savings or even revenue through the sale of excess energy back into the grid or to neighboring buildings, and increasing overall self-sufficiency of the regional or national energy network. These benefits may not necessarily correlate with reduced carbon emissions, but they represent important steps in making the built environment more resilient and sustainable and the building sector less environmentally destructive.

Emissions from the Use of Water

The water we consume in a building produces emissions through the extensive infrastructural system required to move it from its source to the fixtures and appliances we use on an everyday basis. These emissions are mostly associated with the operational energy consumed by pumps and purification systems. We can estimate that consumption statistically, using calculation methods based on the type of use, the number of users, and the properties of water systems. We then multiply the resulting volume by a water consumption emission factor.

SERVICE LIFE

Maintenance

The diligent maintenance of a building optimizes the service life of its component materials and systems. Conversely, if we neglect maintenance, those materials and assemblies may wear out faster than planned and even fail prematurely. This results in shorter intervals of repair and replacement which in turn increases the embodied emissions that accrue over the building life cycle.

There are several building maintenance strategies, each with different life cycle impacts. A *value-adding* maintenance strategy entails ongoing investments that steadily improve the quality and performance of the building over its lifetime. With this approach, the building's emissions may achieve greater than anticipated reductions. A *value-maintaining* strategy is built on maintenance activities that ensure that the building continues to perform as originally designed and that the technical service lives of the building's various materials, assemblies, and systems achieve their intended lifespan. If aging materials or appliances such as exterior cladding, flooring, or lighting fixtures are replaced in accordance with their planned life cycles and the old ones removed and

reused or recycled, then the anticipated carbon balance should not shift significantly. On the contrary, a low or *controlled-decay* maintenance strategy may produce greater-than-projected use-stage emissions, because materials and systems will likely fail before they complete their expected term of technical service. This latter strategy is employed typically where the building is deemed functionally obsolete or in the case where the increase in the land value of the site is significantly greater than the value of the building. This low maintenance strategy will result in poorer-than-anticipated performance of the building's assemblies and systems and accordingly higher carbon emissions.

And, of course, maintenance work itself also creates emissions. We use material and energy to clean and refinish surfaces and to service equipment. In certain building types, such as hospitals, factories, or schools, these maintenance regimens may incur emissions large enough to represent an observable share of the life cycle carbon footprint. Even in those most intensive uses and occupancies, we can control those emissions associated with maintenance by employing low-carbon energy sources for the equipment required (as a part of the energy plan of the building) and by using cleaning agents with verifiably high environmental efficacy.

Repairs, Replacement, and Refurbishment

The repair, replacement, and renovation or refurbishment stages include inputs of material and energy that are similar to those in the initial production and construction phases of the building life cycle, except that the proportions are smaller—unless renovation includes a significant building addition or extension—and the dominance of life cycle impacts will likely differ. In the refurbishment or renovation stage, the processes include many of the same steps associated with the end-of-life stage, namely the dismantling of building assemblies, the transport and handling of waste material, and the management of its dispersal. As the activities of the repair, replacement, and maintenance stages duplicate the activities found in both the production and end-of-life stage of the building life

cycle, so we may use similar assessment techniques to those found in early and late-stage assessments.

It is relatively easy to predict the material inputs that will be required for assembly and system repair or material or equipment replacement. There are readily available tables that describe the average service life of building materials that are often included in assessment software. We can use these references to find estimates of the average technical service life of a material, component, or product each with its own categories of anticipated wear. This allows us to establish the number of life cycles of a given product likely to occur within the building life cycle, measure the material volume required by each of these cycles, and add those to the calculations we make for that product in the initial production phase. Although changes in manufacturing energy mixes may have occurred in the decades that span between the production of the original material and its replacement due to regional efforts to decarbonize energy systems, it's still advisable to use the same emission factors for the replacement materials as we did for those original materials in their production phase. This keeps our impact estimates appropriately conservative.

The energy required for repairs, replacements, and refurbishment can be calculated in a similar manner, using energy estimations from the construction-stage assessment to provide precedent for our replacement scenarios. At the very least, if accurate information on energy consumed during the construction stage in the installation of a building component under consideration is unavailable, we can estimate anticipated energy consumption of its replacement as a share of overall energy consumed during the construction stage. As noted earlier, in this case, it is important to be conservative in our outlook and not incorporate the potential benefits of any potential future upgrades that might decarbonize the energy supply.

Identifying replacement materials and their quantities requires that we create scenarios for refurbishment. We might create, for example, a refurbishment scenario for the building envelope that would reverse the process of its assembly, entailing the removal of surface cladding, the stripping of protective membranes and substrates, the removal of insulation and windows and flashings. Those components would all need to be replaced by new ones. It is possible therefore to quantify those replacement materials by comparing them to the original bill of quantities. Needless to say, the goal would be to minimize the extensiveness of such repair and replacement requirements, through proper maintenance and the replacement of assembly components most vulnerable to wear— the cladding and flashing in the aforementioned envelope to continue the example, before their deterioration leads to more systemic failure.

More difficult to predict than the wear and tear of a building are other forms of obsolescence caused by changes in usage or the occupants' needs. For example, an office space requiring the constant shifting of partition walls may create a cascade of necessary renovations: repairs to affected flooring and ceilings, rerouting of mechanical ducts, and the movement of lights fixtures, electrical outlets, or doorways. These may be the inevitable and often significant results of what might be considered small changes and they are impossible for us to accurately predict, no matter how complex and comprehensive the scenarios we seek to set. Building uses that are subject to regular change, such as a storefront shop space or restaurant, may be refurbished with greater frequency than the life cycle of its constituent materials would require.

It follows then that we should take into account the likely lifespan of the building use we design for and consider whether it's either economically or environmentally appropriate to specify materials that will far outlive their useful life. A replacement phase scenario that synchronizes a material life cycle to the cycles of building refurbishment represents a legitimate approach to both design and to our assessment of impacts and should be reported in the findings of our LCA.

Other Emissions (and Potential Removals) During the Use Phase

In addition to the emissions that arise from the consumption of energy and water, and the repair and replacement of materials and assemblies, use-stage emissions may include incremental leakages of cooling agents (that form fluorinated gases) used in buildings' air conditioning equipment and appliances. As CFCs are extremely strong greenhouse gases, we should seek to reduce such leaks as much as possible. This is mostly a question of proper installation, maintenance, and inspection of equipment that use CFCs and so may fall outside of the design scope. However, a designer may reduce their risk by specifying systems that minimize vulnerable connections, such as using monoblock heat pumps in lieu of "split" heat pumps.

In addition to the range of potential sources of greenhouse gas emissions we've considered during the use stage, a building and its site can also remove carbon from the atmosphere. This may happen through two distinct processes: (1) the carbonation of cement; and (2) the photosynthetic sequestration of carbon by site plantings such as trees, shrubs, and surface plants such as sod.

The *carbonation of cement* occurs slowly over decades, a chemical reaction that binds atmospheric CO_2 to the exposed surfaces of concrete or mortar. In this process CO_2 reacts with moisture in the micro cavities of concrete to turn lime (CaO) back into limestone ($CaCO_3$). Carbonation is thus the reverse process of calcination, a chemical reaction driven in cement production when limestone is burnt to form lime and CO_2 is released into the atmosphere.

That reversal also means that the process represents the slow breakdown of only those cements exposed to the atmosphere.

Carbonation occurs most rapidly within a certain range of relative humidity. Typically, outdoor concrete structures that are protected from rain but not coated in any way have the greatest potential to bind CO_2. The mix of concrete also influences the level of carbonation. Certain cement substitutes, such as fly ash or blast furnace slag enhance the reaction. Although carbonation occurs throughout the use stage, we should note that it is accelerated in the end-of-life stage, when more surface of concrete is exposed when crushed to form rubble and further enhanced when the rubble is laid out in open air to that it more readily reacts with CO_2 [18].

As discussed earlier, biomass, or living plants, *sequester carbon* through the chemical reaction of photosynthesis and store it in their cell walls. In the case of a tree, which may grow during the entire life cycle of a building, its slow accumulation and storage of carbon in its woody matter represent a means to offset some amount of the carbon emitted by the building during the use stage. We can conceivably quantify this storage capacity using growth algorithms available for certain common tree species. In the case of bushes or herbaceous plants, their carbon uptake cycles are much more frequent, lasting in some cases only a few months. However, as leaves fall or grass thatches and they dry, a portion of that plant material accumulates as soil organic matter (SOM). The amount of soil organic carbon (SOC) that may accrue in site soils depends heavily on the soil type and the ambient climatic conditions of the building's location. Although we can estimate SOC mathematically [19, 20], these sorts of calculations are not typically included in building LCAs. They may shed some light, however, on various means we might employ as building designers to decarbonize our buildings while supporting and enhancing the ecosystems that surround them.

Info box 2.6

Estimating the Impacts of Maintenance

Practical calculation of maintenance of a building could include vacuuming the floors, cleaning surfaces manually with cleaning detergents, and washing the floors and mowing the lawn. For cleaning, we would need to know the amount of cleaning fluids consumed and the energy for cleaning per building or per floor area. These calculations could look as follows:

Vacuum cleaning of an office

Weekly time for vacuum cleaning an office	Number of vacuum cleaning weeks per year	Total time for vacuum cleaning per year	Wattage of the vacuum cleaner (data from manufacturer)	Electricity used for vacuum cleaning per year	Local emission factor for electricity	Emissions from vacuum cleaning per year
5 hours	50	5 x 50 = 250 hours	3 kW	250 h x 3 kW = 750 kWh	0.14 kgCO$_2$e/kWh	750 x 0.14 = 104 kgCO$_2$e

Use of cleaning detergents

Amount of cleaning detergents required (per year)	Emissions from the production of the cleaning fluid (data from manufacturer)	Emissions from cleaning fluid (per unit of floor area per year)
30 kg	0.7 kgCO$_2$e/kg of product	30 x 0.7 = 21 kgCO$_2$e

Mowing the lawn

Cutting time per day	Maintenance weeks per year	Total time of lawnmowing per year	Wattage of an electric awnmower	Electricity used for lawnmowing per year	Local emission factor for electricity	Total emissions from lawnmoving per year
2 hours	20	2 x 20 = 40 hours	1.5 kW	40 h x 1.5 kW = 60 kWh	0.14 kgCO$_2$e/kWh	60 x 0.14 = 8.4 kgCO$_2$e

Setting scenarios is also necessary. As there are several cleaning products available—some more environmentally friendly than others—the impacts from the use of these products could change. It is not possible to know which products would be used in the years of maintenance to come, and therefore a conservative assumption would be safe. The same applies to the energy consumption of cleaning machines: as it is not possible to know what type of machines the maintenance companies would use, using the energy consumption of an average machine would be a sound choice. Furthermore, the emissions per unit of energy are likely to change over the study period of the LCA. If reliable decarbonization scenarios are available for energy, they can be used when taking this into account.

In addition to the energy- and fuel-related emissions, also the number of lawnmowers, vacuum cleaners or any other maintenance machines required for the property over the reference study period could be estimated and added to the total sum of emissions from maintenance, if you have chosen to include such products into your LCA. Such data could be retrieved from specific LCA studies or from manufacturers.

According to current understanding, maintenance activities contribute only marginally to the carbon footprint of most buildings. As their calculation is both time-consuming and prone to uncertain scenarios, they are in many cases excluded from building LCAs.

Assessment of the Impacts from Repairs and Replacements

This is a combination of the assessments of production of materials (A1–A3), transport (A4), and construction works (A5). In addition to these, also the impacts from waste management or recycling of replaced building components (C1–C4) need to be taken into account in most cases.

Let´s have an example of replacement of a flooring materials. First, we should get an estimation of the technical service life of the flooring product. The producer may offer such information, but data can also be available from statistics. The calculation of the replacement is done according to formula:

$$Replacements = \left[\left(\frac{Reference\ study\ period}{Product's\ service\ life}\right)-1\right]$$

Most LCA tools offer the possibility of using table values for replacement intervals, so calculating them manually can be avoided. As an example, the calculation of replacements could look as follows:

Products	Technical service life of the product	Reference study period	Replacements	Replacements during the study period
Flooring product A	15 years	50 years	50 / 15 - 1 = 2.333	2
Flooring product B	30 years	50 years	50 / 30 -1 = 0.667	1

Rounding up of the results is based on a methodological choice. Some LCA practitioners prefer to round up the results and others prefer to keep them in decimal format. If your LCA is done for a certification scheme or regulation, instructions on this methodological choice should be given in the respective guidelines. In our calculation example we rounded up the results to the integral number 2 for product A and to integral number 1 for product B. The possible uncertainty and consequences of such a choice can be further considered, if a *sensitivity analysis* is carried out.

Typically included in the use (B1) and maintenance (B2) phases:

- Leakages of cooling agents and other harmful substances from building service installations
- Energy and materials required for scheduled maintenance and cleaning activities
- Uptake of carbon into cement-based surfaces through carbonation (in surfaces that are not protected against it)

Typically excluded from the use (B1) and maintenance (B2) phases:

- Accumulation of organic carbon into the vegetation and soils (although this may have important mitigation potential)
- Daily commuting to and from the building (e.g. office workers or residents)
- Maintenance of municipal infrastructure that serves the building
- Long-term biogenic carbon storages in bio-based materials (these can be reported but not deducted from the emissions in this phase)

Typically included in the repair (B3), replacement (B4) and refurbishment (B5) phases:

- Energy and materials required for producing and packaging new building products
- Energy required from transporting the new materials to the building site and the disassembled of old materials from the site
- Energy required for disassembly of old building components and for assembling new components
- Waste processing and recycling of disassembled construction materials and left-over materials from the repair works

Typically excluded from the repair (B3), replacement (B4) and refurbishment (B5) phases:

- Commuting of construction workers to and from the building site
- Prefabrication of building elements or volumetric units (part of production phase A1–A3)
- Production of construction tools and machines
- Lubricants and oils for tools and machines
- Materials for scaffolding (although required by EN 15978)
- Benefits or loads from the use of recycled construction waste
- Value chains of secondary products from the production

Info box 2.7

What Are the Life Cycle Impacts of the Energy Refurbishment?
In most cases, extending the service life of a building is an essential part of a circular construction economy. However, when considering if a building should be refurbished to save energy—as is often proposed as an environmentally sound option—estimating the embodied emissions may be used to guide the decision-making. This type of an analysis can also be carried out when comparing alternative renovation scenarios (e.g., new windows vs. new insulation vs. new building services).

First, the operational energy consumption will start to decrease, due to the planned energy-saving measures. The reduced amount of energy (kWhs) can be estimated during the initial design phase for scheduled repairs or as larger refurbishments are planned. This sets the first value in the formulation (Exhibit A, Figure 2.15a). These reductions are compared against a baseline, which shows the current (preferably measured) energy consumption of the studied building.

Second, the carbon intensity of consumed energy is also likely to decrease as a function of time, as a serious global effort is being taken into this direction. As a result—and depending on the locally-planned energy decarbonization plans—the emissions from the use of energy will also decrease (Exhibit B, Figure 2.15b). These measures are beyond the control of the building designers, unless capacity for producing renewable energy onsite is being added.

Together the energy efficiency improvements (A) and decarbonization of energy (B) set the new operative emissions trend line (Exhibit C, Figure 2.15c).

However, the process of repairing, adding new components and managing the resulting renovation waste leads to embodied emissions (Exhibit D, Figure 2.15d). The magnitude of these emissions can be estimated based on life cycle analysis. This analysis may also help to determine how much refurbishment is feasible.

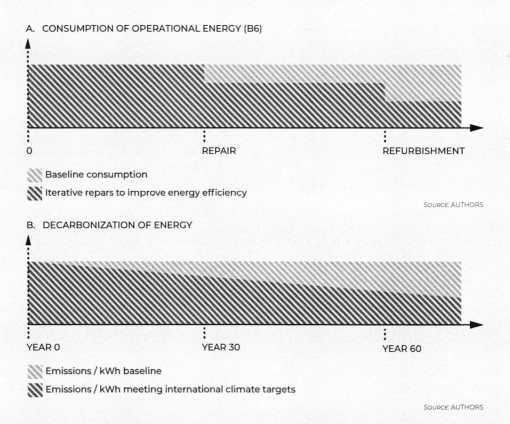

A. CONSUMPTION OF OPERATIONAL ENERGY (B6)

0   REPAIR   REFURBISHMENT

Baseline consumption
Iterative repars to improve energy efficiency

Source: AUTHORS

B. DECARBONIZATION OF ENERGY

YEAR 0   YEAR 30   YEAR 60

Emissions / kWh baseline
Emissions / kWh meeting international climate targets

Source: AUTHORS

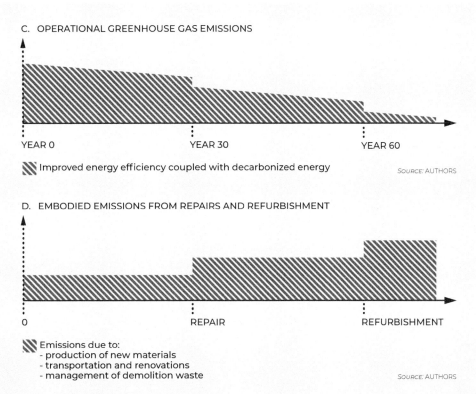

C. OPERATIONAL GREENHOUSE GAS EMISSIONS

YEAR 0   YEAR 30   YEAR 60

▨ Improved energy efficiency coupled with decarbonized energy

Source: AUTHORS

D. EMBODIED EMISSIONS FROM REPAIRS AND REFURBISHMENT

0   REPAIR   REFURBISHMENT

▨ Emissions due to:
   - production of new materials
   - transportation and renovations
   - management of demolition waste

Source: AUTHORS

Finally, as the new operative emissions (C) and embodied emissions (D) are compared, the net emission efficacy of the planned operation can be evaluated (Exhibit E, Figure 2.15e). If embodied emissions (GHG_e) are smaller than the savings from operational emissions (GHG_o), then the repairs and refurbishments can be justified from the climate viewpoint.

However, there are several other reasons that may lead to the need to repair or refurbish. Therefore, emissions are only one parameter in the multi-objective optimization of the feasibility of building´s refurbishment.

Applying a life cycle assessment in this decision-making process will help to avoid causing collateral environmental damage. It can also help to locate most cost and emission optimal means for repairs and refurbishments. This topic is more sensitive in areas where the emission-intensity of energy is already low. There the amortization period for offsetting the embodied emissions may be very long, extending to several decades.

Further information can be found in Lidberg et al. [21], Schwartz et al. [22], and Dodoo et al. [23, 24].

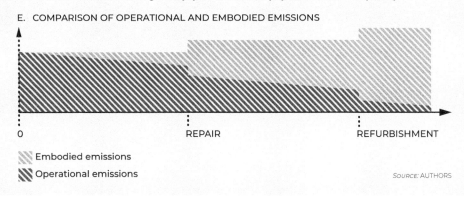

E. COMPARISON OF OPERATIONAL AND EMBODIED EMISSIONS

0   REPAIR   REFURBISHMENT

▨ Embodied emissions
▨ Operational emissions

Source: AUTHORS

END-OF-LIFE STAGE

End-of-Life Scenarios

Just as it is impossible to know in advance exactly when a building will reach the end of its life, it is challenging to predict with any certainty how the fate of the materials that once comprised its assemblies and systems will be managed. To address the inherent uncertainty of the end-of-life phase—the age and condition of the building when it is finally dismantled, the emissions generated by that disassembly process, the extent to which its materials and components can be reused or recycled—we can compile alternative scenarios to describe feasible outcomes which may include:

1. the demolition and partial recycling of waste material into secondary raw materials;
2. the demolition, partial reuse of material components, and partial recycling into secondary raw materials;
3. the partial incineration of waste material for energy recovery and the landfilling of the remaining residues.

The likelihood and extent of recycling in scenario 1 depend on regional or national waste treatment policies and the adoption of circular economy plans. Scenario 1 would require that we ascertain a value for the rate of a country's recycling.

The feasibility of material reuse (scenario 2) heavily depends on both the status of markets for post-construction products and the ease with which our building can be disassembled. In practice, it is very difficult to predict whether a product will have been deemed legally obsolete by the time it is available for reuse. Reasons for a building material's obsolescence might be that its chemical formulation is identified as unsafe, or because its assembly as a system, such as a window, may no longer meet increasingly stringent performance standards. And, of course, a material may no longer be able to perform in its original capacity due to deterioration. Material certification programs, such as the EU's CE mark or the US BCSD material marketplace, signal a material's suitability for reuse. We may, however, assume conservatively that certain building parts

or products are likely to be reused. Bricks, heavy timbers, copper wire, steel structural sections, and even some aggregates may see multiple life cycles. If we seek to apply a percentage value to the potential reuse of all a building's material, then we would ideally design the building to be easily dismantled in order to help ensure that the reuse scenario we set will be feasible to implement and our results, therefore, will prove to have been reliable.

Scenario 3 is unfortunately an entirely likely outcome due to the fact that today's construction economy is so linear. Its incorporation into our LCA is justified by the basic tenet of assessment that one of the scenarios for the building life cycle should reflect existing technologies and current policies. Such a scenario serves an important function—despite its detrimental environmental ramifications—by providing a benchmark with which to compare scenarios 1 and 2.

Most standards typically consider all disassembled materials in the end-of-life stage to be waste. But for our LCA we want to take into account all of the potential impacts (and possible benefits) that may follow the dismantling or demolition of a building. There are two basic options for the fate of a building's constituent components and materials at the end of a building's life: the first, disposal in a landfill, is a profoundly problematic solution, due to a range of impacts it may create in addition to greenhouse gas emissions; the other, is to prepare those materials for reuse or to process them for recycling. Each of these processes associated with the preparation of material for secondary use has its own implications for energy consumption and emissions (although both represent vast improvements over the destructive practices of landfilling waste). The processes of material reuse and recycling bracket a fundamental concept for a circular economic approach to construction, a philosophical (and material) framework that assigns usefulness and value to any material by-product of human activity. Which criteria we use to ensure that materials drawn from the building waste stream are suitable for reuse or recycling and achieve "end-of-waste" status are the subject of subsequent discussion. Suffice to say here, that

FIGURE 2.12 DISASSEMBLY AND WASTE MANAGEMENT. *SOURCE:* AUTHORS

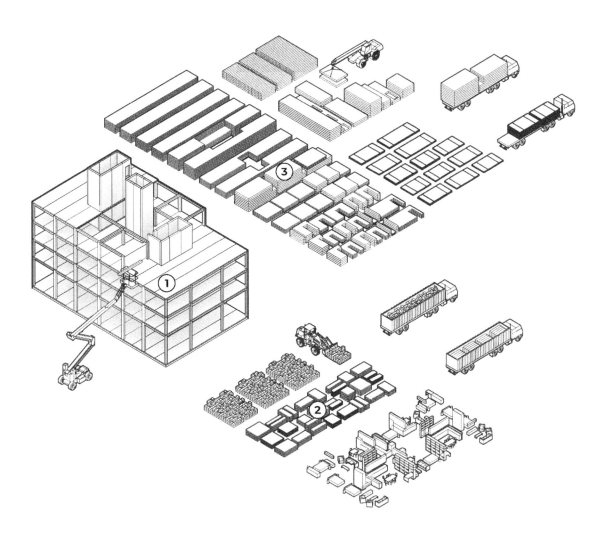

① **DISASSEMBLY**

During deconstruction for end-of-life phase, the building is disassembled non-destructively to maximize the number of components that can be re-used or recycled.

② **WASTE MATERIALS**

Materials that are transported to a landfill or incinerated. Based on the method of deconstruction, this can include furniture, small partition walls, appliances and other small scale, non structural building components.

③ **REUSED/RECYCLED MATERIALS**

Partial reuse of components and partial recycling into secondary raw materials. Some building components such as windows and doors, can be directly reused. Others such as CLT panels and walls can be manipulated, re-manufactured, and reused in other buildings.

the processes required to meet those criteria, will most cases consume energy and generate emissions. In order to create scenarios for those processes and be able to estimate their impacts, we must rely on regional or national protocols and rates for reuse and recycling. If none exists, then we need to make conservative assumptions based on a region's current waste management practices.

Deconstruction

In the best possible case, the dismantling of a building simply reverses the specific steps of its construction. Such a best case requires that the building has been designed for disassembly in the first place, which is to say that its layering of materials and their methods of attachment are detailed and specified in ways that the assemblies can be taken apart methodically and non-destructively, i.e. its components removed without breakage or other damage. This kind of work takes more time than the work of a wrecking ball or a bulldozer, but it usually entails more manual labor so its fuel combustion requirements may be significantly lower.

Given the inherent utilization of manual labor during the dismantlement of a building, we can attribute almost all of the emissions from the deconstruction stage to energy consumption for the operation of lights and fans to protect the safety of workers and for the power tools and equipment they need to use. In this sense, as well as in terms of the order of operations, the energy consumption associated with this stage mirrors the energy required for the initial construction phase or, more accurately, some portion of it.

Transport

Just as the demolition stage mirrors the initial construction phase, the same can be said of the transport energy and emissions associated with the hauling of demolition waste. Accordingly, we use similar methods to predict and calculate transport emissions of materials extracted from the building. We estimate the amount of material to be hauled away from the site by adding those quantities brought to the site from the construction stage to

the materials introduced during replacement (life cycle module B4) and refurbishment (module B5) stages. Put another way, what comes in, must go out. We calculate travel distance from the building site to appropriate waste management facilities and we ascertain the amount and type of fuel consumed per unit of distance.

We can use the same fuel consumption assumptions per unit of distance that we used in calculating for the construction stage. In estimating the emissions incurred during end-of-life stage material transport, however, there is a high level of uncertainty with regard to future vehicle fuel efficiency and the emissions intensity of the fuels they'll use. Decarbonization of vehicle fuel is already underway and is likely to continue to change over the life cycle of a building. Although transportation-related end-of-life emissions per unit of distance traveled will be presumably lower than during the initial construction stage, in order to avoid overly optimistic assessments, we should make no assumptions that rely on predictions of more environmentally friendly future technology, except when regional or national plans call for such a drawdown. In this case, we can use projected fuel emission values as part of our sensitivity analysis.

Landfilling and Decomposition

Emissions in the end-of-life stage arise from two primary sources: through energy consumption, and through the decomposition of material. The energy consumed in the operation of waste management equipment generates emissions and their magnitude depends heavily on the energy sources and fuel types used.

The decomposition of bio-based building material significantly exacerbates life cycle GHG emissions. If the decomposition takes place in anaerobic conditions of a landfill, the organic carbon forms methane (CH_4). Although methane lacks the atmospheric longevity of CO_2, its far greater capacity to absorb energy can make its Global Warming Potential over 30 times more potent. Methane emissions from anaerobic decay place a

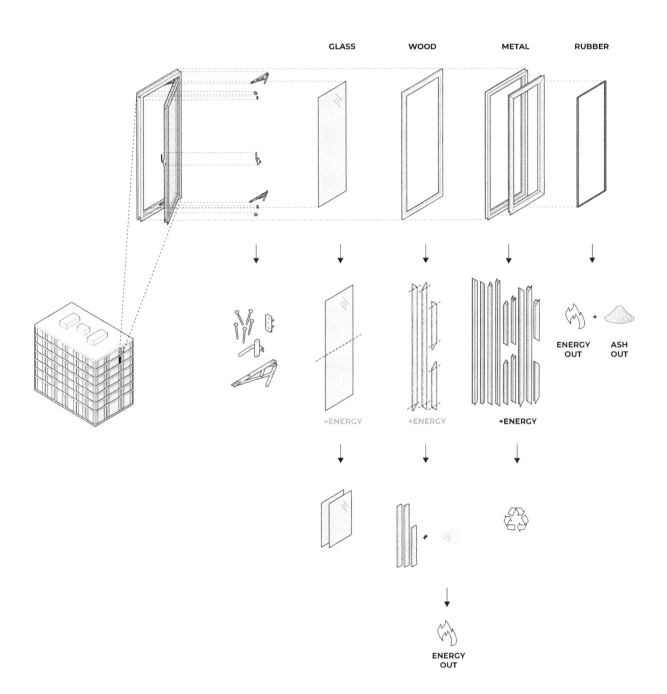

GLASS WOOD METAL RUBBER

+ENERGY +ENERGY **+ENERGY**

ENERGY OUT ASH OUT

ENERGY OUT

far greater burden on the atmosphere than would the incineration of the equivalent volume of biomaterial for energy.

End-of-Waste

The optimum solution to the problem of construction waste during the building life cycle is to turn it into raw materials for new products. Although the processes associated with reusing or recycling material take place at the very end of a building's life, the likelihood that its materials will have a second or third life cycle of use are greatly increased by careful consideration at the inception of the building, its initial design phase. We'll address that potentiality in Chapter 4.

After completing its long trajectory as part of the full building life cycle, a material slated for reuse or recycling must meet "end-of-waste" criteria. This means that the material cannot be harmful, toxic, or inappropriate (from a legal or ethical standpoint) for its intended use as secondary raw material.

Such "end-of-waste" criteria are outlined in legislation or applied on the basis of broadly accepted standards. Typically, these criteria require that the material has completed the requisite steps of waste recovery, preparation, and utilization, that there is market potential for the recycled or reused material, that its technical performance is suitable for the intended next use, and that it doesn't represent measurably greater hazard to human or environmental health than a comparable virgin material. Universal standards and clear legislation that seek to address the implementation of these principles, are only beginning to develop in most jurisdictions.

If we draft a scenario for the end of life of a building that anticipates material recycling and reuse, then we need to include the emissions associated with the preparation processes—separating, cleaning, sorting, and testing—that will ensure the material achieves its "end-of-waste" status. These processes differ for each type of construction material, but their goal is to meet health standards for the workers handling the material as well as for future

users. In addition to these mechanical and material steps, products targeted for "end-of-waste" status must typically undergo a process to certify that the material has been properly handled and prepared.

Although such issues relating to a material's conformance to "end-of-waste" criteria typically fall outside of the methodological bounds of LCA, these processes shed some light on the challenges we face in creating a circular economic flow of material through our buildings and consumer products. And they remind us of the stringency with which we should detail material connections and seek to avoid toxic additives to our buildings if we're truly committed to creating a low carbon building sector.

Closing the Loop

Exactly what ultimately happens to a material that achieves an "end-of-waste" status and is subsequently directed into the process of re-manufacturing is, of course, impossible to know. Those criteria simply set in motion a new set of processes of manufacture and cycles of use that, at the very least, avoid the bulk of the impacts associated with raw material extraction. From the standpoint of an LCA, this all happens beyond the system boundary of our analysis. The philosophy of a "closed loop design" is only beginning to take root in contemporary design and construction practice, but we cannot over-emphasize its potential as a strategy to turn a circular economy from aspiration into reality.

As individuals, as a society, and as an economic system, we can incorporate reused and recycled material streams in a host of technological applications, in construction or any other industrial sector. In order for this to happen, however, we need to transform our behavior, our culture, and a political economy that relies on waste disposal, into one that prizes material durability and quality, the requisite attributes of a material that can have multiple life cycles serving a broad bandwidth of possible applications. Without these basic attributes we cannot hope to develop the markets that would drive a circular economy. Of course, the likelihood of those markets developing and thriving is dependent on several economic factor which include the competitive availability

Figure 2.14
Source: HILDAWEGES PHOTOGRAPHY SHUTTERSTOCK, STOCK ID 284824652

Info box 2.8

Typical Boundaries for End-of-Life Phase: Physical and Action-Based System Boundaries
Calculating the emissions from demolition work (life cycle module C1) is identical to the calculation of construction work (module A5). The amount of energy and electricity for the demolition work needs to be estimated and then multiplied with emission factors for each form of energy. As the demolition work takes place in future, decarbonization scenarios for the emission factors of energy can be applied, if reliable figures are available.

Transporting the demolition waste into waste management (module C2) follows the same steps as calculation for transport in the production phase of the building (module A4). Differences may arise from different distances to waste management facilities and transportation modes. Also the fuels used in the future may have lower emission factors than today. If reliable decarbonization scenarios for fuels are available, they can be considered.

Typically included in the demolition (C1) and transport (C2) phases:
- Energy and materials required in the demolition works
- Transportation of demolition machines to the site
- Transportation of demolition waste from the site to waste management or recycling location

Typically excluded from the demolition (C1) and transport (C2) phases:
- Temporary scaffolding or protection during the demolition (although EN 15978 requires this)
- Commuting of construction workers to and from the demolition site
- Preparation of the site for next use (usually part of next building's life cycle, but dependent on chosen scenario)

Typically included in the waste processing (C3) and final disposal (C4):
- Energy, water, and materials required for various waste processing stages until the waste reaches end-of-waste status or is disposed of (e.g., in landfill)
- Intermediate transportations between different waste processing and recycling sites
- Emissions from the disposal (up to 100 years)

Typically excluded from the waste processing (C3) and final disposal (C4):
- Production of construction tools, machines and facilities for the waste processing and disposal
- Lubricants and oils for tools and machines
- Benefits or loads from the use of recycled demolition waste in further applications

Typically included in module D (additional benefits or loads beyond the system boundary):
- Avoided and caused emissions from the reuse or recycling of components or materials (e.g., steel scrap substituting the need for virgin iron ore)

Typically excluded from module D (additional benefits or loads beyond the system boundary):
- Changes in the markets due to reused or recycled products entering the markets
- Benefits arising from long-term biogenic carbon storages that extend into the next product system (although these can be assessed based on EN TR 16957)

and price of virgin raw materials, economic incentives for the use of recycled materials, and penalties for virgin material extraction, and finally, the exposure of the relative externalities (shadow costs) of both virgin or recycled materials and their careful comparison.

RESULTS, INTERPRETATION, AND COMPARISON

Describing the Dominance of Life Cycle Phases

Once we've completed our calculations, it's a good idea to describe the dominance of the emissions across the building life cycle. This reveals the environmental "weak" points of the design at which notable impacts occur and it offers us an opportunity to address those stages of the life cycle where we might achieve the most significant reduction of environmental impacts.

Some potential pathways to improvement may be closed to us due to reasons that are beyond the control of designers or builders. A site that requires significant soil stabilization, such as spread footings or sheet piling, may generate large emissions in the production and end-of-life stages. These emissions may be unavoidable if a site with more stable soil conditions is not available and, in many cases, by the time we are conducting our analysis, the site may already have selected and purchased. Our next step would be then to look at other sources of significant emissions in their order of relative dominance and target those that are practically and economically feasible to mitigate through design attention. The case study buildings we describe in Chapter 3 will illustrate the relative dominance of different life cycle stages.

Functional Units

In certain cases, we may be better able to communicate the results of our analysis by employing alternative *functional units* in our calculations. The purpose of employing different functional units would be to make the results more comparable and comprehensible. A functional unit typically used is the measurement of our building's usable or mechanically conditioned floor area. This, however, does not capture the efficiency of the way the building is to be used. A better functional unit than floor area for the life cycle assessment of a university dormitory might be the number of beds it provides. In this case, we'd divide the net life cycle carbon impacts by the building's *functional capacity*. A more illustrative functional unit in an office building might be the number of desks it might provide for employees. For the specific analysis of a structural member, we might consider not simply comparing the dead weight of its structural material, but instead the amount of that material required to span between supports. The careful selection of our functional units increases the relevance of our comparisons and better illustrates the true performance of our building and direct us to the ways we might reduce our impacts.

Sensitivity Analysis

As discussed earlier in this chapter, it's also good LCA practice to conduct and report our sensitivity analyses. Our calculation of a building's life cycle carbon footprint relies heavily on scenarios we have created which brings with it a level of uncertainty. This uncertainty is rooted in the challenges of predicting, for example, when a repair may need to take place and its extent, or whether a change in the daily schedule of a building use will drive increased mechanical system operation and energy consumption. Hardest to know in advance, are what the waste management practices or laws governing material reuse and recycling will be at the end of a building's life.

To address these sources of uncertainty, we perform sensitivity analyses. These analyses are comparisons for which we change specific parameters of the initial carbon footprint calculation. One end-of-life scenario may be that we plan and detail for the disassembly and reuse of the chords of our buildings steel roof trusses for use in the structure of another building. Our sensitivity analyses then might examine the environmental "vulnerabilities" of the proposed solution based on the variability of impacts incurred in the transport of those components over different distances to their final site of reprocessing or reuse. Our sensitivity analysis would ideally expose the point at which the potential carbon benefits of our roof truss reuse scenario would be counteracted by the emissions incurred in excessive transport distances.

Comparing Impact Estimates

As we've discussed throughout this chapter, comparative assessment is fundamental to the LCA and the carbon footprint calculation process. Our ability to compare design options and their relative life cycle impacts—whether they are a more localized analysis of a structural component or surface cladding or the study of the bulk and massing of an urban district—is what makes the LCA such a valuable tool in our toolset as designers rather than simply something we do to grade our building after its completed and the course of its environmental impacts is firmly established. As we apply these techniques with increasing frequency to a range of questions about the potential environmental consequences of any set of decisions we might need to make, our facility with the method increases and our familiarity with the nuances of the process and what it may have to tell us grows, we start to see how the LCA can serve as a valuable interactive design tool, one that offers the design team measurable criteria for making systemically low carbon design decisions and buildings.

What is critical to the process, however, is that in comparing equivalent design alternatives we're sure to use the same analytical approach, applying the same system boundaries, the same databases, the same functional units, the same degree of precision with which we compile an inventory. Without that methodological equivalency, the differences embedded in the assumptions and subsequent calculations may distort our results beyond legitimate comparison. Just as important is our awareness that what creates potential impact is the design context in which a solution is deployed, rather than the product, material, or energy source alone.

This is why our understanding of the calculation process is so critical, why we should be extremely cautious in comparing only the raw numerical

summary of different LCAs conducted by different assessors, and possibly why varying claims of the environmental benefits or impacts of certain design solutions or building products may be so contested. It's a good idea, therefore, when setting our own benchmarks for our building performance, that we do so based on comprehensive statistical sample sizes of similar LCAs, rather than one or two.

Limits of a Life Cycle Approach

The metabolism of a building depends on processes and material that lie both "upstream" and "downstream" from even the most expansive system boundaries of life cycle assessment. Upstream impacts are those that take place as a prerequisite for all of the building's life cycle phases. Even discounting the geo-physical, geo-biological, and geo-chemical processes involved in the formation of the raw materials that we extract for the purposes of building, we rely on the construction of factories, the manufacture of machinery and the installation of vast infrastructural systems that serve as conduits for energy, networks for transport, and even hardware for communication. These temporally (and often spatially) remote processes and networks and their associated impacts or benefits may lie far beyond our capacity to measure them. A share of the impacts created in the manufacture and installation of a factory production line could theoretically be attributed to the product that it creates, but in practice such a calculation would be nearly impossible and its effect on our overall estimate of impacts would be likely to have little consequence.

Downstream impacts are those that occur well after the physical structure and systems of the building we've designed have been dismantled and its constituent materials dispersed. We can barely predict, let alone calculate, the impacts incurred as those materials make their way back out into the environment. Whether as a piece of plastic floating in some remote ocean, as an effluent chemical with ozone-depleting or mutagenic properties or in a second life as a recycled component of a well-built new building or a durable and useful consumer product, these impacts may unfold over the course of decades. They may have deleterious chemical and biological consequences that we would never intend if given the choice, or they may serve to mitigate the ongoing damage most human technological activity causes the environment. Either outcome—ecological burden or benefit—is rooted in the choices we make as designers. Our ability to conceptualize the building life cycle and to project beyond it to its material past and its likely future gives us agency in minimizing harmful impacts or, ideally, avoiding them all together.

This is the key to a circular construction economy, a philosophical framework and future prospect we'll consider in subsequent chapters. As the conceptualizers and creators of large complex physical objects and systems with significant lifespans, we can make choices and engender processes that significantly reduce our building's carbon footprint today and make it much more likely that the carbon footprint remains small well into the future. This is where the work of quantifying the impacts that we can actually predict and estimate with sufficient certainty gives way to the larger conceptual questions we should ask and the strategies we should craft. This is where even the broadest system boundaries within which we make our LCA calculations give way to larger systemic frameworks—political, economic, and ecological—and appropriately comprehensive principles and objectives [25] encompassed boundaries that are *planetary* in philosophical scope and spatial and temporal extent [26].

THE STREAMLINED LIFE CYCLE ASSESSMENT FOR BUILDINGS

In this chapter, we have had a look at the standards-based LCA. We can see that the many steps we're required to take and the many crossroads at which we face critical choices make the contemplation of such an undertaking daunting. In reality, even if we have the interest, few of us feel we have the time to delve deeply into the intricacies of life cycle assessment or systems analysis. The pace of today's

building design projects barely gives room for much other than quickly identifying the most feasible solution to meet our clients' needs and schedules. So, we should take advantage of the shortcuts that have already been coded into building LCA or BIM software [27].

These applications don't require a PhD degree in environmental science. We're simply prompted to enter a set of parameters. In this final section of the chapter, we offer a brief overview of the main steps of a streamlined LCA. It's important to note, however, that although much can be automated with existing digital LCA tools, an understanding of the underlying principles and methods is critical to their effective use. Software for building LCA or plug-ins to building information modeling software requires, at a minimum, that we provide information from two major components of the building life cycle: a bill of materials and a quantification of operational energy consumed. As these create the majority of greenhouse gas emissions, data on emissions from transport, construction or repair work, and from demolition and waste management processes are usually available as preset statistical values that have been predefined for the scope of the assessment. Furthermore, many of those parts of an LCA may be difficult to estimate and play only a marginal role in the outcome and we can draw them from data sources and tables and thereby avoid the unnecessary waste of time. An example of such a component of the building system might be electrical wiring or ventilation ducts, which can be assessed using given average values per floor area of the building.

We can retrieve a bill of materials from a BIM model, assuming that the model has been built in such a way as to enable us to identify individual materials. This means that we should avoid modeling structure and interstitial voids as solid blocks but instead model all of the layers and geometries of individual assembly components with as much fidelity as possible. Without describing every nut and bolt or the area or volume of plastic packaging, this initial care in modeling the building will provide a sound basis for generating material lists and quantities directly from BIM. By adopting more precise modeling practices, different material substitutions and alternative design solutions become easily comparable during the LCA process.

We can then export our bill of materials directly from our BIM to our LCA tool. Current trends in the development of BIM software suggest that our ability to calculate inventories and their respective carbon footprints directly through our models will evolve quickly. This would make iterative testing of design solutions and the real-time assessment of their potential impacts possible with leaving our building information model.

The quantity of operational energy our building will consume is another story. In many countries and regions an energy declaration is already mandatory in any application for a building permit. This declaration is based on the calculation or simulation of required operational heating, cooling, and electricity usage in a standard operating scenario of the building. If we already have such a document to

hand, we can enter the estimated amount of energy (in kilowatt-hours or mega joules) directly into our LCA tool. If we have not estimated the operational energy usage, then a simulative energy model lies ahead. Some BIM tools already include built-in basic-level energy simulation features. We can use these to generate a ballpark figure in advance of performing more sophisticated energy simulations. Average, statistical values for typical consumption of energy in a given building type are not suitable for describing the energy performance of an individual design, and we should not use them to estimate the impacts of operational energy usage in our LCA.

In this ideally digitized process, a building LCA is much less a scientific process than an exercise in data entry. And though our reliance on building information models and LCA tools will inevitably save us time and frayed nerves, it has the drawback of distancing us as building designers from the concepts of the process we're undertaking and also the facts that really have an impact on the carbon emissions and the potential economic and material circularity of our design solutions.

Info box 2.9

Quantity Take-Offs from the BIM to LCA Software

Most commonly used BIM software include inventories of the building parts, products, and materials used in a design. They also offer possibilities for adjusting the contents and breakdown of such schedules. Creating a bill of materials in BIM typically includes the following steps:

Route 1

1. Check the system boundary of the model with the LCA assessor. Discuss the required building parts and the level of detail. Check if the LCA tool has an interface for the import of the inventory or instructions for preparing the inventory into a spreadsheet format.
2. Coordinate the inventory with the design team. Agree on consistent material labelling and Industry Foundation Classes (IFC) for classifying the elements of the design. If possible, use an integrated BIM that contains the required amount of data from architecture, structures, interiors as well as building service and automation systems.
3. Build or update the model(s) correctly using real material and geometries. Avoid modeling structure types as solid objects, use correct layers of materials and possible voids instead.
4. Check the quality of the model with an appropriate model checker tool.
5. Prepare the inventory for the LCA. Adjust the contents of the inventory according to the requirements of the assessment.
6. Export the inventory into the LCA tool for the actual assessment.

Partial LCA in the BIM: Route 2

The BIM software can also be used for performing parts of the LCA. This route is still maturing, and requires that environmental product data are available. Some material producers already provide BIM design objects that include information on e.g., the carbon footprint of the product, based on an EPD.

1. Coordinate the requirements for the partial LCA with the LCA assessor of the project. Define which parts of the LCA will be done within the BIM tool. Agree on the used EPDs or generic databases.
2. Make use of the BIM objects that have environmental information included. Check that their environmental data are in accordance with the requirements of the LCA study.
3. Define material-related environmental factors for structures that do not contain the information yet. By using the material or structure type settings, define the environmental indicators for BIM. Input the required environmental data (e.g., carbon footprint) into the material or structure-type settings. Retrieve the environmental data from a database or EPD that has been agreed to be used in the project.
4. Coordinate the assessment with the design team and prepare the model(s) as described in steps 2–4 of Route 1.
5. Develop an inventory of environmental impacts within the BIM software. Adjust the inventory to fit the requirements of the LCA study.
6. Provide the LCA assessor with the results of the partial LCA for completing the assessment.

3 CASE STUDIES IN DECARBONIZATION

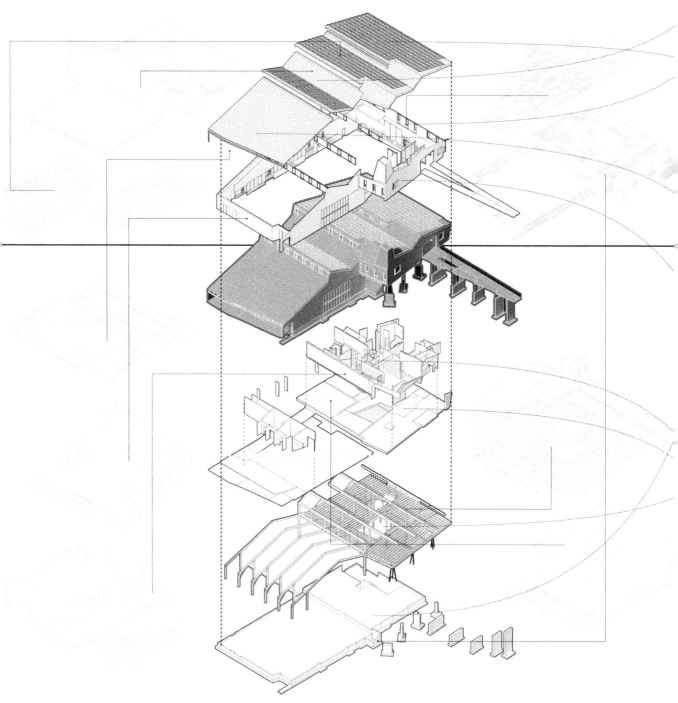

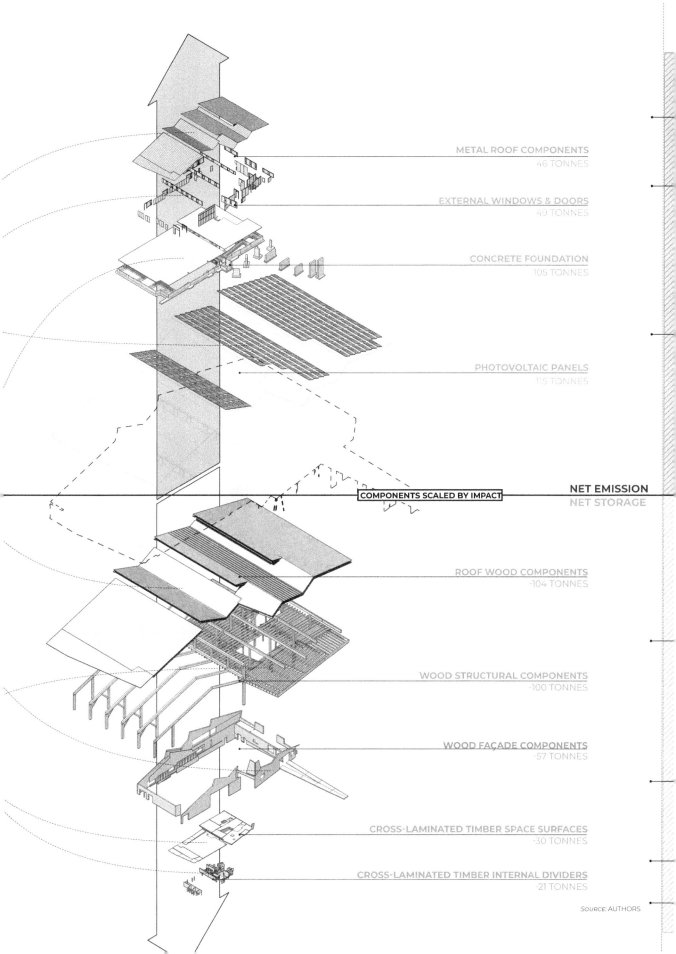

METAL ROOF COMPONENTS
46 TONNES

EXTERNAL WINDOWS & DOORS
49 TONNES

CONCRETE FOUNDATION
105 TONNES

PHOTOVOLTAIC PANELS
115 TONNES

NET EMISSION
NET STORAGE

COMPONENTS SCALED BY IMPACT

ROOF WOOD COMPONENTS
-104 TONNES

WOOD STRUCTURAL COMPONENTS
-100 TONNES

WOOD FAÇADE COMPONENTS
-57 TONNES

CROSS-LAMINATED TIMBER SPACE SURFACES
-30 TONNES

CROSS-LAMINATED TIMBER INTERNAL DIVIDERS
-21 TONNES

Source: AUTHORS

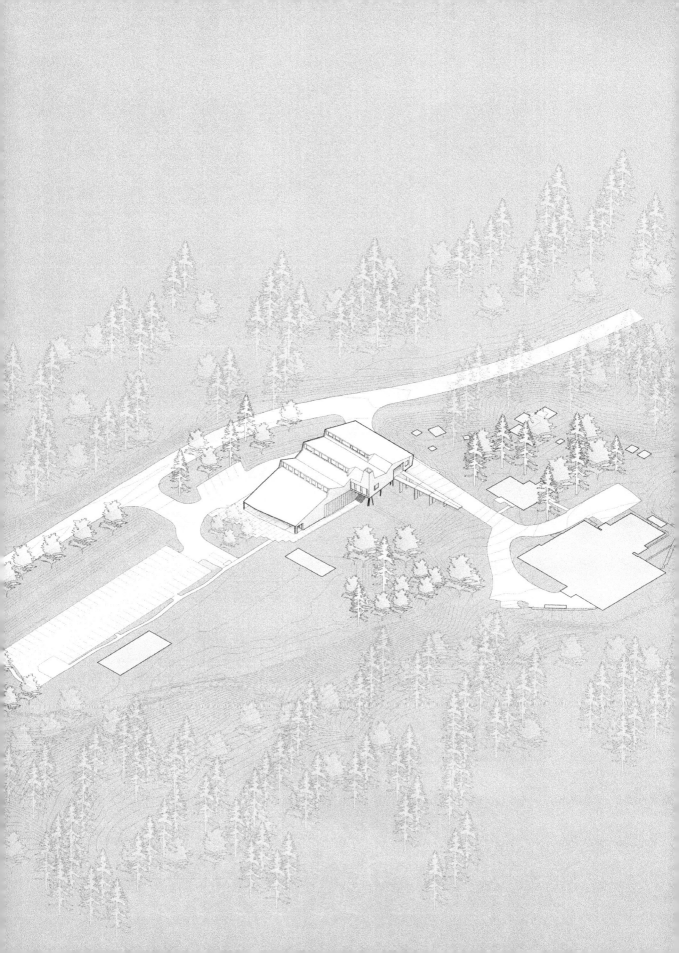

CHAPTER THREE
CASE STUDIES IN DECARBONIZATION

NOTES FROM THE FIELD

Tracking and arresting the flows of carbon in building will inevitably present repeated challenges to the building designer, given the specific conditions and constraints of each project and, more broadly, the well-established and slow-to-change activities of the building sector, the habits of its participants, and the complexity of its supply chains. A field manual seeks to describe conditions that one might face in the day-to-day conduct of one's work and to offer an orderly set of operations to address those conditions. These prescribed steps are typically prioritized to counter the difficulties, even chaos, that one might encounter in the field in order to ensure that the objectives of a mission, such as the decarbonization of a building, might be achieved in spite of those challenges. But a field manual is no substitute for experience. So we offer the following case studies, described through the analytical lens of life cycle assessment (LCA), that we hope will make manifest some of the more theoretical discussions of the preceding chapters.

We've chosen two buildings—Common Ground High School and Puukuokka Housing Block—that represent recent efforts. The buildings were designed by two different architecture, engineering, and construction teams, working in distinct building economies from opposite sides of the Atlantic Ocean. One example is from the New England region of the United States; the other is set in the north-eastern corner of Europe in Central Finland. Despite their different contexts and distinct programs, both case study buildings share similar approaches to decarbonization. Both are formed primarily from engineered timber and other bio-based materials. Both employ significant degrees

of industrial prefabrication in their manufacture and assembly. These parallels reflect two biases. The material bias stems from the ongoing research by the authors into the substitution benefits of renewable, carbon-storing building products and systems. Both buildings were familiar analytical subjects with detailed building information models. As such, they offered our assessment process robust data sets and comprehensive quantity surveys. The methodological bias lay in our conviction that techniques of prefabrication and industrial building manufacture are growing trends in construction with many potential benefits to the decarbonization of building: a high degree of manufacturing precision which creates tighter assemblies with better thermal performance, waste reduction through material optimization, and reversibility of the assembly process making circular economic reuse of the buildings' components and materials more feasible. In a sense, the choice of these two buildings for analysis reflects an attempt to assess recent efforts to establish best practices for decarbonized design rather than simply critique building practice that has ignored the impacts of embodied emissions and would therefore make for easy targets. As we've noted, the time frame for an effective response by the building sector to climate change is closing. We must look to forward-thinking models to move the discourse further faster.

It goes without saying, however, that two case studies—whether they reflect similar or polar opposite approaches to decarbonization—are insufficient illustration of all of the potential particularities and carbon-related nuances that shape the building life cycle and its assessment—the variability of material economies, manufacturing methods, available energy systems, and cultures and

FIGURE 3.1 COMMON GROUND HIGH SCHOOL SOURCE: AUTHORS

behaviors of building occupants and managers—and that we have outlined thus far in this book. An exhaustive survey of building types, sites, and assemblies, their political, economic, and cultural contexts and their relative carbon impacts is beyond the scope of this book and analysis. Instead, these two case studies illustrate the relationship between intention and outcome, expose the challenges of two specific places, building programs, and construction methods, and quantify where both benefits and impacts accrue. With the help of these case studies, we hope to demonstrate the way in which different building types, climatic conditions, and policy frameworks can influence the carbon footprints of building.

In this chapter, we illustrate how the principles of life cycle assessment—as presented in Chapter 2—have been applied in practice, and which types of results one can generally expect to find. A word of caution is, nevertheless, worth noting at the outset. Different buildings are built for different needs and, especially when situated in different locations, cannot be directly compared to each other. Depending on the typology, occupation, size, shape, orientation, energy class, and many other distinctive features, a building's environmental, social, and economic impacts are given very different starting points. Therefore, it is not necessary to memorize the details or carry our LCA calculations three decimal places to the right of the decimal point. Instead, we recommend a focus on the general findings, the underlying design strategies and logics, and the lessons learned from the implementation in the construction process. Which solutions proved they support a low carbon footprint? How do these solutions square with your expectations?

HOW WERE THE CALCULATIONS PERFORMED?

Material Inventories

Fortunately, we had access to the drawings and building information models of the case study buildings, as well as to some of their technical documentation. This provided us a wide range of data for the materials, products, and systems used in each building. Based on this information, we calculated the quantities and weights of each product, further breaking down the figures into separate materials.

The buildings were divided into component classes and categories based on their design and construction, rather than on a universal classification of construction materials and systems. This means that the building component classifications are not identical for each of the case studies. Rather than speculate how to unify the material categories between each project, we chose to accept this difference. For example, Common Ground High School was mostly built on-site with flat-packed structural and enclosure components, whereas the Puukuokka Housing Block was mostly built from prefabricated volumetric units. Thus, it was more logical to make a division of the building's components based on which portions of each project were built on-site and which were prefabricated at a remote location. Despite these differences in material categorization, the overall carbon analysis results are comparable.

Carbon Footprints

The carbon footprints were calculated according to the life cycle methodology presented in Chapter 2 of this book, following the approach of standard EN 15 978 [1]. We have estimated most of the relevant life cycle stages of the buildings and their parts, but excluded some marginal or uncertain stages.

To calculate the environmental impacts of building materials, we used both Environmental Product Declarations and the open-source dataset "Inventory of Carbon and Energy" [2], supplemented with other representative national datasets when possible. Replacement rates for building products were based on typical technical service life estimations of building parts [3].

We calculated the transportation distances based on an analysis of the location of the building and potential warehouses and factories nearby. We also measured distances to existing waste management facilities and estimated the transportation of construction and demolition waste accordingly. As different types of transportation emit GHGs at different rates, we made assumptions about the vehicles used (mostly trucks and trains, a few ships, and some air freight).

The emissions from the construction work, repair work, and demolition work could not be recovered from the project reports. Therefore, we used reference values from the literature [4, 5] and adapted them to their regional context.

Biogenic Carbon Neutrality of Wood

Both of the case study buildings include a significant amount of wood in their structures and surfaces. Wood contains atmospheric carbon for half of its dry weight, which can be calculated and translated into corresponding units of emissions using the calculation method of standard EN 16 449 [6]. In addition, the production of the wooden material leads to CO_2 emissions from three main sources: fossil emissions (the result of burning fossil fuels for energy, for example), biogenic emissions (the result of burning wood or other bio-based materials for energy as another example), and emissions related to land use and land use change (for example, system-wide climate impacts are different, if harvested forest is reforested, or if it is converted into a parking lot after the harvesting).

In the examples provided, we applied the principle of biogenic carbon neutrality based on standard EN 16 485 [7]. In this approach, the biogenic component of the CO_2 emissions of wooden construction products is calculated as a negative value, if the wood is sourced from a sustainably managed forest. An equivalent amount of CO_2 accounted for in the beginning of the life cycle as a negative value (environmental asset) must be amortized within the same system boundaries as an emission (environmental load) occurring at the end-of-life stage of the product, thereby reflecting a biogenic carbon balance over the full building life cycle. As the wood material comes from sustainable sources, we assumed land-use related emissions to be neutral as well, because the harvested forests would be reforested. However, depending on the energy and processes needed to manufacture and fabricate particular wooden components, there may be fossil hydrocarbon emissions for wood-based products at some point in their life cycle.

Carbonation of Concrete

Concrete can sequester atmospheric carbon as it undergoes a slow chemical process called carbonation during its service life, as described in Chapter 2. In our example we have calculated the carbonation of concrete surfaces in the yard and exposed building parts according to the method advocated by Lagerblad [8], which takes into account the weather exposure conditions and cement types of different cement-based building parts.

Accumulation of Carbon in Plants and Soil

As plants grow, they absorb CO_2 from the atmosphere. There are both trees and herbaceous plants on the sites of both case study buildings. We have estimated their growth during the reference study period of 50 years and calculated the uptake of carbon in the plant biomass. Also, the removal of carbon in the removed trees has been taken into account. The amount of carbon in the trees has been estimated using growth algorithms and stem volume functions [9].

Carbon stored in tree trunks and branches is assumed to stay intact for the duration of the study period. Leaves and herbaceous plants decay seasonally and thus release the organic carbon back into the atmosphere. However, a fraction of this organic carbon stays in the soil as soil organic carbon. The amount of this carbon varies based on soil types. We have estimated the accumulation of the soil organic carbon based on the methods outlined in earlier research [10, 11].

Mitigation Potential

The mitigation potential was estimated by only considering which building materials or appliances could be replaced with alternatives with a lower carbon footprint. We did not consider the mitigation potential that would have required redesigning the building, changing its location or changing the technical service lives of its components. The results are therefore indicative only.

In reality, not all of the speculated emission savings could be realized. Changes in materials cause changes in costs, replacement rates, architectural appearance, fire safety, acoustic properties, and other functional features. Furthermore, the studied

---

Info Box 3.1:

Units and Scales of Emissions

The calculation results are given in carbon dioxide equivalents (CO_2e). This unit includes all greenhouse gas emissions translated into the warming potential of carbon dioxide.

It is also possible to show the results as carbon (C). Based on the molecular weight of carbon and oxygen, CO_2 is 3.67 times heavier than bare carbon [6]. For clarity, the units in these calculations are constantly given in CO_2e.

The units are in metric tons or tonnes. Is one metric ton too little or too much? It can be compared to the average per capita carbon footprint of Americans, Europeans or Africans. As discussed in this book, the average per capita carbon footprints today are 16.5 metric tons for Americans, 6.4 for Europeans, and 0.8 for Sub-Saharan Africans [12]. This helps to make comparisons, especially of the emission mitigation potential.

---

buildings have a very low carbon footprint and are good examples of low-carbon design. The speculative mitigation potential is, however, a useful example to illustrate which parts of the building could be rethought and how those material interventions would affect the emissions.

CASE STUDY 1
COMMON GROUND HIGH SCHOOL

The new building at the Common Ground High School is located in New Haven, Connecticut, in the northeastern United States. The campus stands at the foot of West Rock Ridge, a 700-foot-high trap rock cliff ensconced in second-growth mixed hardwood forests that is today a city-owned park. The campus itself occupies a former farm in which extensive excavation and reshaping of the land have resulted in artificially steep banks and poor draining soils and surfaces.

Over the course of twenty years, educators and administrators have transformed the complex of farm buildings into a high school with a curricular focus on environmentalism and sustainable agriculture. Today the school operates as a public charter program open to teenagers from New Haven and the surrounding towns. Its primary program comprises two science classrooms, an art studio, a gymnasium with a half basketball court and administrator's and teacher's offices.

The superstructure of the building was prefabricated from a mixture of engineered wood fiber: cross-laminated timber panels, glue-laminated timber beams and trusses, I-joists, cellulose fiber insulation, and oriented strand board (OSB) panels. The primary structural components were made from black spruce, harvested and manufactured into mass timber elements in northern Quebec. That material was then shipped approximately 1 050 kilometers to southern New Hampshire in the US where it was fashioned into structural assemblies and then flat-packed and shipped another 100 miles south to the building site for installation. The rapid installation of prefabricated elements served to offset the conventional schedule of site and foundation works. The construction took place over 14 months while the school remained in session.

Designed by Gray Organschi Architecture, the new Arts and Sciences Building at the Common Ground High School received an American Architecture Award for 2017.

ARCHITECTURAL OBJECTIVES
(by Gray Organschi Architecture)

The new building at Common Ground High School offered our design team the rare opportunity to work closely with dedicated teachers and deeply engaged students to craft a special architectural design. Their challenge to us was to make a building that was healthy for both the school community and our global environment; durable in its construction using sustainable systems and renewable materials in a legible and innovative way; flexible enough to adapt to the school's rich and constantly evolving curriculum; self-sufficient, largely, in its use of energy and increasingly precious and limited resources on our planet; respectful of the existing buildings and campus landscape that give the institution its distinct character. We felt that the Common Ground's brief for the new building was in itself an eloquent manifesto for sustainable, low impact architecture.

The curriculum of Common Ground is rooted in ecological systems thinking. Its public charter school facilities serve 225 high school students, mostly from New Haven's inner city. Its umbrella organization, the New Haven Ecology Project, engages over 12,000 children and adults from the surrounding metropolitan community in a range of farming and environmental research and restoration activities across their campus throughout the year. A building committee comprised of Common Ground faculty, administrators, and students commissioned our design team to collaborate with their school to develop a new art studio, science classrooms, and a community meeting and recreation facility bordering the educational farm complex that lies beneath New Haven's West Rock Park. Over the course of four years of planning, design, funding, and finally construction, our design team's special collaboration with teachers, administrators, and students enabled us to develop and refine a master plan for the campus and to design the nearly 15,000 square feet of new science and art classrooms, administrative office spaces and large multipurpose community space in a high performance, energy-optimizing building that provides healthy and beautiful spaces for learning.

In addition to providing much-needed classroom and community space for this growing institution, the new building was to knit together a working landscape of existing classroom and administration buildings with the gardens, forests, and wetlands that serve as Common Ground's campus and "outdoor classroom." The aspiration was that the building and its site would teach about the complex and potentially convivial relationship between the built and the natural environment.

As a basis for design, the school's building committee called for a functional, durable building that would support their broad range of activities while reducing long-term maintenance costs, one that would perform at the highest levels of energy efficiency in order to curtail greenhouse gas emissions over its service life. Their greatest challenge to our team was that the new structure should serve as a pedagogical tool, legible in its use of physical resources and committed not just to the regenerative ecological function of its immediate site but also to the protection and promotion of the health of distant landscapes. Just as the school's faculty and students sought to understand the potential downstream impacts from their daily farm and school activities on the Mill River watershed and the ecological health of Long Island Sound 4 miles to the south—the effects of their use of water, the disturbance of soil and associated hydrologic function, and the introduction of effluent waste—they also hoped to acknowledge and explore the upstream impacts of their construction project.

The study and practice of agriculture and land management place an emphasis on Common Ground's curriculum; the fields, hoop houses, forest, and wetlands that serve as outdoor classrooms are the focus of their campus. In that spirit, our collective design process embraced the premise that the new building—or at least much of the material that comprised it—could be grown rather than geologically extracted. Although our architecture and engineering team

had a strong background in wood construction and extensive experience with large-scale, laminated timber structural components, in particular, we had yet to scrutinize specific silvicultural practices, assess the industrial inputs and emissions of biogenic material processing, and quantify the resulting storage of carbon in the molecular structure of the harvested wood products and building components we specified. To engage and optimize the transcalar properties and ramifications of this biological resource, became a focus of our design.

Operational Energy and Water Use

In addition to that bio-based material approach, we also sought to reduce operational energy and "waste" water generation. The building's interior spaces are heated and cooled by a synergistic system of solar photovoltaic panels and ground-source heat pumps served by geothermal wells lying in an array beneath the school's parking area.

Through careful analysis of classroom light levels and our subsequent design of windows and skylights, we sought to optimize day-lighting that would supplement and, at certain times in the day and year, entirely eliminate the need for artificial illumination. We oriented the building and sculpted its massing and roof overhangs to reduce solar heat gain in summer months, while allowing ample northern light to wash its interior spaces. A combination of high venting clerestories and operable windows at floor level promoted natural ventilation in order to further reduce mechanical cooling loads.

We sought to reduce water consumption through the specification of low volume fixtures and the monitoring of water consumption. And the roof is designed to serve as its own "watershed" shaped to collect and funnel storm water into and through a series of rain gardens and bio-remediation pools that filter and clean it and feed low-energy agricultural irrigation systems. These constructed wetlands serve simultaneously as a habitat that promotes the site's biodiversity, outdoor classrooms to facilitate hands-on learning, and a preventative measure to minimize any additional burden on the city's antiquated storm sewer system.

All new and renovated exterior and interior spaces maintain the natural integrity and biological and hydrologic processes of the site and are built using low-impact techniques and environmental best practices to minimize immediate construction disturbance and long-term ecological impacts to area eco-systems.

This brings us back to the material make-up and structural assembly of the new building at the Common Ground High School.

There are two solar energy systems at work in the school. In addition to the photovoltaic energy generation system, an increasingly common sustainable technology that proved essential to the building's low-energy operation, we sought to exploit a second solar source—photosynthesis—as manufacturing energy, the same biochemical process that students learned about in biology class but understood more deeply as they worked the school's farm fields or hiked through the school's forested landscapes.

Structural Biomass

Like many modestly sized buildings in the US, the art and science building at Common Ground High School is comprised of an array of commercially distributed forms of structural biomass, harvested wood products manufactured from wood lamellae, fiber, flakes, pulp, and furnish, industrially agglomerated, adhered, and compressed through lamination or extrusion into sheets, boards, batts, and structural shapes. Each plant-based product has its own identifiable geographic source, a method and means of processing that entails the input of energy and raw material and the generation of waste and emissions to soil, water, and air. In contrast to other classes of

FIGURE 3.2 COMMON GROUND HIGH SCHOOL. *Source:* DAVID SUNBERG/ESTO PHOTOGRAPHICS

structural material that are extracted, sintered, and smelted from raw materials and industrial fuels drawn from deeper geological strata and in which material formation cycles are measured on a geological timescale of tens of millions of years, structural biomass will regenerate within the relatively rapid time frame. This "fast domain" of photosynthetic building material production and harvest, dependent on the species of plant, the climate zone and microclimatic context, and the degree to which forest soil media are disturbed during harvest, can be measured in decades. Although it is an exercise in extrapolation to measure the quantity of atmospheric carbon taken up through that continuing photo-biochemical reaction in plant fiber and accumulated in the soils and woody matter across forest landscapes, we can measure with great specificity the weight of carbon in wood of a particular species and moisture content. If we fairly account for the CO_2 emissions entailed in the harvest, processing and transport of the wood products and assemblies we specify for our buildings, we can understand the net carbon sequestration potential of the built environment. We can optimize future cycles of sustainably managed forest sources. We can consider photosynthesis, with its relatively low energy density compared to fossil fuels, as a readily available, non-emitting form of manufacturing energy. And we can transform the constructed environment from an emissions source into a carbon sink.

A critical structural decision in the design of the prefabricated system of wall and roof components that shape the new Common Ground High School building structure and envelope was the use of glue-laminated timber beams (GLBs) and cross-laminated timber (CLT) panels. Three-ply black spruce CLT forms the tension surface in the cellulose-insulated stressed skin panels that span the school's classrooms and circulation spaces. CLT also forms the shear walls and elevator and stair cores that resist lateral wind and seismic loading as well as the large open stairway in the center of the building. The wood was harvested in a 60-year rotation of patch clear-cutting and replanting within a 5-million-acre area of black spruce forests in the Canadian province of Quebec. Processed into structural elements in a nearby production facility in Chibougamau, it was then shipped to a fabrication plant in Walpole, New Hampshire, where it was fully prefabricated as an integrated system of structure and insulated wall and roof components. Those components were trucked south where they were installed as the shell and structure of the new school in New Haven. Visible in the public spaces, these mass timber elements and surfaces serve as a reminder to the faculty and students, who use the spaces, of the regional forest landscapes 600 miles to the north that generated that material.

Other species of wood are represented throughout the building: laminated Southern Yellow Pine planks, pressure-treated for durability, form the primary path between the upper and lower campus; strands, veneers, strips and fibers from aspens, poplars, and longleaf pines comprise the engineered joists, studs, and panels that make up the hollow prefabricated wall and roof assemblies, densely packed with recycled cellulose pulp insulation. In addition to the usual array of hardwoods that serve as trim and cabinetry in a building of this type, wood strand-based acoustical panels line the walls of classrooms and roof of the gymnasium to mitigate sound reflection while compressed bamboo flooring lines the upper circulations spaces as wearing surface.

The transparent nature of the entire process—from the earliest aspirational discussions, through the increasingly detailed but always participatory design collaboration and a pedagogically curated construction process supported by the project's construction managers, the ongoing monitoring of its energy, water, and maintenance served this innovative group of teachers and students as an opportunity to teach and to learn about global ecology and sustainable human behavior.

FIGURE 3.3 INSTALLING PREFABRICATED ROOF COMPONENTS AT COMMON GROUND HIGH SCHOOL. *SOURCE:* GRAY ORGANSCHI ARCHITECTURE

Summary of Total Carbon Emissions, Storages and Circulation Potential

The total life cycle emissions of Common Ground High School reached 1600 tonnes during the selected study period of 50 years. In this case, the share of operational and embodied emissions was evenly split: 51% of the emissions are associated with the use of operational energy, and 49% is attributed to embodied sources. From the latter, the production of building materials and products accounts for largest share, with close to 60% of all embodied emissions.

All other life cycle phases played a marginal role. The joint impact of construction and demolition processes—including related transport—remained below 10%.

The most significant carbon storages (long-term deposits of carbon removed from the atmosphere) in the case study building were established during the production stage. Wooden components in the roof and frame structures had a storage capacity equal of 460 tonnes of CO_2.

The building and its site also function as a carbon sink during the use stage. Ground vegetation, trees, and soils sequester almost 56 tonnes of CO_2 over the course of 50 years. Furthermore, the slowly carbonizing concrete surfaces of the building store an additional tonne. When calculated together, the carbon storages and sinks account for over 510 tonnes of CO_2e, offsetting one-third of the building's life cycle emissions.

Because of the uncertainties related to future emissions, the greatest opportunity for emissions reduction and therefore the most relevant area of focus during the design process lay in the selection of the building's material palette. In addition, designing the building for high energy efficiency—without shifting consequential emissions to other life cycle stages (e.g., by requiring more emissions-intensive materials or appliances)—will likely pay off in the future, regardless of what the exact energy-related emissions or energy mixture will be. In this case study the emissions that arise from operational energy and material use are those that designers can directly influence through thoughtful design work.

The construction products of the studied building are made from a variety of raw materials. Some can be reused, many can be recycled, but certain products remain a challenge for a potentially circular construction economy. The reason for this low reuse potential lies partly in the assembly of the components (difficult to disassemble separately), partly in their specific dimensioning (designed for a specific, bespoke building), but mostly in immature reuse policies: we lack clear quality control mechanisms for most reusable construction products, the legal risks for the technical performance of the reused products are considered significant, and the logistics for designing and constructing with reused products are complicated.

However, the potential for recycling of the products is more promising. Metals are commonly recycled and concrete commonly downcycled into road construction. Wood has the potential to be downcycled into secondary wood products—such as particle boards—but is very subject to economic feasibility of the recycling value chain. Plastics are still a challenge to the recycling processes of today, because there are numerous plastic types used in construction and they can contain several additives that make their mechanical recycling difficult. For both wood and plastics, the option for energy recovery is the second option, if recycling cannot be considered. From the viewpoint of avoiding greenhouse gas emissions, energy recovery cannot be seen as the most sustainable alternative. Both wood and plastics release their embodied carbon when burnt.

We also had another look at the material selection of the building and tried to identify ways to lower emissions through greener material choices. We did this without changing the size, shape or energy efficiency of the building. As a summary, we could identify a reduction potential of 158 tonnes of CO_2, which is 10% of the total life cycle emissions of the building.

In the following sections we will further explain how the overall life cycle emissions arise during the life cycles of building's materials. Furthermore, we will also study the emissions from its operational energy use and the volume of emissions that can be avoided by generating renewable energy on the building site.

FIGURE 3.4 EXPOSED CROSS-LAMINATED TIMBER STRUCTURAL PANELS AT COMMON GROUND HIGH SCHOOL. *Source:* DAVID SUNBERG/ESTO PHOTOGRAPHICS

COMMON GROUND HIGH SCHOOL: KEY FIGURES

MATERIALS

The material-related emissions in the production phase of the Common Ground High School arise from two major sources: site and ground elements, and—perhaps surprisingly—electrical elements. Looking at the distribution of production phase emissions, almost half of the emissions are attributed to these two sources.

In the following, the calculation results are presented for each category of building components.

Table 3.1

Common Ground High School: emissions and $kgCO_2e$/building.

Emissions		$kgCO_2e$/building
A	**Production and construction**	
A1–3	Production of materials	477,156
A4	Transport to site	44,903
A5	Construction work	41,267
		563,326
B	**Use**	
B1	Use in building	(not assessed)
B2	Maintenance	(not assessed)
B3–4	Repairs and replacements	169,146
B5	Refurbishment	(not assessed)
B6	Use of energy	794,783
B7	Use of water	(not assessed)
		963,929
C	**End-of-life**	
C1	Deconstruction work	37,669
C2	Transport to waste management	18,783
C3–4	Waste management and final disposal	23,065
		79,517
A–C	**Full life cycle**	**1,606,772**
Storages, sinks, and climate benefits		
bio-CO_2	Carbon storages in bio-based products	-463,098
B1	Carbonation of cement-based products	-1,723
B1	Uptake of carbon into plants and soil	-55,604
D	Net benefits from reuse and recycling	(not assessed)
D	Surplus renewable energy	0
	Full life cycle	**-520,424**

FIGURE 3.5 COMMON GROUND HIGH SCHOOL CARBON EMISSIONS, SINKS, AND STORAGES. *SOURCE:* AUTHORS

EMISSIONS AND STORAGES FOR BUILDING PARTS (kgCO₂e/m²)

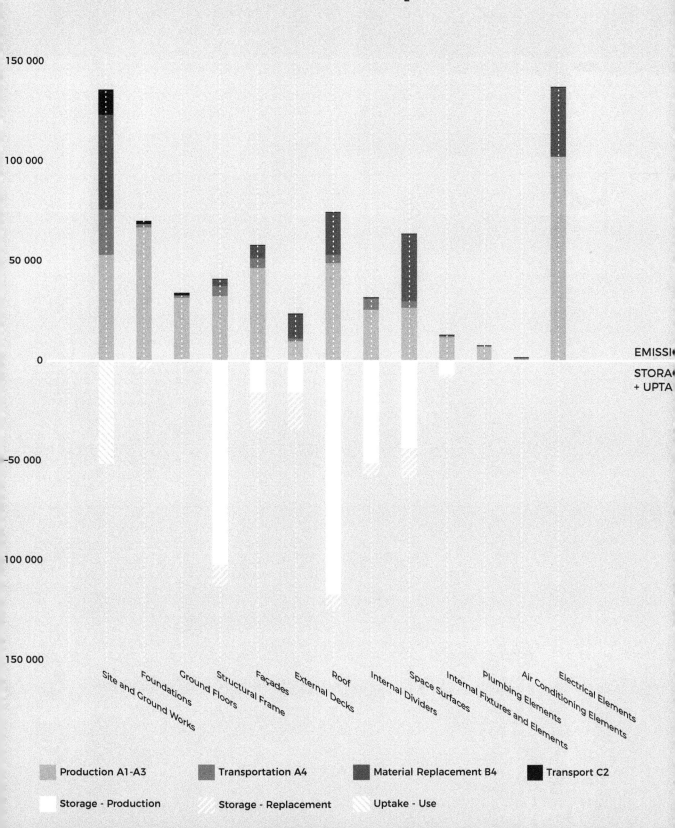

EMISSI[...]

STORA[...]
+ UPTA[...]

Scale	
150 000	
100 000	
50 000	
0	
-50 000	
100 000	
150 000	

Site and Ground Works
Foundations
Ground Floors
Structural Frame
Façades
External Decks
Roof
Internal Dividers
Space Surfaces
Internal Fixtures and Elements
Plumbing Elements
Air Conditioning Elements
Electrical Elements

- ■ Production A1-A3
- ■ Transportation A4
- ■ Material Replacement B4
- ■ Transport C2
- □ Storage - Production
- ▨ Storage - Replacement
- ▨ Uptake - Use

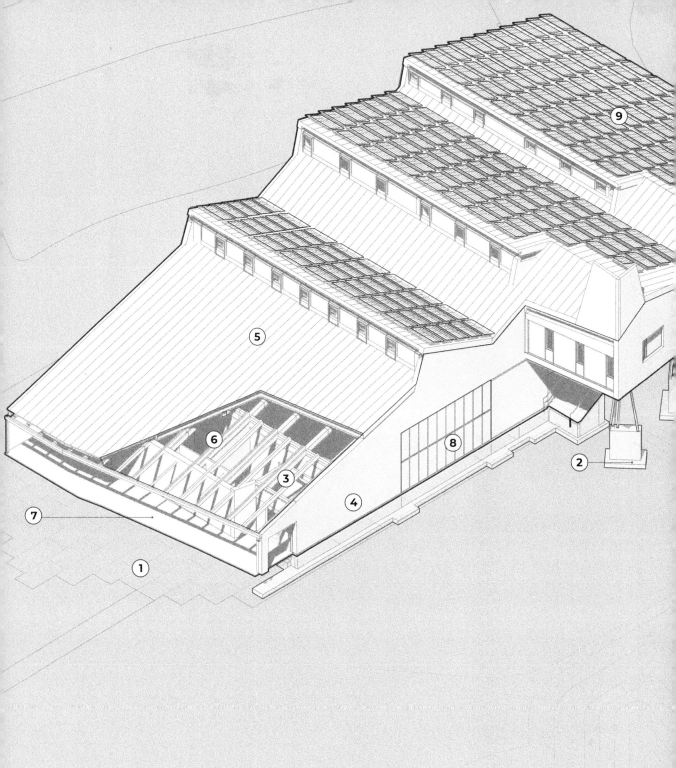

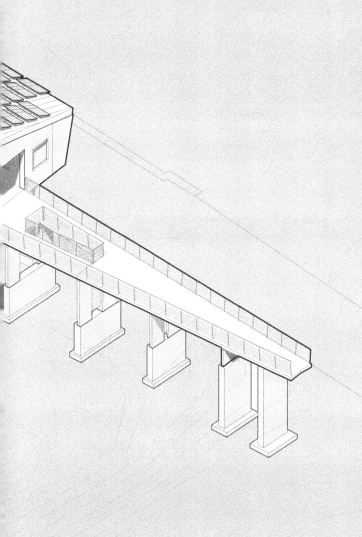

TOTAL EMISSION

698 TONNES

TOTAL STORAGE + UPTAKE

514 TONNES

① SITE & GROUNDWORKS

EMISSIONS: 142 TONNES
UPTAKE: 58 TONNES
MITIGATION: 50 TONNES

② FOUNDATIONS & GROUND FLOOR

EMISSIONS: 109 TONNES
UPTAKE: 1,4 TONNES
MITIGATION: 35 TONNES

③ STRUCTURAL FRAME

EMISSIONS: 39 TONNES
UPTAKE: 122 TONNES
MITIGATION: 2 TONNES

④ FAÇADES & EXTERNAL DECKS

EMISSIONS: 81 TONNES
UPTAKE: 77 TONNES
MITIGATION: NONE IDENTIFIED

⑤ ROOF

EMISSIONS: 78 TONNES
UPTAKE: 134 TONNES
MITIGATION: NONE IDENTIFIED

⑥ INTERNAL DIVIDERS

EMISSIONS: 32 TONNES
UPTAKE: 56 TONNES
MITIGATION: 7 TONNES

⑦ SPACE SURFACES

EMISSIONS: 65 TONNES
UPTAKE: 64 TONNES
MITIGATION: 7 TONNES

⑧ INTERNAL FIXTURES

EMISSIONS: 11 TONNES
UPTAKE: 8 TONNES
MITIGATION: 1 TONNES

⑨ BUILDING SERVICE INSTALLATIONS

EMISSIONS: 145 TONNES
UPTAKE: NONE
MITIGATION: 65 TONNES

SITE AND GROUND WORKS

The construction materials used for the site were mostly concrete, gravel and asphalt. Plastics were also used for the drainage pipes underground. In addition, soil and vegetation cover large areas of the site. All these materials create both emissions, but some do also absorb them. Growing vegetation uptakes carbon from the air and some of that carbon accumulates into the soil. The same happens as concrete paving carbonates.

Emissions

Most of the emissions from sitework arise from the site's manufactured paving surfaces. Their industrial production incurs significant volumes of emissions, totaling 95 tonnes. Asphalt parking and road surfaces, together with concrete paving, account for over 60% of the emissions in this category. We assumed that the asphalt surfaces and concrete paving would be replaced once during the service life of the building, which almost doubles the emissions from this building category.

During the initial sitework, 16 trees were removed from the site. Later, new trees were planted. We estimated that the CO_2e emissions caused by the removal of trees is close to 11 tonnes, although it was not possible to weigh them. Should the removed trees have been used for a good purpose—for furniture or other long-lasting products—their organic carbon would have continued to be bound into their biomass.

Carbon Storages

We found that the uptake of carbon through newly planted trees and vegetation, in addition to the accumulation of organic carbon into soil has the potential to exceed 55 tonnes during the study period. Carbonation of the concrete surfaces will also remove close to 2 tonnes during this time. This means that the site continues to function as a carbon sink, thanks to the preserved and enhanced ecosystem services.

Mitigation Potential

If emissions were intended to be mitigated through material choices for sitework and landscaping, the greatest potential can be found in the surfaces. Altogether, 41 tonnes of emissions of site and ground works could have been avoided, which would be a significant improvement.

Using a concrete mix that included more cement substitutes, such as fly ash or blast furnace slag, would lower the emissions during the life cycle of concrete paving and concrete pipes. The estimated impact of replacing half of the used cement with blast furnace slag would yield 26 tonnes savings.

Furthermore, the emissions from the production of asphalt could be reduced by approximately 15%, if reclaimed asphalt with warm mix technology had been available [13]. This would reduce the emissions by 7.5 tonnes over the study period, during which the asphalt would be replaced once.

Although the production of plastics for the storm sewer pipes causes rather a lot of emissions, it is difficult to make these pipes from alternative materials and they are vital for the function of the drainage system.

Circulation

Some of the components of the site can be reused. Concrete paving requires very little additional effort before reuse—as long as its transportation does not become too expensive or emissions-intensive.

The remainder of the site materials are likely to be recycled after their initial service life. It is typical to downcycle concrete into road construction after it has been demolished. Asphalt can also be recycled into new asphalt, even on the site. Plastics used for drainage pipes may be recycled as well. In order for this recycling to happen, however, there need to be markets for recycled materials and the costs need to be tolerable.

750

500

250

+142 TONNES

C2

B2

A4

A1
A3

EMISSION
STORAGE
+ UPTAKE

-58 TONNES

250

500

Source: AUTHORS

FOUNDATIONS AND GROUND FLOOR

The building rests on a concrete slab and frostwall foundation made with concrete made from a mix in which 15% of Portland cement was substituted with fly ash. No piling or stabilization of the soil was required.

Emissions
The foundation walls and slabs had the greatest impact on the carbon footprint of the foundations. Constructed from reinforced concrete, their emissions were mainly attributed to the manufacturing of cement. Foundations were not estimated to be replaced or repaired during the reference study period. Although the materials for these components of the building are rather heavy, their transportation to the building site and again away from the building site after the building has been demolished in distant future will account for only around 5% of the emissions associated with their manufacturing.

Carbon Uptake and Storages
The potential uptake of CO_2 through the carbonation of concrete is limited in the foundations, as they are mostly underground and this slows the process considerably. Through the carbonation of the foundation, some 0.9 tonnes of CO_2 may be removed during the study period. Concrete floor slabs inside the building are sealed and therefore carbonation is not likely to happen. Wooden building materials used for the forming of the foundations store a further 0.5 tonnes of CO_2.

Mitigation Potential
Using more cement substitutes would have lowered the emissions from the production of the concrete foundations. If half of the used cement had been replaced with blast furnace slag—a share which is often a practical maximum—the emission reduction during the study period of 50 years would have been 35 tonnes. This would be a critical improvement.

The use of cement substitutes would in most cases lead to dual benefits: most substitutes also enhance carbonation. However, the use of cement substitutes usually requires a longer duration for the concrete to reach its design strength. If cast on-site, this could slow the construction schedule.

Circulation
Concrete foundation walls are not likely to be reused, as they are cast on-site. If prefabricated foundation elements had been used, there would have been a theoretical reuse potential. However, downcycling concrete into aggregate is a common practice and the most likely alternative for foundation and ground floor materials.

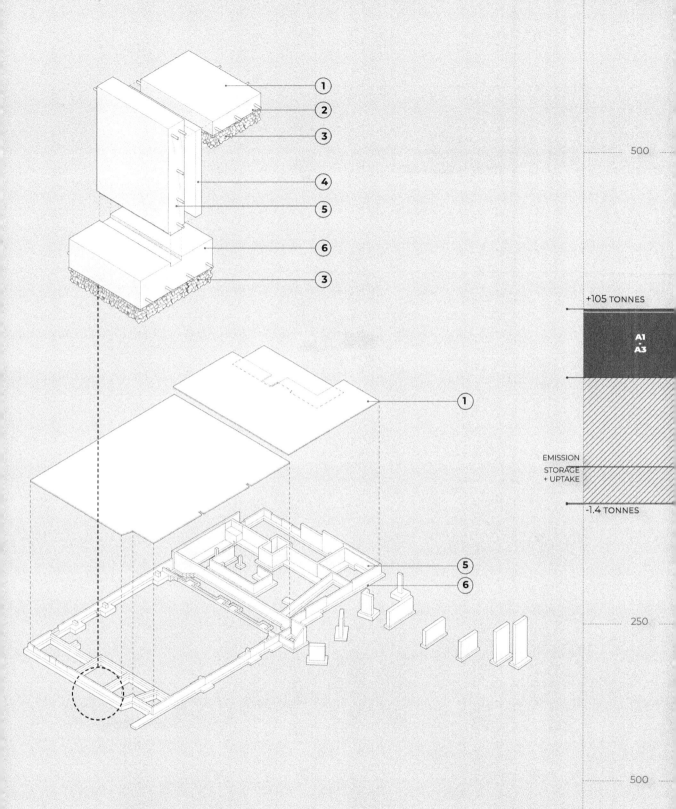

750

500

+105 TONNES

A1
·
A3

-1.4 TONNES

EMISSION
STORAGE
+ UPTAKE

250

500

1	CONCRETE SLAB ON GRADE	**4**	RIGID INSULATION
2	REINFORCED STEEL BAR	**5**	FOUNDATION WALL
3	COMPACTED STONE	**6**	CONCRETE FOOTING

Source: AUTHORS

STRUCTURAL FRAME

The load-bearing frame is made from wooden panels and timber. Cellulose fiber is used as insulation material and gypsum boars as sheathing in parts of the walls.

Emissions
The load-bearing frame is made entirely of timber and thus most of the emissions from the processing of materials for the frame are associated with wood material.

Gypsum boards create almost 10% of the life cycle emissions of the structural frame, although they are not assumed to be replaced during the study period.

Carbon Storages
These wooden frame materials also store approximately three times as much carbon than the emissions from their processing during the production phase. The atmospheric carbon that is stored in the wooden frame for its long use phase is a viable asset from the climate mitigation viewpoint.

Mitigation Potential
As the wooden building parts store more carbon than their production emits, the available mitigation potential is modest. Reducing transportation distances may offer potential for emission reduction, although wooden components are light to transport. Therefore, part of the mitigation potential lies outside of the system boundaries. A harvesting method for the logs and the continued use of disassembled frame components—instead of burning them for energy or applying energy-intensive recycling processes—can increase this potential.

Circulation
Many parts of the structural frame seem to have a potential for reuse. To unleash this potential, the parts should be easy to dismantle. Although mechanical connections are reversible, having too many of them in a structure will increase the disassembly costs. In addition, the reuse of structural elements for future structural application is highly dependent on the design. As the exact load-bearing capacity of a reused building part is difficult to assess (and few designers are willing to take the risk of ensuring it), a relevant option would be to reuse them again for a secondary purpose that requires a reduced load-bearing capacity.

Wooden components can also be recycled into other wood-based products, such as boards. To make this possible, the quality of the secondary recycled raw material has to be sufficiently equivalent to virgin primary raw material. Legislation that addresses this is in development in several jurisdictions. The development of *end-of-waste* criteria for different construction and demolition waste streams will likely ease the recycling of timber waste.

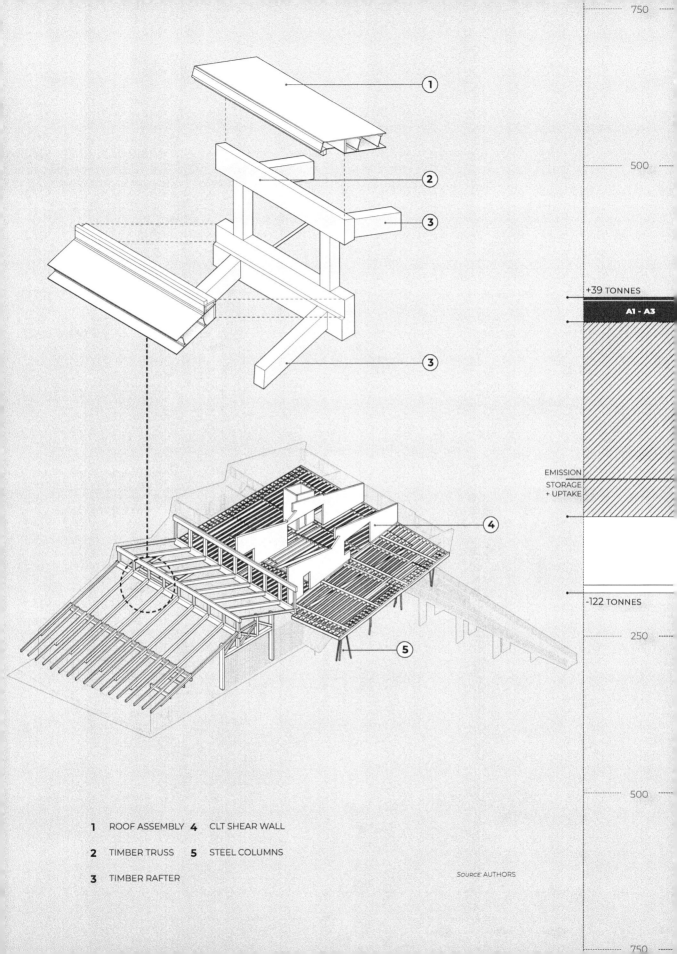

750

500

+39 TONNES

A1 - A3

EMISSION
STORAGE
+ UPTAKE

-122 TONNES

250

500

750

1 ROOF ASSEMBLY   **4** CLT SHEAR WALL

2 TIMBER TRUSS   **5** STEEL COLUMNS

3 TIMBER RAFTER

Source: AUTHORS

FAÇADES AND EXTERNAL DECKS

Façades were constructed from cedar wood siding untreated with either paint or preservatives. Windows were framed with thermally broken aluminum extrusions and double glazed. Doors were mostly insulated metal panels. External decks were pressure-treated yellow pine.

Emissions

Windows and doors create the major share of the emissions associated with the building enclosure. Their frames and especially glass account for around 60% of the emissions of the façades. The yellow pine glulam panels also account for 12% and siding material 11% of those enclosure's emissions.

Carbon Storages

Although the production glulam panels create emissions, these structural components store almost four times as much carbon as they emit. The same is true of the external decking material: pine boards store almost five times more carbon than their production emits.

Mitigation Potential

The potential for the mitigation of emissions for the wooden components is moderate, as already discussed. Using massive solid timber beams instead of glulam structures would have reduced the emissions slightly, but the availability of over-sized massive sawn timber component is very limited and they have less structural capacity than glulam components. Beyond the system boundaries of our analysis, we can assume that the harvest of larger, more mature trees would be required to achieve the required member size.

Circulation

Windows and doors could in theory be reused after their first service period in the school. This would require, however, that they still meet the technical standards and regulatory requirements of future building. Exterior siding boards can be reused, if they remain free of decay. This would require that their attachment methods make them easy to disassemble without breakage and that they have not been treated with harmful chemicals.

The aluminum frames of the windows are recyclable, assuming that their alloy is suitable for their next intended use. Glass from the windows can be recycled as well. Wood from exterior siding boards can be re-engineered into wooden new siding profiles. The pressure-treated decking, however, will likely prove problematic for recycling. This depends entirely on the chemicals that comprise the treatment.

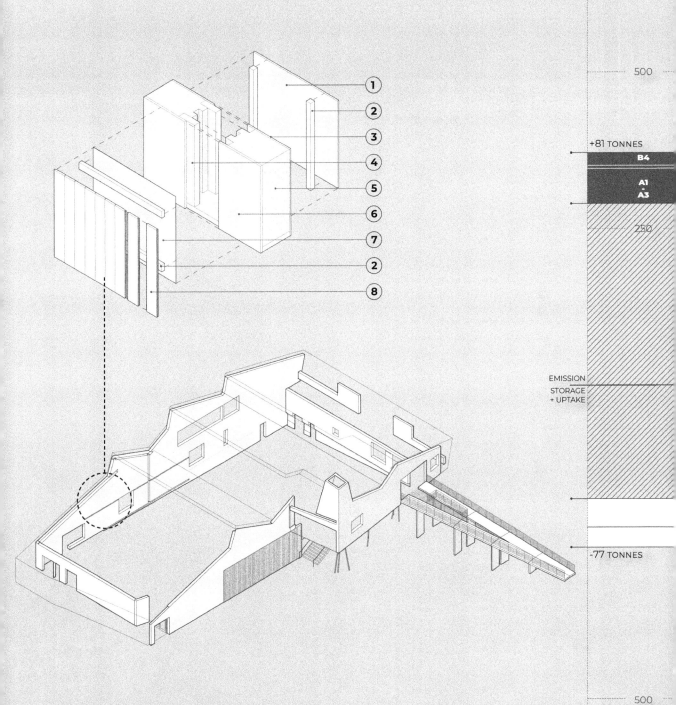

1 GYPSUM BOARD	**4** ENGINEERED WOOD STUDS	**7** INSECT SCREEN
2 WOOD FURRING	**5** CELLULOSE INSULATION	**8** VERTICAL CEDAR RAINSCREEN
3 OSB SHEATHING	**6** OSB WITH WATER BARRIER	

Source: AUTHORS

ROOFS

The roofs of the building were mostly made of timber structural members with metal roofing and oriented strand board sheathing. Cellulose fiber was used as the thermal insulation material.

Emissions
When assessing the emissions incurred during the production and replacement of the materials, the metal components dominate. Their production accounts for over 60% of the emissions of the roof and one cycle of projected replacement during the study period accounts for another 30%.

Carbon Storages
The wooden structure of the roof stores a large amount of biogenic carbon. This storage is almost twice the volume of emissions from the production of all the materials that comprise the roof assembly.

Mitigation Potential
For the components of the roof, there are very few options for mitigating the emissions. Wooden components and wood-based insulation offer only marginal potential, and steel roofing has good inherent potential for future re-circulation, making its substitution with other alternative materials less attractive.

Circulation
The components of the roof are not likely to be reused after disassembly. All of their materials, however, have good potential for being recycled into new products. Steel roofing is easy to circulate, the only possible issue being the amount of copper in the steel alloy that may in the future set certain limitations to the recycling. The same applies to timber parts, if they have not been treated with harmful coatings. In addition, the cellulose insulation may be recycled or incinerated for energy.

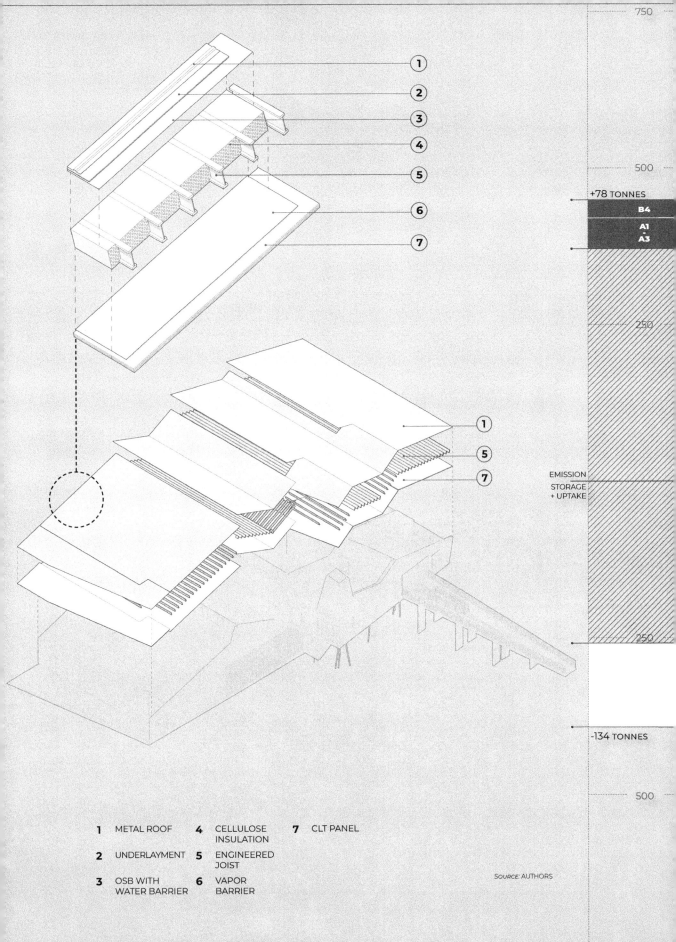

750

1
2
3
4
5
6
7

500

+78 TONNES

B4

A1
+
A3

250

1

5

7

EMISSION

STORAGE
+ UPTAKE

250

250

-134 TONNES

500

1	METAL ROOF	4	CELLULOSE INSULATION	7	CLT PANEL
2	UNDERLAYMENT	5	ENGINEERED JOIST		
3	OSB WITH WATER BARRIER	6	VAPOR BARRIER		

SOURCE: AUTHORS

750

INTERNAL DIVIDERS

Internal partitions of the building were made from exposed cross-laminated timber and glass.

Emissions
Over 40% of the life cycle emissions of internal partitions come from the manufacturing of gypsum board. Additionally, some 24% of their emissions are attributed to manufacturing of cross-laminated timber parts.

Storages
Wooden components in the internal dividers store around 1.3 times the volume of emissions that their production creates.

Mitigation Potential
Substituting gypsum boards with wood paneling—if realistic from the viewpoints of economic, architectural, and technical requirements—would lead to the avoidance of up to 6.9 tonnes of emissions from this portion of the building. This potential depends heavily on the fire safety requirements of the building assemblies and, if pursued as an alternate solution, might require other measures of fire protection that could actually increase emissions. Furthermore, gypsum boards are an inexpensive alternative to most fire-resistive wall surfaces. For these, this particular mitigation potential is only theoretical.

Cross-laminated timber elements consume more energy in their processing than light-frame timber wall panels would create, but the carbon storage capacity of massive wooden walls is an asset. For these reasons, their substitution with functionally comparable light panel walls does not appear to create any improvement. Although transparent and shock-proof polycarbonate could be used instead of glass, its typical per unit production emissions can be over seven times greater than the comparable areas of glass.

Circulation
The fate of the internal partitions in their end-of-life seems a potential benefit. Wood and glass are easy to recycle or even reuse. The feasibility of recycling the gypsum wall board that lends the internal partition their fire and acoustical rating remains a concern. Technological advances and especially increased environmental commitments of some of the leading gypsum board producers may improve the likelihood of their reuse in the future. Reclaimed gypsum can also be used in other industrial processes and applications that lie outside the circulation loops of the construction sector.

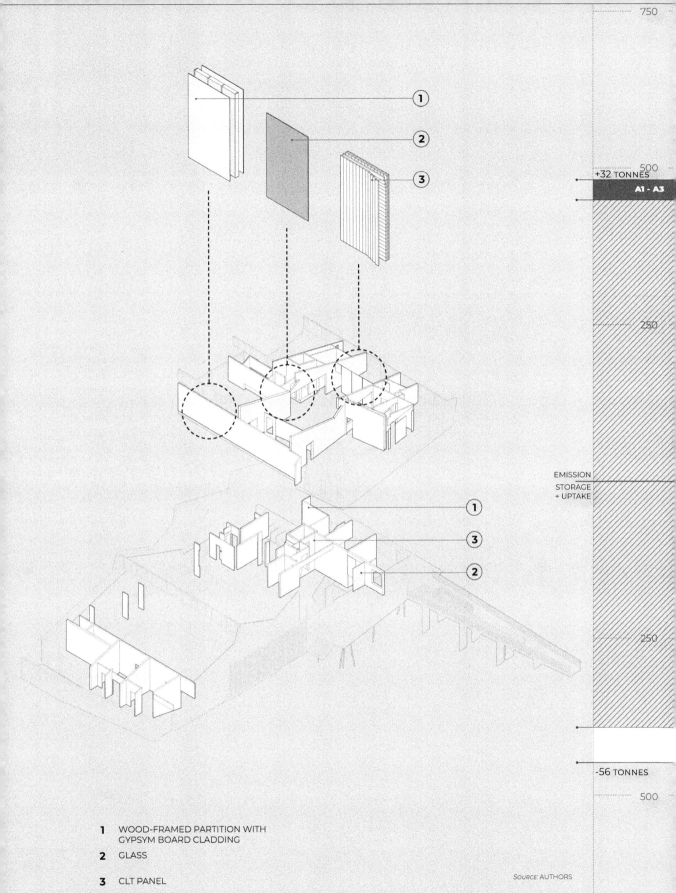

750

500
+32 TONNES
A1 - A3

250

EMISSION
STORAGE
+ UPTAKE

250

-56 TONNES

500

1   WOOD-FRAMED PARTITION WITH
      GYPSYM BOARD CLADDING

2   GLASS

3   CLT PANEL

Source: AUTHORS

750

750

SPACE SURFACES

In this building, the surfaces were made from a variety of different materials. A large proportion of them were formed from bio-based and recycled materials. This makes the overall carbon footprint in this building category small. Cross-laminated timber was used as the primary surface of upper-level ceilings. Smaller areas of the lower floor ceilings were surfaced in gypsum board. Recycled rubber was used for flooring along with ceramic tiles in the bathrooms.

Emissions
Emissions from the production of the surfaces are relatively small during the study period of 50 years. In total, they account for some 9% of the material-related life cycle emissions. Were we to extend the reference study period, the role of replaceable surface materials would grow in importance.

Most of these emissions arise from the life cycle of the flooring. The resilient multilayer floor in the multipurpose room—made from polyvinylchloride—and the rubber sheet flooring together account for almost half of the emissions of the space surfaces. In addition, the gypsum board creates approximately 12 tonnes and the cross-laminated timber panels around 11 tonnes for that category of emissions.

Storages
Although the manufacture of cross-laminated timber panels produces a fifth of the emissions, it stores carbon in quantities that represent more than four times the amount emitted. Additionally, the bamboo flooring stores biogenic carbon.

Mitigation Potential
In theory, some part of the ceramic tiles used in the restroom walls could have been replaced with water-resistant membrane covered with glass fiber wallpaper and layers of paint. This treatment offers the same level of moisture protection (moisture will diffuse through the tile seam mortar to the underlying moisture buffer anyway) but is more prone to physical wear and therefore less usable in a school.

The remaining practical mitigation potential in the internal partitions would have been replacement of the gypsum boards with wooden panels. If all gypsum boards were replaced, the theoretical maximum savings in the production phase would be 7.2 emissions tonnes. However, as with the space dividers, this potential is only theoretical due to possible consequential disadvantages in terms of fire safety, acoustic performance, and life cycle cost.

Circulation
There is an array of likely end-of-life uses for the interior's surface materials. If no harmful chemical coatings were applied or used later over their long service life, wooden and bamboo flooring surfaces can be recycled. To make their recycling feasible, the designer can make recommendations for the maintenance of the surfaces with only such treatments that do not risk the future reuse of the material.

The multilayer and rubber floorings can also be recycled as aggregates in secondary products, considering that there is already a demand for this type of recycled content as long as the composition of the material is toxin-free Again, chemicals used in the maintenance of the flooring may play an important role in this respect.

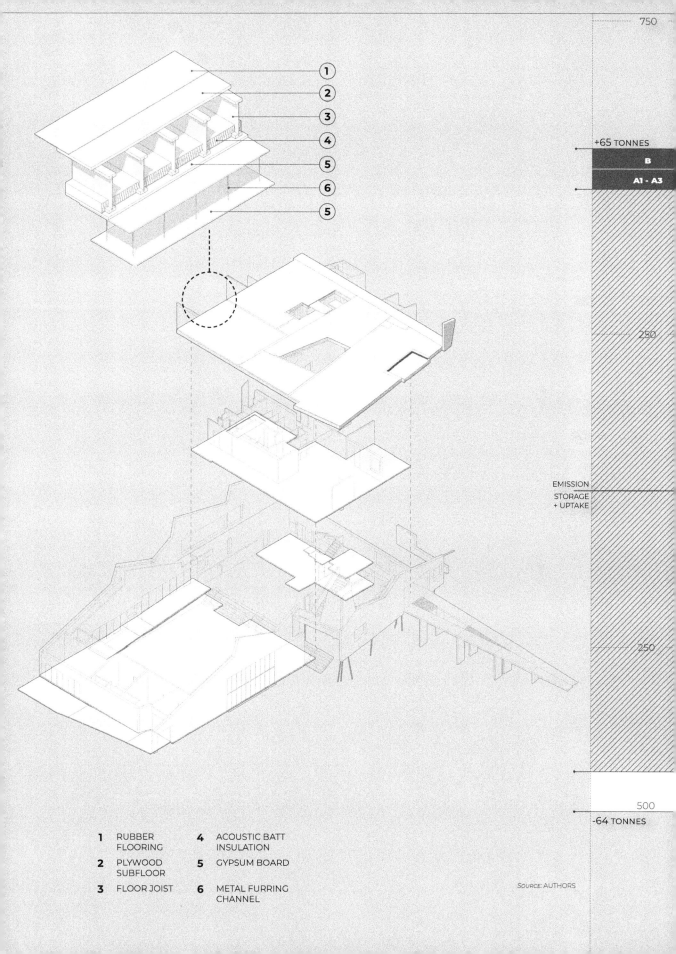

750

+65 TONNES

B

A1 - A3

250

EMISSION
STORAGE
+ UPTAKE

250

500

-64 TONNES

1	RUBBER FLOORING	**4**	ACOUSTIC BATT INSULATION
2	PLYWOOD SUBFLOOR	**5**	GYPSUM BOARD
3	FLOOR JOIST	**6**	METAL FURRING CHANNEL

Source: AUTHORS

INTERNAL FIXTURES

Internal fixtures of the building consist of internal doors and staircases. The materials used for the doors were in some cases wood and, in others, metal. Of the two stairs, one was constructed from concretes and the other cross-laminated timber. The overall role of these internal components in the carbon balance of the building is marginal, only around 2% of all material-related emissions.

Emissions
Of all the internal fixtures measured, the doors created the highest emissions. This is due to the production of metals that are used in layups of door leaves. The concrete stair treads cause one-fourth of the emissions of the internal fixtures.

Storages and Uptake
The wood used for the stairs stores over 5 tonnes of CO_2. As the stairs are made from massive engineered timber, this storage is most likely secure for the entire service life of the building.

During the service life of the stairs, some of the production emissions could be reabsorbed by the exposed concrete through carbonation. In a school building, however, it's likely that the concrete surface of a staircase is kept well sealed throughout its life cycle, as it is otherwise very prone to staining. Sealing prevents the air from reacting with cement and therefore we assume no carbonation will occur to provide additional emissions offsets.

Mitigation
The largest potential for mitigation is in the concrete components of the fire stair. Using 50% blast furnace slag to replace ordinary Portland cement would reduce the production phase emissions by 0.8 tonnes.

Circulation
Both doors and stairs hold great potential for reuse in some future new building, after their removal at the end of this first building life cycle. In order for this to happen, treatment with chemicals that are harmful or toxic and that would disqualify them from reuse, would need to be avoided. This responsibility would fall to the building managers. In addition, future technical criteria and regulatory requirements may be stricter, rendering them obsolete or, at the very least, making some future reapplication of doors and stair components more limited. Less likely in such a case, or if there were no markets for these types of building parts, they would undergo recycling. Both the metal and wood from the doors offer real potential for this outcome. The down-cycling of concrete into aggregates for road construction is also a very common practice. Cements, unfortunately, are very difficult to recycle once they have reacted in the concrete mix. There are as yet no practical technological innovations in cement reuse on the horizon

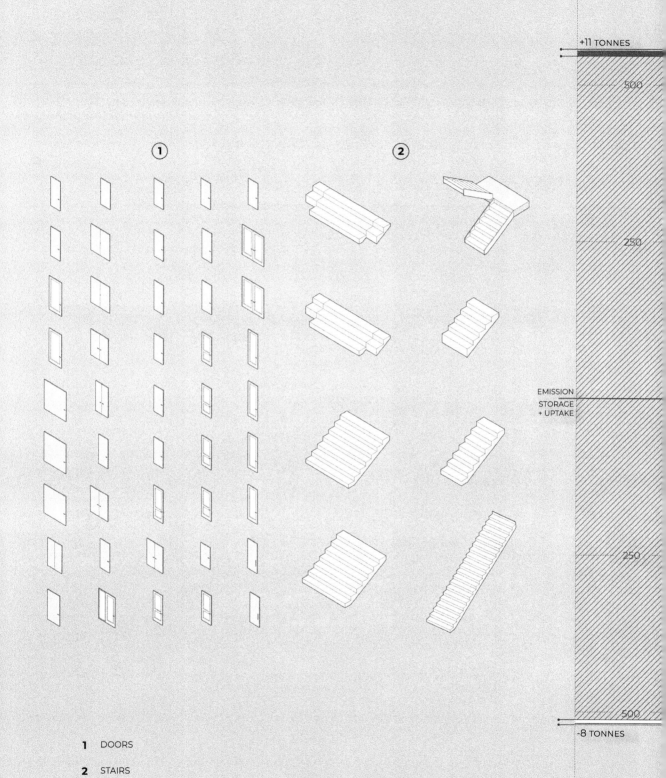

750

+11 TONNES

500

① ②

250

EMISSION
STORAGE
+ UPTAKE

250

500

-8 TONNES

1 DOORS

2 STAIRS

SOURCE: AUTHORS

BUILDING SYSTEM INSTALLATIONS

The materials that make up the building systems included several metals (steel, aluminum, copper) and plastics (polyvinylchloride, polyethylene, and polystyrene). These materials were energy-intensive to manufacture and the technical service life of most building systems installations are considerably shorter than the life of the building. This means their replacement at some point is extremely likely. The technological development of building environmental control and systems, however, is rapid. The materials and, especially, their associated production processes are likely in the future to be more environmentally friendly than the products we use today. When looking at the emissions and replacement periods of building systems, it has to be kept in mind that they play an essential role in the overall energy efficiency of the building, along with many of its critical technical functions. Therefore, for those savings in these materials to be properly considered, they should be evaluated from the standpoint of the functional value they add in enabling the building to operate with the intended efficiency.

Emissions
The overall impact of the building systems is considerable in a public building. In the case of the Common Ground School systems, the total sum of life cycle material-related emissions was 20%. There are large differences in the life cycle emissions of the plumbing, air-conditioning, and electrical elements. And because the building is equipped with solar photovoltaic panels, which will need to be replaced in less than 30 years, their share of the emissions of building service installations dominates. In fact, the solar panels alone account for almost 15% of the entire life cycle emissions of the whole building. However, when comparing the embodied impacts of the panels into the emission savings that provide through the production of carbon neutral renewable energy, they are still an investment worth making (see section "Energy" for further details).

Mitigation
The greatest potential for reducing emissions from the building elements is in the selection of the solar panels. Depending on the panel type, the production emissions may range from 67 $kgCO_2e/m^2$ (thin film PV panels) to 242 $kgCO_2e/m^2$ (mono-crystalline silicon panels).

The case study building is equipped with mono-crystalline PV panels that are a fundamental component of producing carbon-neutral renewable electricity for the school. Should thin film panels have been used instead, the production emissions would have been 65 tonnes less.

However, with this potential saving, there are a few drawbacks. First, the efficiency of thin-film panels has traditionally been slightly lower (11–13%) than in silicon panels (15–16%). This means that mono-crystalline panels help to offset more emissions than thin-film panels. During 50 years, however, this difference is only less than a tonne in favor of mono-crystalline panels. Second, the thin-film panels may contain cadmium, which is carcinogenic. If not treated properly, this can be a risk to construction workers and also constrains the recyclability of the panels.

Circulation
Because innovations in the components of building system develop rapidly, it's challenging to plan for their reuse after their first service life. This suggests recycling as a more viable option. Most of their elements are made from metals and plastics, materials with a significant potential for recycling.

Metals have high degree of recyclability and can circulate almost indefinitely. Plastics, however, remain something of a challenge to keep in circulation. Depending on the plastic type, its additives, wear, and potential contamination, there are alternatives for its mechanical or chemical recycling. Although the market demand for recycled plastics is modest, a promising market potential may boost the feasibility of plastic recycling.

If building system components could be collected by an operator with the capacity to separate their materials they are comprised of, the door to their recycling is opened. This requires, however, that the building system components have been designed and manufactured in a manner that makes it easy to identify and separate each constituent material. Plastics contain a high energy potential so if recycling is feasible, energy recovery remains an option.

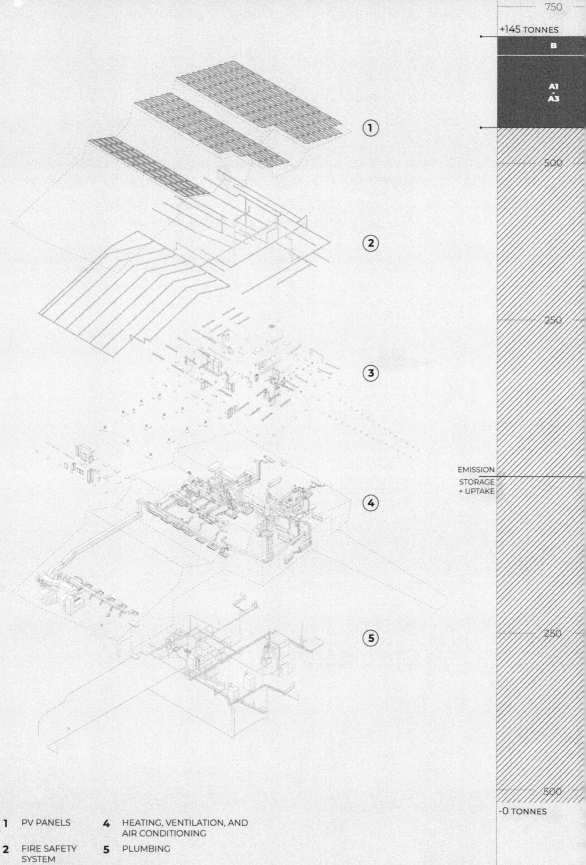

750

+145 TONNES

B

A1
-
A3

500

250

EMISSION
STORAGE
+ UPTAKE

250

500

-0 TONNES

1 PV PANELS   4 HEATING, VENTILATION, AND
                     AIR CONDITIONING

2 FIRE SAFETY   5 PLUMBING
   SYSTEM

3 ELECTRICAL

Source: AUTHORS

Table 3.2

Site and ground works:
material inputs and outputs, expected technical service life, and likely end-of-life scenarios.

Material inputs	Expected technical service life	Likely end-of-life scenario
311 tn gravel	Building's lifetime	Recycling: aggregate for infrastructure works
116 tn asphalt	20 years	Landfill or recycling for asphalt
35 tn concrete	25 years—building's lifetime	Recycling: aggregate for infrastructure works
5 tn plastic	50 years	Energy recovery Recycling: Mechanical recycling into new products
3 tn vegetation (grown)	Over 100 years	Landfill (or natural decomposition)
468 tn total inputs		
Material outputs		
3,196 tn soil (removed)		Landfill
4 tn trees (removed)		Landfill
3,200 tn total outputs		

Table 3.3

Site and ground works:
emissions, uptake of carbon and further mitigation potential.

Emissions during 50 years	Uptake during 50 years	Further mitigation potential
142 metric tons	58 metric tons	50 metric tons
• Asphalt 52 tn • Concrete paving 26 tn • Plastic drainage pipes 17 tn • Removal of trees 11 tn (interpreted as a biogenic carbon emission) • Gravel 7 tn • Concrete pipes 5 tn	• Organic carbon into soils 56 tn • Carbonation of concrete 2 tn	• Greener cement mix 26 tn • Reclaimed asphalt 8 tn • Recycled concrete rubble 7 tn

123

Table 3.4

Foundations and ground floor:
material inputs, expected technical service life, and likely end-of-life scenario.

Material inputs	Expected technical service life	Likely end-of-life scenario
728 tn concrete	Building's lifetime	Recycling: aggregate for infrastructure works
2 tn steel	Building's lifetime	Recycling: secondary raw material for steel production
0.3 tn wood	Building's lifetime	
730 tn total		

Table 3.5

Foundations and ground floor:
emissions, uptake and storages, and further mitigation potential.

Emissions	Uptake and storages	Further mitigation potential
109 tonnes	1.4 tonnes	35 tonnes
· Concrete foundation 106 tn · Steel 3 tn · Wood 0.01 tn	· Concrete carbonation 0.9 tn · Wood 0.5 tn	· Greener cement mix 35 tn

Table 3.6

Structural frame:
material inputs, expected technical service life, and likely end-of-life scenarios.

Material inputs	Expected technical service life	Likely end-of-life scenario
67 tn wood and cellulose	Building's lifetime	Recycling: wood-based boards or bioenergy
9 tn gypsum	Up to 50 years	Recycling: secondary raw material for gypsum production
3 tn steel	Building's lifetime	Recycling: secondary raw material for steel production
0.2 tn plastics	Up to 50 years	Energy recovery
79 tn total		

Table 3.7

**Structural frame:
emissions, storages, and further mitigation potential.**

Emissions	Storages	Further mitigation potential
33 tonnes	122 tonnes	2 tonnes
• Wooden components 22 tn • Steel 5 tn • Gypsum 4 tn • Insulation materials 2 tn	• Wooden components 122 tn	• Gypsum to wood 2 tn

Table 3.8

**Façades and external decks:
material inputs, expected technical service life, and likely end-of-life scenario.**

Material inputs	Expected technical service life	Likely end-of-life scenario
23 tn wood and cellulose	Building's lifetime	Recycling: wood-based boards or bioenergy
7 tn glass	Up to 50 years	Recycling: secondary raw material for gypsum production
7 tn metals (steel, aluminum, zinc)	Up to 50 years	Recycling: secondary raw material for metal production
1 tn components (multi-material doors)	Up to 50 years	Reuse or recycling into secondary raw materials
378 tonnes total		

Table 3.9

Façades and external decks:
emissions, storages, and further mitigation potential.

Emissions	Storages	Further mitigation potential
81 tonnes	77 tonnes	None identified
· Windows and doors 49 tn · Wood components 20 tn	· Wooden components 77 tn	

Table 3.10

Roofs:
material inputs, expected technical service life, and likely end-of-life scenario.

Material inputs	Expected technical service life	Likely end-of-life scenario
88 tn wood and cellulose	Building's lifetime	Recycling: wood-based boards or bioenergy
5 tn steel	Building's lifetime	Recycling: secondary raw material for steel production
0.2 tn plastics	Up to 50 years	Energy recovery
93 tonnes total		

Table 3.11

Roofs:
emissions, storages, and further mitigation potential.

Emissions	Storages	Further mitigation potential
76 tonnes	134 tonnes	None identified
Metal parts 46 tn Wooden parts 30 tn	Wooden parts 134 tn	

Table 3.12

Internal dividers:
material inputs, expected technical service life, and likely end-of-life scenario.

Material inputs	Expected technical service life	Likely end-of-life scenario
32 tn wood	Building's lifetime	Recycling: wood-based boards or bioenergy
28 tn gypsum	Up to 50 years	Recycling: secondary raw material for gypsum production
2 tn glass fiber	Building's lifetime	Recycling into new glass fiber or landfill
0.3 tn cement	Building's lifetime	Landfill or recycled aggregates
0.2 tn steel	Building's lifetime	Recycling: secondary raw material for steel production
67 tonnes total		

Table 3.13

Internal dividers:
emissions, storages, and further mitigation potential.

Emissions	Storages	Further mitigation potential
32 tonnes	56 tonnes	7 tonnes
Gypsum boards 13 tn Cross-laminated timber 9 tn	Cross-laminated timber 30 tn Other wood parts 26 tn	Gypsum to wood 7 tn (theoretical)

Table 3.14

Space surfaces:
material inputs, expected technical service life, and likely end-of-life scenario.

Material inputs	Expected technical service life	Likely end-of-life scenario
28 tn wood	Building's lifetime	Recycling: wood-based boards or bioenergy
10 tn gypsum	Up to 50 years	Recycling: secondary raw material for gypsum production
3 tn plastics	20–30 years	Energy recovery, landfill
3 tn rubber	20–30 years	Energy recovery, landfill
1 tn bamboo	20–30 years	Recycling: secondary materials or bioenergy
1 tn ceramics	Building's lifetime	Recycling: secondary raw material for steel production
46 tonnes total		

Table 3.15

Space surfaces:
emissions, storages, and further mitigation potential.

Emissions	Storages	Further mitigation potential
65 tonnes	64 tonnes	7 tonnes
• Multilayer PVC flooring 20 tn	• Cross-laminated timber 42 tn	• Gypsum to wood 7 tn (theoretical)
• Gypsum boards 12 tn	• Plywood 17 tn	
• Cross-laminated timber 11 tn	• Bamboo 7 tn	
• Rubber sheet flooring 10 tn		

Table 3.16

Internal fixtures:
material inputs, expected technical service life, and likely end-of-life scenario.

Material inputs	Expected technical service life	Likely end-of-life scenario
25 tn concrete	Building's lifetime	Recycling to aggregates or landfill
4 tn wood	Building's lifetime	Recycling: secondary materials or bioenergy
1 tn doors	30–50 years	Reuse or recycling into secondary raw materials
0.5 tn steel	Building's lifetime	Recycling: secondary raw material for steel production
0.2 tn bamboo	Up to 50 years	Recycling: secondary materials or bioenergy
30 tonnes total		

Table 3.17

Internal fixtures:
emissions, storages, and further mitigation potential.

Emissions	Storages	Further mitigation potential
11 tonnes	8 tonnes	1 tonnes
· Doors 4 tn · Concrete 3 tn	· Cross-laminated timber 4 tn	· Greener cement mix 0.8 tn

Table 3.18

Building system installations:
material inputs, expected technical service life, and likely end-of-life scenario.

Material inputs	Expected technical service life	Likely end-of-life scenario
5 tn solar panels (multi-material)	20 years	Recycling into secondary raw materials, treatment of hazardous waste
3 tn steel	20–50 years	Recycling: secondary raw material for metal production
2 tn copper	20–50 years	Recycling: secondary raw material for metal production
2 tn plastics	20–50 years	Energy recovery or landfill (where allowed)
0.1 tn aluminum	20–50 years	Recycling: secondary raw material for metal production
12 tonnes total		

Table 3.19

Building system installations:
emissions, storages and uptake, and further mitigation potential.

Emissions	Storages and uptake	Further mitigation potential
145 tonnes	None	65 tonnes
· PV panels 115 tn · Electric cables 21 tn · Steel pipes 6 tn		· Thin-film PV panels instead of monocrystalline 65 tn

MITIGATION POTENTIAL FROM MATERIALS AND SYSTEMS

We've found that the mitigation potential from the construction materials in Common Ground High School could reach as much as 158 tonnes of CO_2e and we've located the greatest potential for reducing material-related emissions in the solar panel selection and the concrete mix.

If the solar panels used for the building had been produced using thin-film technology. it would have yielded 65 tonnes of emission savings, a significant reduction. The consequences of this saving could come with a cost of increased toxicity. This single example demonstrates just how multi-faceted the sustainability of system optimization can be. Making choices from among the many options and weighing up their implications are a value-based, subjective and difficult proposition.

Other mitigation measures include alternatives for cement in the concrete foundation and stair structure. If half of the ordinary Portland cement used were to be replaced with blast furnace slag, the CO_2 savings would amount to 62 tonnes. Replacing the gypsum board with wood paneling would avoid 16 tonnes of emissions—but this potential is only theoretical, as it may not solve the technical and regulatory requirements, as noted earlier. More realistic options

for impact reduction avail themselves, if we replace asphalt surfaces with reclaimed asphalt, saving 8 tonnes. If we use recycled concrete aggregate instead of natural gravel, we further avoid 7 tonnes of emissions. Altogether, these theoretical measures have the potential to reduce the material-related embodied emissions by 20%. Over the full life cycle of the building, the mitigation potential would be 10%.

The overall mitigation potential using simple material substitution is promising, but still not that significant. Further reductions would require the complete reconsideration of most of the metals, plastics, glass, and concrete used in the building, as these materials account for most of the global industrial emissions [13]. It's clear that the urgency to reduce emissions from the construction sector generally demands strong policies and innovative approaches that might more forcefully mitigate impacts.

Part of the solution may be achieved through the decarbonization of industrial energy However, emissions inherent in certain processes (e.g., calcination of clinker in cement production) are unavoidable. Curbing these emissions demands either radical innovation in the decarbonization of cement manufacture or offsets achieved through carbon capture and storage technology. These technologies, at a practical scale, remain

---

Table 3.20

Mitigation potential from materials and systems.

Measures	Mitigation Potential		
	Avoidable emissions (tn CO_2e)	Share of material-related emissions (%)	Share of life cycle emissions (%)
Greener solar panels	65	9	4
Greener cement mix	62	8	4
Gypsum to wood	16	2	1
Reclaimed asphalt	8	1	0.5
Recycled concrete rubble	7	1	0.4
Total	158	20	10

expensive, somewhat untested, and therefore unreachable in the short term. That being said, it appears unavoidable that we will need to rely on the "tailpipe" technologies that capture carbon, despite their current cost and the challenges of their implementation.

Other radical solutions, such as offering incentives that favor renovation over new construction, an increase in space usage through multi-functionality and scheduling, the reduction of the weight of structures and components or building volume and floor area reductions seem inevitable, all things considered. These sorts of measures lead inevitably to profound changes in the value chains of design, construction, and the industrial production of construction materials and components and across the real-estate development sector.

ENERGY-RELATED EMISSIONS

Background of Energy Calculations

The energy that the case study building consumes was based on measurements during its first few operating years. We assume, therefore, that the energy consumed accounts for both operational energy and for the embodied energy for scheduled maintenance activities. We assume that the energy demand would remain stable for the reference study period. The electricity consumed is sourced from the local grid, electricity is mainly produced with natural gas and nuclear power with a carbon footprint of 0.273 kg CO_2/ kWh [14]. During the study period of 50 years, it's highly likely that the production of electricity will change its source. When the fuels used for electricity change, the carbon footprint per kWh will change.

The changes in the carbon footprint of the electrical supply are difficult to estimate. If international climate goals were the target, or if local electricity companies voluntarily invest in renewable energy, the rapid decarbonization of energy might be feasible. If the normative

framework is not bound by international goals or if local utility companies do not take voluntary steps to achieve these goals, then the emissions during the study period may not decrease. To provide an example of the impact of these various scenarios, we have calculated the energy emissions of three alternative scenarios:

1. A baseline scenario with no changes.
2. An incremental decrease scenario with an assumption of 10% reduction of emissions every decade until 2050.
3. A rapid decarbonization scenario with an assumption of halving the emissions every decade until 2050.

As we'll see, the selection of this scenario is crucial to the results of the entire life cycle assessment.

The case study building is equipped with photovoltaic panels that produce solar electricity. In our example, we calculate this energy as carbon-neutral. However, the full life cycle of solar panels that are required for production of this renewable energy is not carbon-neutral. The production of the panels in fact causes significant emissions, but we've estimated those impacts for the production phase of the building. The amount of solar energy captured is based on the recorded data during the first years of operation. As the productivity of the solar panels may decrease during their service life, we've also accounted for that by using a reduction factor.

Results: Energy-Related Emissions

The energy-related operational emissions are a direct result of the production of energy that is used in the building. During the first operational year of the building it consumed 238 MWh electricity. From this overall sum, 70% (167 MWh) were purchased from the grid.

The solar panels integrated into the building were metered to produce 71.6 MWh electricity during the first year of the building's operation. This amount of renewable electricity is subtracted from

COMMON GROUND HIGH SCHOOL ENERGY DEMAND (MwH)

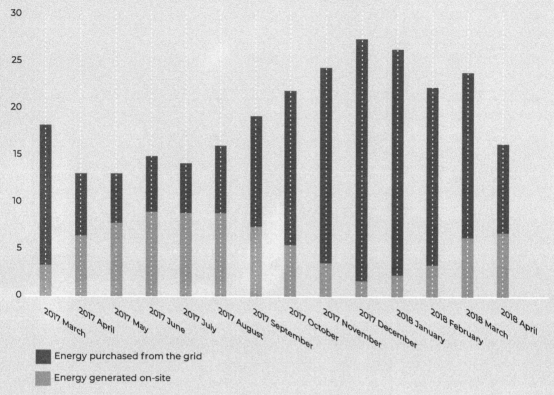

■ Energy purchased from the grid
■ Energy generated on-site

ALTERNATIVE ENERGY SCENARIOS (kgCO$_2$e/m^2)

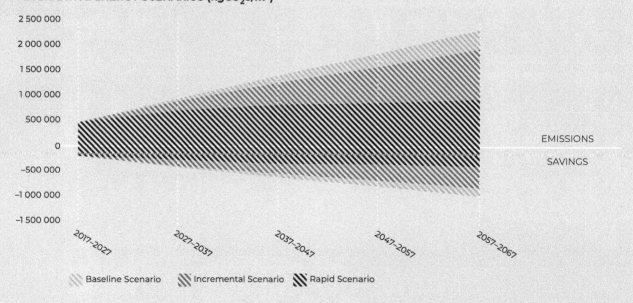

EMISSIONS

SAVINGS

▨ Baseline Scenario   ▨ Incremental Scenario   ▨ Rapid Scenario

SOURCE: AUTHORS

the purchase of electricity from the grid. From this subtraction, we can approximate that 19.5 metric tons of CO_2 emissions could be avoided.

The share of generated renewable electricity fluctuates seasonally between 6% (December) to 64% (July). The annual average share for renewable solar electricity is around 30%.

We should evaluate the significance of the avoided emissions from a life cycle perspective. As described in the previous section, the manufacturing of the solar panels for the building accounted for some 4.6 metric tons of CO_2. As these panels have a technical service life of approximately 25 years, they are likely to be replaced once during the reference study period of 50 years. This replacement may double the emissions from the production of the solar panels to almost 10 metric tons of CO_2. During the same period, assuming that the efficiency of the panels remains intact, their use would substitute for some 3 580 MWh of purchased electricity. Depending on the carbon intensity scenario for grid electricity, this substitution would lead to CO_2 emission savings ranging from 977 to 391 metric tons, respectively.

Although the production of solar panels is very emissions-intensive, they are an investment worth making if the emissions of the purchased grid electricity do not decrease rapidly over the life cycle of the building. If the carbon intensity of the purchased electricity drops according to a rapid decarbonization scenario, the replacement of solar panels after their initial service life should be reconsidered. It is, however, likely that the production of new solar panels in 25 years' time would also consume less energy and create fewer emissions.

The accumulation of emissions in the rapid decarbonization scenario is only 40% of the emissions of the baseline scenario. As can be understood, this level of variance is crucial to the results and the dominance of various stages in a life cycle assessment. Therefore, it is not recommended basing the emission calculation from energy use on only one scenario. However, regardless of which scenario for energy-related emissions is applied, it is still important to aim for energy-efficient design solutions.

Furthermore, it can be argued that the great uncertainty surrounding energy-related emissions in fact underlines the importance of mitigating those parts of a building's life cycle emissions that a designer can control. This means that we need to pay attention to material-related emissions and their mitigation at the beginning of a building's life cycle.

Because of the different emission scenarios, the potential for emission savings through the use of on-site renewable energy varies. The lower the emissions from energy use, the lower the respective emissions savings. We should keep in mind that these avoided emissions are in fact imaginary. Rather than actually having been removed from the atmosphere, they illustrate the consequential benefit of choosing renewable energy. Their relative importance is less than that of actual energy-related emissions. Moreover, we should by no means misinterpret this to mean that we should aim for greater emission savings in the baseline scenario. The magnitude of the emissions savings is directly tied to the energy-related emissions in each of the different scenarios.

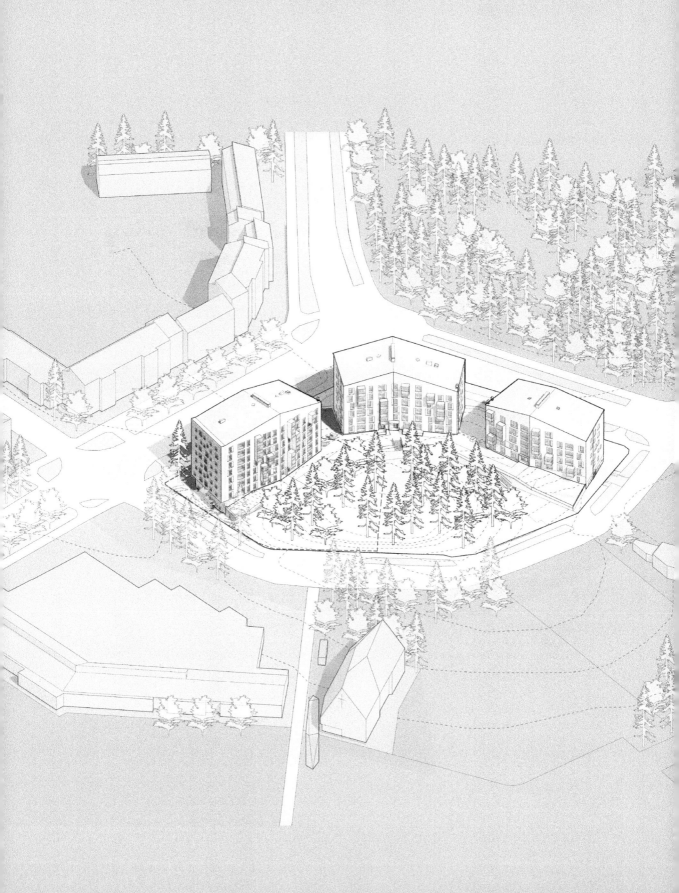

CASE STUDY 2:
PUUKUOKKA HOUSING BLOCK

Puukuokka One Apartment Building

The Puukuokka block is situated in central Finland, in the city of Jyväskylä, which is famous for many of the works by Alvar Aalto. Built from massive wood components, the block consists of three buildings that range from six to eight storeys. The entire block houses 184 apartments. The case study focused on Puukuokka One, which has 58 apartments in eight storeys. The structural system of the three buildings in the block consists of a concrete foundation, which serves as a platform for modular timber-framed units that were prefabricated and transported to the site in nearly turn-key status. The prefabricated volumetric modules form the structural frame for the buildings.

The high degree of prefabrication led to a short construction time on site. The modular units included frames, insulation, windows and doors, building service installations, as well as final surfaces. The façade was also prefabricated and attached to the modular units on site as they were stacked on top of each other layer by layer. Hallway elements and roof trusses were also prefabricated. The concrete foundation was the only building element that was built on site.

A typical single apartment of the building consists of two modular units: one for the living room and bedroom, and the other for the kitchen, bathroom, and entrance hall. All the building service ducts were integrated into one of the walls of the modular units that faces the hallway in the core of the building. Wooden surfaces are visible in the façades and inner surfaces of the building to the extent permitted by fire regulations.

The Puukuokka Block sits on a hilly landscape where a natural pine forest grows. During the design and construction, care was taken not to excavate the bedrock and to preserve as much natural forest on the site as possible.

Designed by OOPEAA Office for Peripheral Architecture, the Puukuokka Housing Block won the national Finlandia Prize for Architecture in 2015.

FIGURE 3.17 PUUKUOKKA HOUSING BLOCK SITE *Source:* AUTHORS

ARCHITECTURAL OBJECTIVES
(by OOPEAA Office for Peripheral Architecture)

In 2011, when the fire regulations in Finland were adjusted to allow for the use of wood in multistorey apartment buildings, OOPEAA was eager to take the opportunity to explore the potential of cross-laminated timber (CLT) in urban housing. As a growing city committed to promoting environmental sustainability in its development, Jyväskylä was interested in embracing the new possibilities that have opened up as a result of the change in the fire regulations. This led to a fruitful collaboration between the architects, the city, and the builder in creating the Puukuokka Housing Block. Jyväskylä is one of the growth centers in Finland and there is a strong commitment to providing good quality affordable housing in an environmentally responsible and socially sustainable way. As a natural, locally available, renewable and recyclable material, wood has great potential in the effort to reduce the burden on the environment caused by construction. Therefore, wood was a natural choice for a building material for the new housing block to be built in Jyväskylä.

Completed in 2015, Puukuokka One was the first eight-storey-high wooden apartment building in Finland. With Puukuokka Two built in 2017 and Puukuokka Three the following year, the entire block was completed in 2018. Puukuokka served as a pilot case to develop and test a CLT-based system of volumetric modules. It explores the potential of modular prefabricated CLT construction to meet the goal of providing high quality, environmentally responsible and affordable housing with a mix of different household types, ranging from single dwellers of all ages to families with children. The aim was to find a solution that makes the best possible use of the technical and aesthetic qualities of CLT and to create a wooden building on a large scale with a distinct architectonic expression of its own. The design builds on the natural qualities of wood to create an esthetic that is not simply borrowed from that of traditional small-scale wooden housing nor from that of typical apartment buildings made of concrete elements. The aspiration was to create a building that combines the sense of warmth and privacy of a single-family dwelling with the semi-public character of the shared spaces of an apartment building.

Puukuokka is located in Kuokkala, a neighborhood by Lake Jyväsjärvi, which was originally planned and initiated in the 1980s. The neighborhood was already familiar to the architects as they had already designed the Kuokkala Church there. Completed in 2010, the church serves as an identifying landmark for the district and provides a meeting place for the community with a broad range of programs, from kindergarten and theater clubs to performances and sacral services. The town plan for the extension of the neighborhood comprising the Puukuokka Block was developed in close collaboration between the City of Jyväskylä and the architects and it was tailored to meet the needs of the Puukuokka building complex. Together with the nearby Kuokkala Church, the Puukuokka Block, built on a hill, provides a sense of distinct character to the neighborhood. The Puukuokka housing has been extremely well received by the residents who praise it for creating a comfortable living environment with an excellent framework for a friendly and socially stable neighbourhood.

To support social sustainability, Puukuokka pilots an innovative lease-to-own financing strategy that aims to promote stable communities. A 7% down payment on the purchase price of an apartment allows the purchaser to secure a state-guaranteed loan, and, through rental payments over a period of 20 years, the purchaser gradually acquires full ownership of the unit. The sales price is negotiated and agreed upon when the lease is signed. In contrast to the typical arrangement of offering affordable housing through rental units, this model promotes a sense of ownership and a long-term commitment to the community. The range of apartments of different sizes to suit the different needs of residents in their different life phases further supports a balanced mix of residents of various ages and promotes the possibility to transition from one type of apartment to the next without necessarily moving out of the community. It is possible, however, to sell your share even before you have acquired full ownership of the unit, so the arrangement is flexible and doesn't necessarily bind the residents to a full 20-year term.

Choice of CLT as Building Material
An interest in the special characteristics and qualities that different materials possess and a desire to find solutions that take advantage of the natural qualities of the material chosen, while also optimizing the process of building and construction, informed the architects' approach in developing the system of using volumetric CLT modules to construct

FIGURE 3.18 PUUKUOKKA HOUSE ONE. *Source:* OOPEAA/MIKKO AUERNIITTY

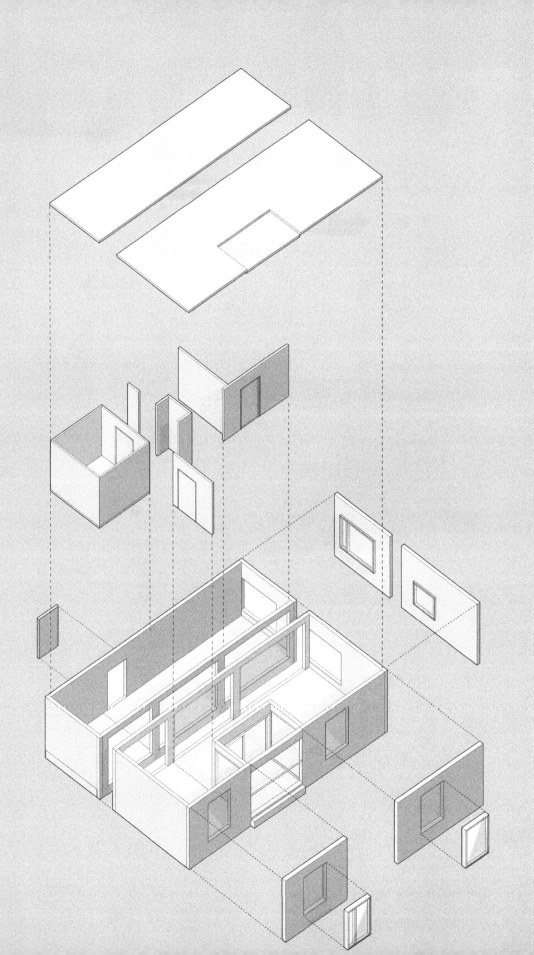

the Puukuokka Housing Block. The choice of CLT as a material for the building complex was carefully evaluated to find a solution that best suits the context of the site and the goal of providing affordable housing of high quality for the residents of the growing city of Jyväskylä.

Wood has several important advantages as a building material. In addition to being locally available and suited to the local climate, it also easily lends itself to modularity. Even the traditional log structure functions like a system of reusable building components that can be added to or taken apart and reassembled again in a different place or in a different order for a different use. In a similar manner, the prefabricated volumetric modules made of CLT can be taken apart and reassembled. Wood is also a material that ages well and that has a sense of warmth to it. Thanks to its excellent heat insulation qualities, it is also an energy-efficient material that makes it possible to lower the energy needed for heating, which is a key concern in the northern climate in Finland. An interest in exploring the potential of using the new wood products as a sustainable solution to urban housing and in developing new systems of flexibly customizable modularity led to the decision to choose CLT as the building material for the Puukuokka Housing Block.

The entire load-bearing structure and frame are made of massive wood composed of prefabricated volumetric CLT modules made of spruce. The modules were prefabricated in a local factory less than two hours away from the site. Prefabrication made it possible to prepare the modules in controlled indoor conditions. This helped to cut down the construction time on site to six months per building and to reduce the exposure to weather conditions during construction. That made it possible to achieve a higher quality of the end result.

Working with CLT enabled several important aspects in the project: It made it possible to create a spacious hallway and atrium space with a lot of light realized in an energy-efficient manner as a semi-warm space. The insulating qualities of massive wood allow the temperature of the individual units to be controlled independently without the temperature of one unit affecting that of the others. The system of using prefabricated volumetric CLT modules made it possible to integrate the piping for heat, water, electricity, and ventilation in the wall structure in the hallway, making it easily accessible for maintenance and repairs. This arrangement also allows for an efficient organization of the plan.

Optimizing the Production and Working with the Natural Conditions of the Site

The entire process of production, transportation, construction, and assembly for the Puukuokka Block was carefully optimized to take best advantage of the potential provided by the use of prefabricated modules. The prefabricated modules were brought to the site in batches for installation, one level at a time, and the prefabricated wooden façade elements were attached when lifting the modules in place, one floor at a time. This made the protection of wood during construction easy to manage. It also made it possible to keep the disturbance to the terrain caused by the construction as small as possible while taking into account the biodiversity of the nature of the site and minimizing the long-term ecological impact.

Responding to the natural qualities of the site and working in harmony with the conditions of the local climate, also the façades are made of wood. Dark tinted spruce is used on the external side of the block while on the interior yard side, the façades are made of larch, which has intentionally been left untreated. It will weather well and acquire a silvery gray patina over time.

The buildings follow the contours of the site to minimize the disturbance to the underlying bedrock and existing vegetation. The presence of the forest landscape and the nearby lake has been further emphasized by the carefully framed and generous views that open up in the shared lobby and hallway spaces as well as in the apartments. Each apartment unit also has a balcony, either a recessed one or a protruding one. Both have been deliberately planned so that they help to extend the views into the surrounding landscape.

Placing the parking indoors in the basement level of the buildings made it possible to save the backyards for communal outdoor space for the residents to use. To preserve the naturally hilly landscape of the site, as much of the bedrock has been left untouched as possible. In the design of the buildings and the backyard, special attention has been paid to the conveying, detention, and infiltration of storm water. For energy needs for heating and cooling, the Puukuokka Housing Block relies on the city's district heating system that uses green energy.

FIGURE 3.19 Prefabricated CLT apartment modular units in the Puukuokka Housing Block
Source: AUTHORS

Summary of Total Carbon Emissions, Storages, and Circulation Potential

The total sum of GHG emissions at the Puukuokka One housing block is 4 280 tonnes of CO_2e. Of this total, operational energy use represents 46% and embodied emissions 54%.

The largest single contributor to the emissions during the chosen study period was operational energy with 1 979 tonnes of CO_2e. However, the production of the building materials came close to this figure with 1 838 emission tonnes.

In this case, the construction, repair and demolition work had quite a small impact on overall emissions. Their joint contribution was 540 tonnes. This is partially due to the applied scenarios, which differ from the scenarios used for the Common Ground High School. In both cases, however, the share of these life cycle phases was less than that of energy and materials.

As the buildings in the Puukuokka block are made mostly from massive timber, substantial amounts of biogenic carbon are stored in their construction material. The wooden building components of Puukuokka One store almost 1 600 tonnes of CO_2e. As the site has lots of vegetation, growing plants and soils sequester over 253 tonnes of CO_2e. In addition, its concrete foundations and pavements will slowly absorb 6 tonnes of CO_2e through the slow carbonization process during and after the life cycle of the building. Altogether, carbon storages and sinks in the project represent 78% of the building's material-related emissions over a 50-year study period.

Although the building's climate impacts are moderate, we tried to identify further possibilities for mitigating them. By replacing certain construction materials, we found an emission reduction potential of over 560 tonnes. Using a greener cement mix would have enabled this environmental improvement. Interestingly, if the full mitigation potential were to be reached and the building's carbon storages and sinks kept intact, the latter would offset 98% of those reduced material-related emissions, almost half of all life cycle emissions.

With respect to the circular economic potential of the Puukuokka One, its modular units offer the possibility of easy reuse when disassembled from the building at the end of its functional life. The building is built by stacking ready-made modules on top of each other, and therefore it is realistic to assume a similar disassembly and relocation scenario for them as well. Although we cannot exactly quantify this potential—much depends on the process of disassembly, transportation, and retrofitting the modules for next use—their structure appears to be ideal as a means of providing for another life cycle in a future building.

When looking at the material that comprises the building, the wooden parts would either be burnt for bioenergy, or recycled into secondary products—if an industry that can process recycled wood has evolved by the time of the theoretical demolition of the building. Concrete and gravel materials could be circulated into aggregates and used in infrastructural projects.

In the following analysis, we'll take a closer look at the life cycle emissions and storages at Puukuokka One. First, we'll provide an overview of the LCA results. Then, we'll show them for each building category. We'll offer the results in terms of material inputs, their emissions, and sinks, along with their potential for further emissions mitigation. Finally, we'll present the use of energy and its associated emissions.

FIGURE 3.20 INSTALLING THE PREFABRICATED MODULAR UNITS FOR THE PUUKUOKKA HOUSING BLOCK. *Source:* OOPEAA/STORA ENSO

PUUKUOKKA ONE: KEY FIGURES

Materials

Most of the material-related emissions arise from the modular units and from the foundations of the building. These two building parts represent nearly 70% of all embodied emissions. Regarding carbon storages and sinks, the modular units dominate with close to 70% of all stored and sequestered carbon. In the following, we present the results of this assessment by building category.

Table 3.21

Puukuokka One: key figures.

Emissions		kgCO$_2$e/building
A	**Production and construction**	
A1–3	Production of materials	1,508,456
A4	Transport to site	146,658
A5	Construction work	164,181
		1,819,295
B	**Use**	
B1	Use in building	(not assessed)
B2	Maintenance	(not assessed)
B3–4	Repairs and replacements	330,324
B5	Refurbishment	(not assessed)
B6	Use of energy	1,978,749
B7	Use of water	(not assessed)
		2,309,073
C	**End-of-life**	
C1	Deconstruction work	43,469
C2	Transport to waste management	24,513
C3–4	Waste management final disposal	86,939
		154,921
A–C	**Full life cycle**	**4,283,289**
Storages, sinks and climate benefits		kgCO$_2$e/building
bio–CO$_2$	Carbon storages in biobased products	-1,589,913
B1	Carbonation of cement-based products	-5,781
B1	Uptake of carbon into plants and soil	-253,456
D	Net benefits from reuse and recycling	(not assessed)
D	Surplus renewable energy	0
	Full life cycle	-1,849,150

Figure 3.21 Puukuokka Housing Block carbon emissions, sinks, and storages. *Source:* AUTHORS

EMISSIONS AND STORAGES FOR BUILDING PARTS (kgCO$_2$e/m^2)

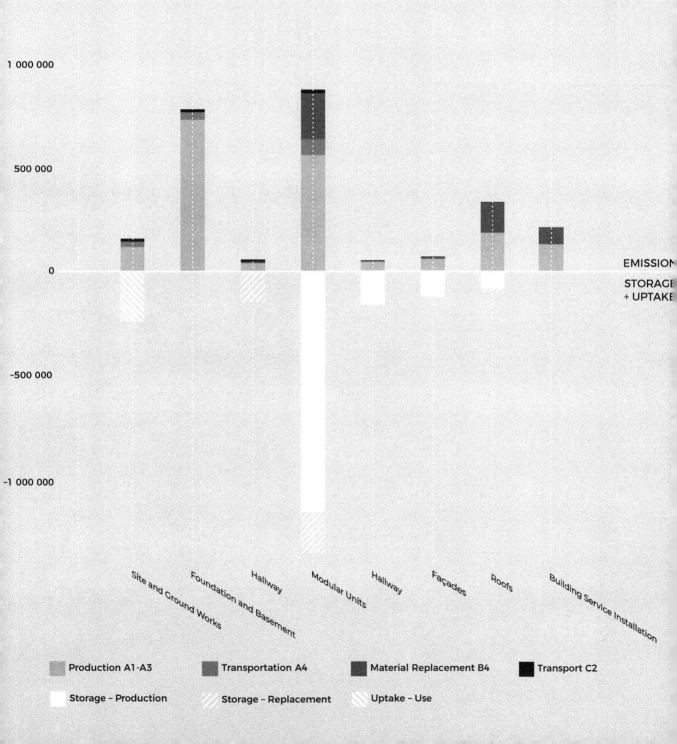

EMISSION

STORAGE
+ UPTAKE

Legend:
- Production A1-A3
- Transportation A4
- Material Replacement B4
- Transport C2
- Storage – Production
- Storage – Replacement
- Uptake – Use

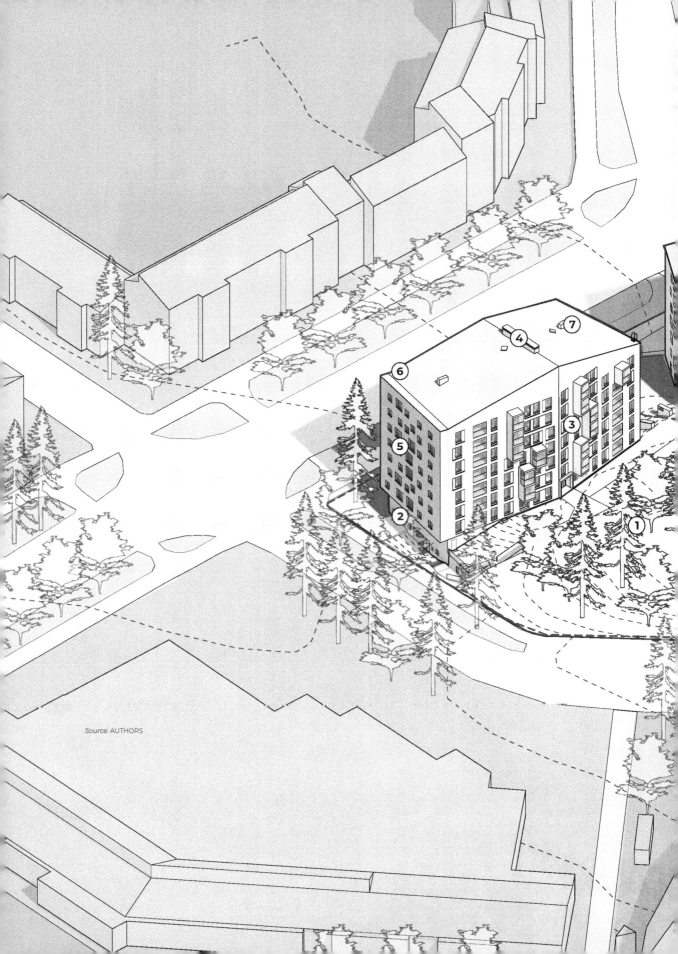

Source: AUTHORS

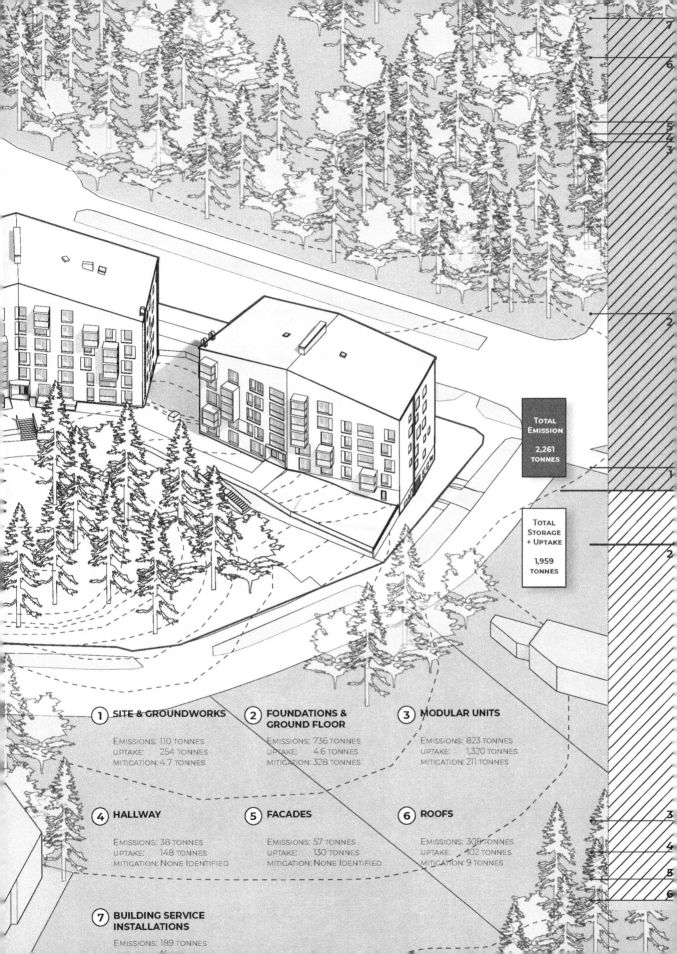

TOTAL EMISSION
2,261 TONNES

TOTAL STORAGE + UPTAKE
1,959 TONNES

① SITE & GROUNDWORKS

EMISSIONS: 110 TONNES
UPTAKE: 254 TONNES
MITIGATION: 4.7 TONNES

② FOUNDATIONS & GROUND FLOOR

EMISSIONS: 736 TONNES
UPTAKE: 4.6 TONNES
MITIGATION: 328 TONNES

③ MODULAR UNITS

EMISSIONS: 823 TONNES
UPTAKE: 1,320 TONNES
MITIGATION: 211 TONNES

④ HALLWAY

EMISSIONS: 38 TONNES
UPTAKE: 148 TONNES
MITIGATION: NONE IDENTIFIED

⑤ FACADES

EMISSIONS: 57 TONNES
UPTAKE: 130 TONNES
MITIGATION: NONE IDENTIFIED

⑥ ROOFS

EMISSIONS: 308 TONNES
UPTAKE: 102 TONNES
MITIGATION: 9 TONNES

⑦ BUILDING SERVICE INSTALLATIONS

EMISSIONS: 189 TONNES

SITE AND GROUND WORKS

Emissions
The greatest source of emissions was the removal of trees and soil. We calculated the biomass of the trees as direct emissions although in practice it is possible that they could have been processed into products, thereby extending the carbon storage over secondary product life cycles. Furthermore, the removal of soil and its transport from the site incurred relatively large emissions. We did not calculate the organic carbon content of the removed soil as direct emissions but assumed instead that the carbon dynamics of the soil would be sustained, albeit in a different location, and that the organic matter in the soil would not start to decompose anaerobically and cause methane emissions.

Uptake of Carbon
In considering the potential uptake of carbon by the site itself, the accumulation of organic carbon in the planted vegetation—mostly pine trees—was found to have a remarkable climate mitigation potential of 254 tonnes. This is almost 2.5 times the amount of embodied carbon of the soil and ground works. This does not include the accumulation of organic carbon in the existing forest trees and soil that were maintained in areas of the site. The total impact of ecosystem services is probably even larger, yet hard to quantify reliably.

Mitigation Potential
The components of the foundation offer theoretical potential to mitigate emissions. If the concrete structures had been made from a greener mix of concrete, in which 50% of the cement was replaced with blast furnace slag, the emissions would have been reduced by 4.5 tonnes. The replacement of gravel with recycled concrete rubble did not appear to offer notable emission reductions. Had fewer trees and less soil been removed, the consequent emissions would have been smaller. The geometry and dimensions of the building and site, however, do not make this a feasible alternative.

Circulation
It would be entirely possible to reuse the site's concrete paving panels at the end of the building life cycle, if they had not been damaged during their service life. Alternatively, demolished concrete paving and concrete stairs could be recycled into concrete rubble and used to replace natural stone aggregate or gravel in future building, landscape, and infrastructure projects. Similarly, site gravel and aggregates when ultimately removed from service could be reused as well. The only materials that would present challenges are the plastic drainage pipes and catch basins. If uncontaminated by impurities, their polyethylene and polypropylene plastics could be mechanically recycled into new raw material. As a last option, they could be burnt for energy, but in that case their fossil carbon would be released, only to further accelerate climate change.

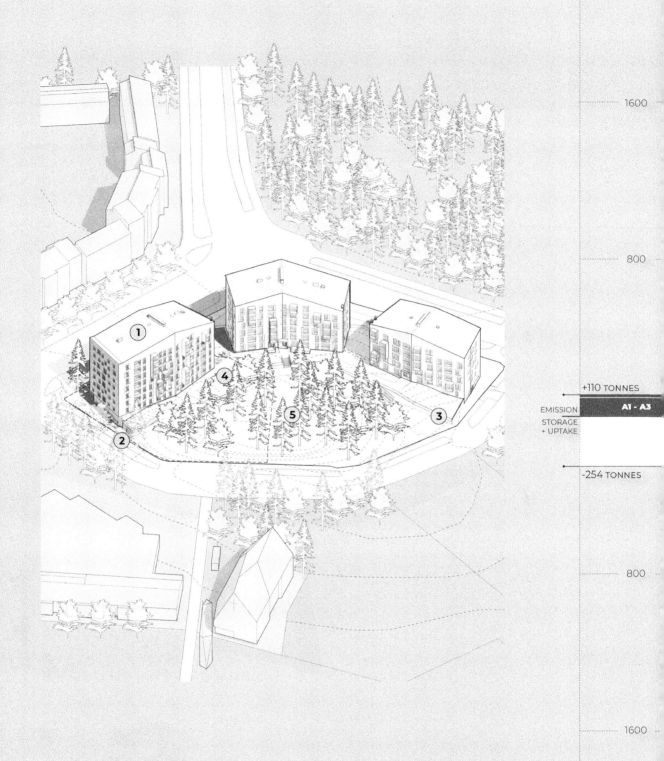

2400

1600

800

+110 TONNES

EMISSION   A1 - A3
STORAGE
+ UPTAKE

-254 TONNES

800

1600

1 PUUKUOKKA   **4** GRAVEL
HOUSE 1

2 ASPHALT   **5** VEGETATION

3 CONCRETE

Source: AUTHORS

FOUNDATIONS AND GROUND FLOOR

Emissions

Most of the emissions associated with the production of the building's foundation would be hard to avoid. They result from the limited option of building materials that—despite their carbon intensity—ensure that the building superstructure will have a long service life.

Concrete has been used for the load-bearing frame and retaining walls of the entire foundation and basement level. Although a necessarily durable feature of the building, its production created a significant volume of emissions. The total for the production of the foundation represents 28% of the embodied emissions of the entire building. These emissions, however, would be challenging to abate, given the position of the building on a slope. The same applies to the second most influential source of embodied emissions in the foundation: the EPS foam insulation, which is an essential component of the foundation assembly that avoids frost damage and heat loss in the cold Finnish climate. The resulting 36 tonnes of emissions can, then, be considered as a necessary carbon investment that ensures the longevity of the building's service life and the performance of its thermal envelope. Moreover, the galvanized steel anchoring system was essential for securing the foundation to the underlying rock but it added some 32 tonnes of CO_2e emissions to the foundation's embodied impacts. Although there are numerous doors throughout the basement level, the amount of emissions of these highly processed components was a marginal 2.7 tonnes of CO_2.

Carbon Uptake and Storages

The only potential for carbon sequestration in the foundations lies in the mineralization of its concrete structures. With the future demolition of the foundation structure, the concrete that comprises it can absorb, in ideal conditions, some 4 tonnes of CO_2 from the atmosphere. The wooden components of the basement level doors offer biogenic carbon storage of only 0.6 tonnes.

Mitigation Potential

Using cement substitutes would have lowered the emissions from the production of the concrete foundations. If half of the cement used were to have been replaced with blast furnace slag, the embodied emissions of the foundation materials would have been reduced by a significant 326 tonnes. Furthermore, if recycled aggregate, such as concrete rubble, had been used instead of natural gravels, the emissions would have been 2 tonnes less.

Circulation

Given the unique shape of the building, it does not seem very likely that its foundation elements could be reused. As noted above, the most likely reuse scenario is that they would be crushed and used as aggregate for infrastructure works substituting for natural gravel. The same applies to the crushed stone that provides the base for the building footings and slabs.

The EPS foam insulation could be reprocessed into new insulation materials as long as it was handled carefully and remained clean enough during the demolition process and if the mechanical recycling processes for plastics had by the end stage evolved into economically feasible direction. It is unlikely, however, that the polypropylene plastic that has been used as geotextile stabilization mat would be recycled, as it would most likely be badly damaged when the overlying soil is removed. The geotextile, therefore—despite its critical reinforcing function—may ultimately end up in some part as particulate plastic that pollutes the soil.

The mineral wool batts that serve as insulation can be recycled into new insulation products, or alternatively reprocessed into geopolymers. In the latter case, as a substitute for Portland cement in concrete, those geopolymers can serve to help decarbonize concrete. But in the case of Puukuokka One, the small quantity of mineral wool used makes this opportunity marginal, when considered in isolation within the life cycle of the building.

In the case of the doors that are used throughout the basement level, their panels could be reused in whole, or their metal and wood components recycled into new products.

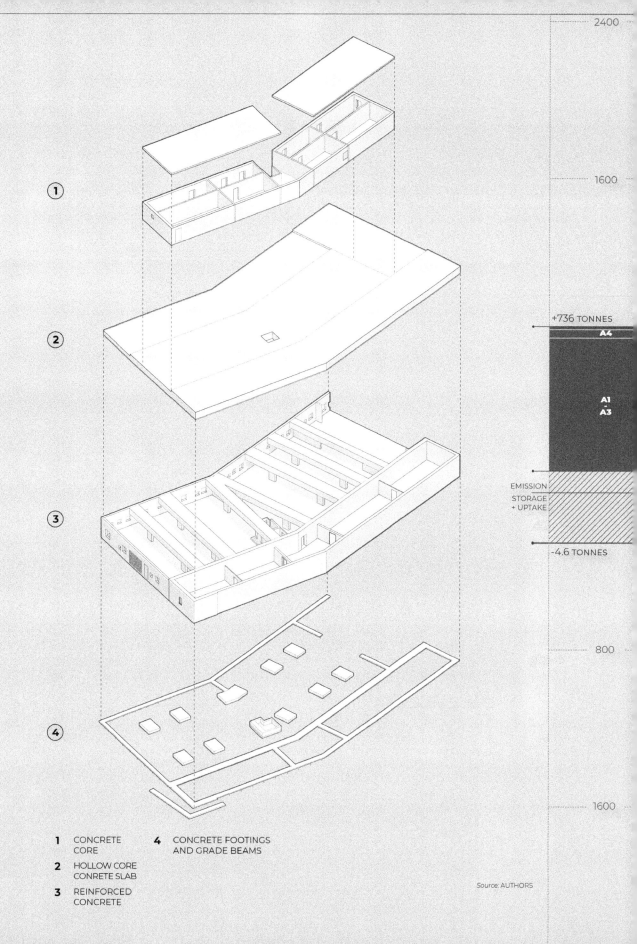

2400

1600

①

②

+736 TONNES

A4

A1
–
A3

EMISSION
STORAGE
+ UPTAKE

③

-4.6 TONNES

800

④

1600

| 1 | CONCRETE CORE | 4 | CONCRETE FOOTINGS AND GRADE BEAMS |

1 CONCRETE
   CORE

2 HOLLOW CORE
   CONRETE SLAB

3 REINFORCED
   CONCRETE

4 CONCRETE FOOTINGS
   AND GRADE BEAMS

Source: AUTHORS

MODULAR UNITS

Emissions

For the modular units, we should note the different technical service lives of the various materials that comprise them. The typical, inexpensive flooring material—laminate made of high-density fiberboard will likely need to be changed every 15 years. Although its initial input to the global warming potential of the modular units is only 67 tonnes, the replacements over our 50-year study period lift it to the top of the emission list. Laminates create one-third of the emissions of the modular units. They even surpass the emissions of the cross-laminated timber, the load-bearing frame material, although the latter constitutes nearly half of the entire weight of the modular units and the laminates only 2%. The concrete toppings slabs, on the other hand, contribute only about 10 tonnes of CO_2e over the building life cycle because they are assumed to last for the entire service life of the building.

Storages

The frames and panels of the modular units store remarkable amounts of biogenic carbon. The storage capacity of the cross-laminated timber panels and other timber components is 1 319 tonnes, which is 1.6 times more than the production emissions of the modular units themselves Altogether, these storages account for close to 70% of the total storages of the entire building. In addition to the timber components, there is a potential additional uptake of carbon at the end of life of the modular units: the cement-based materials can sequester some 1.7 tonnes of CO_2.

Mitigation Potential

As wooden components represent over half of the weight of the modular units, the only relevant mitigation potential for lowering emissions can be found in the flooring selection. If an average laminate were to be replaced with the market's most environmental laminate, emissions would drop over 190 tonnes. This huge figure clearly demonstrates that the way similar products are made can have significant implications for their impact. A factory that uses renewable energy, optimizes the raw materials it consumes, and avoids long transport distances can produce functionally comparable products with considerably less emissions than a manufacturing facility that relies on fossil energy, has not yet introduced efficiency measures and waste practices designed to reduce raw material consumption. One could also read this result with a critical eye. The initially large emissions associated with the laminate flooring are partly a result of the LCA scenario selected in which the material was anticipated to be replaced every 15 years. Although this is a typical estimate of the service life for laminate flooring, it could last longer. There may be no physical need to change it. The role of that particular material, then, might well deserve a sensitivity analysis of its own.

Circulation

Within the framework of currently available technology and the legal requirements and policies that guide it, most of the timber parts of the modular units would probably be burnt for bioenergy in the end-of-life stage of the building life cycle. Although the emissions created by this energy recovery process might be legitimately understood as a climate-neutral result in a simple accounting of biogenic carbon flows, the emissions are still a problem, in spite of their organic origin. In terms of helping to offset emissions within a broader system boundary, say, one that considers the building sector as a whole, a much more preferable option would be to reuse the modular units by incorporating them in another building, of course after remodeling them once they have been removed from the original building assembly. Herein lies significant potential for modular building units. In many cases, the *designed* reuse potential—for the concrete sandwich panel systems of the 1960s, for example—has remained mostly theoretical, although the buildings might originally have been designed with this option in mind. In the case of modular units like the ones at Puukuokka One, however, the ease of their disassembly and reuse could turn that potential into reality. In such a case, most of the components that fitted inside the modular units would travel to the site of their next use as well. Building systems and fixtures which have a shorter technical service life, might be the exception.

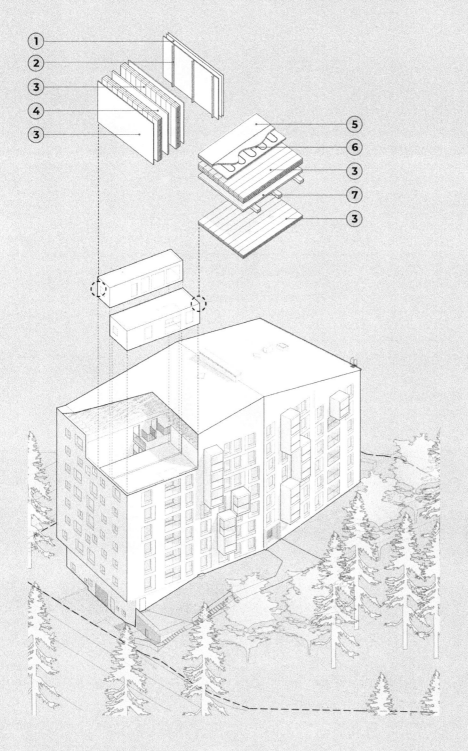

2400

+823 TONNES

B4

A4

A1 + A3

800

EMISSION
STORAGE
+ UPTAKE

1600
-1,320 TONNES

1	LARCH AND SPRUCE SIDING	**4**	INSULATION	**7**	ACOUSTIC INSULATION
2	WOOD FURRING	**5**	OAK FLOORING		
3	CLT PANEL W/ GYPSUM BOARD	**6**	CONCRETE SCREED		

Source: AUTHORS

HALLWAY

Emissions and Storages

The building's shared circulation corridor, that connects one volumetric dwelling -module to the next, is comprised primarily of wood. Its emissions, therefore, are low compared to the amount of carbon it stores. The cross-laminated timber structure accounts for 22 tonnes of emissions but store almost five times more CO_2, and the rest of the wooden components add close to 50 tonnes to that storage. Gypsum boards and acoustic panels together account for close to 7 tonnes of emissions, but this is marginal compared to the importance of the acoustical privacy and comfort and fire resistance they provide.

Mitigation Potential

There is hardly any potential to mitigate the rather minor emissions associated with the construction of the connector corridor. Most of the materials—some 80% of the mass—are wood-based. Changing the gypsum board for material that has fewer emissions would not be relevant for this more public part of the building, as there are no feasible alternatives that offer the fire safety that the gypsum board provides.

Circulation

As discussed in earlier sections of this chapter, the wood-based products that comprise the structure of the Puukuokka One corridors could be reused, but in this case, their unique shape may reduce this potential. Instead, recycling them into secondary wood products would be more feasible and therefore the desired option. This would require stripping the cross-laminated timber panels of any potential accumulated surface treatments which would likely be both technically reasonable and economically feasible. As a last option, the wooden components could be burnt for bioenergy, or in a better scenario, processed through pyrolysis into biochar, which could then be used for landscaping and storing carbon in soils.

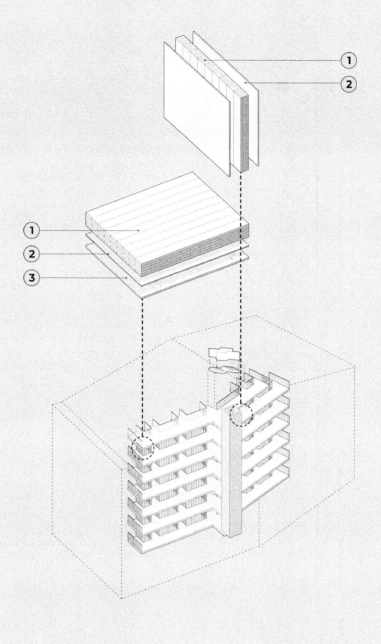
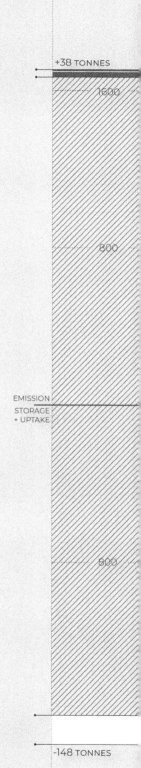

2400

+38 TONNES

1600

800

EMISSION
STORAGE
+ UPTAKE

800

-148 TONNES

1 CLT PANEL

2 GYPSUM BOARD

3 ACOUSTIC
PANEL

Source: AUTHORS

FAÇADES

Emissions and Storages

The primary areas of Puukuokka One's façades are made from spruce and larch claddings. During the selected LCA study period, these claddings would not require replacement and therefore their production stage emissions remain low. The highest individual contributor to the emissions of the façades are the metal components, which add some 30 tonnes of emissions to the project and account for close to 40% of the emissions attributed to the façades.

Naturally, the wooden elements act to store carbon. Of the different wood façade components, the cross-laminated timber panels contain one-third of the stored carbon and the rest is stored within the spruce and larch cladding.

Mitigation Potential

The façade assembly offers very little potential for further emissions mitigation. If the areas of metal cladding had been replaced with plywood panels, for example, there might have been some initial emissions reductions, but this would have changed the architectural intent, and the reuse of that substitute cladding, unlike the metal paneling it would presume to replace, would have a shorter service life, be more subject to damage, and therefore be less likely to be reused in the end-of-life stage.

Circulation

As most of the materials—in terms of weight—are wood-based, their likely end-of-life scenario is either energy recovery or recycling into new secondary raw materials. However, as parts of the façade planks are left untreated, they could be suitable for carpentry after being disassembled from the façade. The patina that would have gathered over the years of their technical service life might be considered a value-added material property. The metal parts of the façade would likely maintain their value and be reused or recycled.

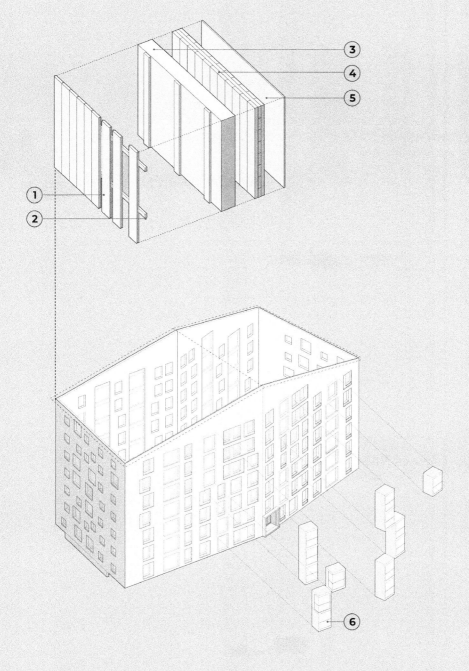

2400

+57 TONNES

1600

800

EMISSION
STORAGE
+ UPTAKE

800

1600

-130 TONNES

1	LARCH AND SPRUCE SIDING	4	CLT PANEL
2	WOOD FURRING	5	GYPSUM BOARD
3	CLT PANEL W/ GYPSUM BOARD	6	CLT BALCONY

Source: AUTHORS

ROOFS

Emissions and Storages

The roofing material is of critical importance. By protecting all of the systems that lie beneath it from weather and the primary point of water infiltration, the roof prevents the slow breakdown of secondary and tertiary structures within the building assembly. In Puukuokka One, the roofing material installed is bitumen, which is inexpensive and suitable for relatively low-slope roofs. The production of bitumen roofing, however, is emission-intensive, and the expected technical service life is less than 40 years. The need to replace the roofing once during our study period produces significant emissions—15 tonnes of CO_2e—and represents over 40% of the roof assembly emissions. Oriented strand boards which serve as roofing underlay produce an additional 7.5 tonnes of emissions, and the mineral wool insulation another 6 tonnes.

The wooden components, on the other hand, store over 100 tonnes of CO_2. Although the roof is large, its carbon storage accounts only for 5% of the entire building's storages, due in large part to the multiple storeys of timber dwelling units below it that occupy a relatively small footprint.

Mitigation Potential

As the bitumen roofing causes most of the emissions, any significant mitigation potential would be achieved through its potential replacement. There are, however, few alternatives for low slope roofs with significantly smaller production phase emissions. Finding a bitumen sheet supplier whose product was manufactured with lower embodied emissions seems the only feasible alternative. The "greenest" bitumen on the market, however, has less than half the emissions of the typical products on the market. As the bitumen layers would be replaced during our study period, this simple switch to a "greener" product would have provided a benefit of nearly 9 tonnes.

Circulation

The wooden roof trusses are engineered specifically to correspond to the building's geometries and spans and the loads it must withstand. It is therefore less likely that they would be reused in their current configuration. Instead, the wooden elements could feasibly be recycled into secondary products. The insulation materials—if they have not suffered damage from moisture infiltration at any point during the building's long service life—could be recycled into new insulation materials or even into geopolymers. Similarly, gypsum could be carefully disassembled and sent for recycling into new gypsum products,

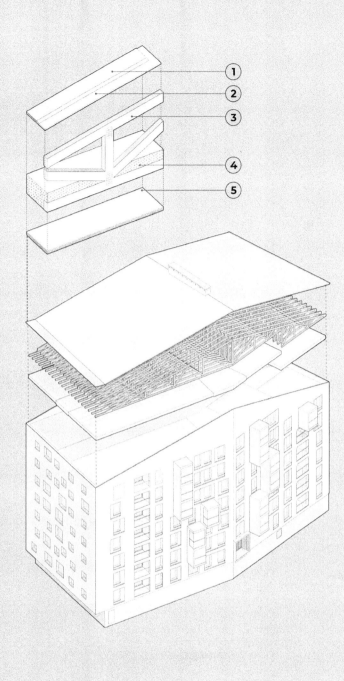

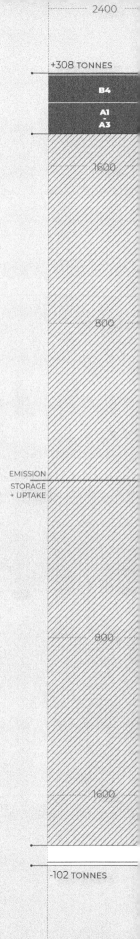

2400

+308 TONNES

B4

A1 – A3

1600

800

EMISSION
STORAGE
+ UPTAKE

800

1600

-102 TONNES

1	BITUMEN ROOFING	4	MINERAL WOOL INSULATION
2	ORIENTED STRAND BOARD	5	CLT PANEL
3	TIMBER TRUSS		

Source: AUTHORS

BUILDING SERVICE INSTALLATIONS

Emissions

Building system components are made mostly from plastics and metals. As these materials are emission-intensive to manufacture, they also account for considerable amounts of emissions per unit. In this case, the total input to building's carbon footprint was estimated to be 185 tonnes, which is 8% of the entire project. Plastics are the largest contributor to this emission. Polyethylene, polyvinylchloride, polypropylene, and polycarbonate are among the most commonly used types of plastic in the building systems' components and equipment.

The building is connected to a district heating grid and does not employ renewable energy systems. This is because the carbon footprint of the local district energy is already very low, due to the use of renewable energy sources.

Mitigation

The current design of the building systems represents the assembly of a typical residential building. Because it has been optimized to meet the legal minimum requirements of indoor air quality and thermal comfort, it seems realistic that there would be possibilities for achieving the same level of service with fewer material inputs. If the building had been designed to employ natural ventilation techniques, the size of the ventilation ducts would have been reduced and possibly the production and maintenance of the air handling units avoided. This would have had, however, a significant influence on the design of the building, as well as on the building's-physical performance, so the mitigation potential is hard to quantify and would likely have increased material expenditure elsewhere in the design.

Circulation

As noted in the case of the Common Ground High School, the metals that comprise the Puukuokka One's building systems have a high degree of recycling potential, even in the current state of the industry. It is safe to assume, therefore, that over 90% of that material would be recycled. The same cannot be said for the plastics and rubber. For these classes of materials, both mechanical and chemical recycling processes remain inadequate, and, in the case of rubber, would be far from carbon-neutral. Thus, a realistic, yet conservative assumption about their fate would be that they would be incinerated for energy.

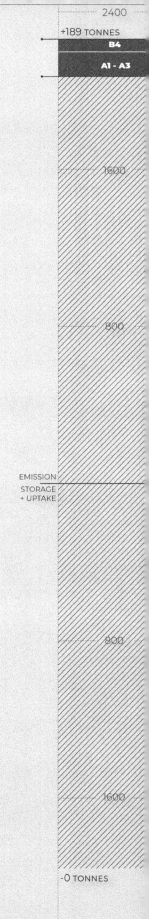

2400

+189 TONNES
B4
A1 - A3

1600

800

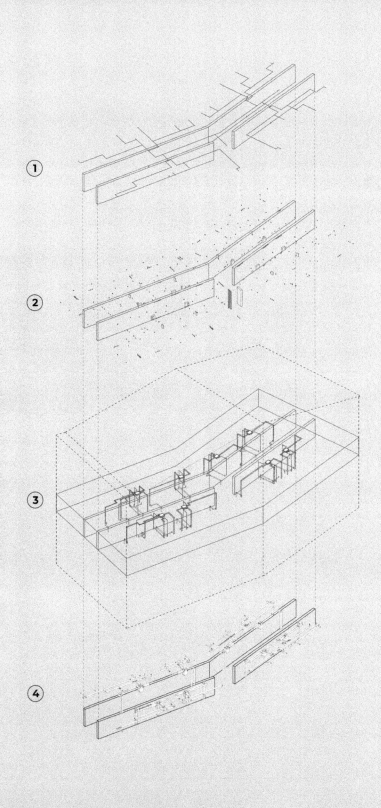

EMISSION
STORAGE
+ UPTAKE

800

1600

1   UNDERFLOOR   4   VENTILATION
    HEATING   SYSTEMS

2   ELECTRICAL
    FIXTURES

3   RESIDENTIAL
    PLUMBING

Source: AUTHORS

-0 TONNES

Table 3.22

Site and ground works:
material inputs and outputs, expected technical service life, and likely end-of-life scenario.

Material inputs	Expected technical service life	Likely end-of-life scenario
135 tn vegetation (grown)	Over 100 years	Landfill
84 tn gravel	Building´s lifetime	Recycling: aggregate for infrastructure works
80 tn concrete	Building´s lifetime	Recycling: aggregate for infrastructure works
1.2 tn plastic	50 years	Energy recovery Recycling: mechanical recycling into new products
Material outputs		
5,940 tn soil (removed)		Landfill
46 tn trees (removed)		Landfill
6,284 tn total		

Table 3.23

Site and ground works:
emissions, storages, and further mitigation potential.

Emissions	Storages	Further mitigation potential
110 tonnes	254 tonnes	4.7 tonnes
· Removal of trees 84 tn (interpreted as biogenic carbon emission) · Removal of soil 11 tn · Concrete stairs and paving 11 tn · Gravel 1.5 tn	· Trees and vegetation 254 tn · Carbonation of concrete 0.06 tn	· Greener cement mix 4.5 tn · Recycled concrete rubble replacing natural gravel 0.2 tn

Table 3.24

Foundations and ground floor:
material inputs, expected technical service life, and likely end-of-life scenario.

Material inputs	Expected technical service life	Likely end-of-life scenario
3,429 tn concrete	Building's lifetime	Recycling: aggregate for infrastructure works
1,447 tn gravel	Building's lifetime	Recycling: aggregate for infrastructure works
11 tn steel	Building's lifetime	Recycling: secondary raw material for steel production
11 tn plastic	Up to 50 years	Energy recovery Recycling: mechanical recycling into new products
4 tn gypsum	Up to 50 years	Recycling: secondary raw material for gypsum production
1.2 tn components (doors)	Up to 50 years	Reuse or recycling as secondary raw materials
0.5 tn mineral wool	Up to 50 years	Landfill, possibly recycling into new insulation or geopolymers
4,904 tn total		

Table 3.25

Foundations and ground floor:
emissions, storages, and further mitigation potential.

Emissions	Storages	Further mitigation potential
736 tonnes	4.6 tonnes	328 tonnes
· Concrete 637 tn · EPS insulation 36 tn · Steel 32 tn · Gravel 11 tn	· Carbonation of concrete 4 tn · Wooden parts in doors 0.6 tn	· Greener cement mix 326 tn · Use of recycled aggregate instead of natural gravel 2 tn

Table 3.26

Modular units:
material inputs, expected technical service life, and likely end-of-life scenario.

Material inputs	Expected technical service life	Likely end-of-life scenario
605 tn cross-laminated timber	Building's lifetime	Recycling: wood-based board or bioenergy
226 tn cement screed	Up to 50 years	Recycling: aggregate for infrastructure works Landfill
76 tn mineral wool	Building's lifetime	Landfill, possibly recycling into new insulation or geopolymers
72 tn gypsum	Up to 50 years	Recycling or landfill: secondary raw material for gypsum boards, other industrial uses or landfill
66 tn windows and doors (containing metals, wood, glass, plastics, and rubber)	Up to 50 years	Reuse or recycling into secondary raw materials
60 tn concrete	Building's lifetime	Recycling: aggregate for infrastructure works
45 tn timber	Building's lifetime	Recycling: wood-based board or bioenergy
29 tn floor and wall tiles, cement surfaces	30 years	Recycling: aggregate for infrastructure works Landfill
28 tn laminate	15 years	Energy recovery
5 tn EPS sound insulation	15 years	Energy recovery
2 tn steel	Building's lifetime	Recycling: secondary raw material for new steel products
1,214 tn total		

Table 3.27

Modular units:
emissions, storages, and further mitigation potential.

Emissions	Storages	Further mitigation potential
823 tonnes	1,320 tonnes	211 tonnes
· Laminate 269 tn · Cross-laminated timber 206 tn · Windows and doors 131 tn · Mineral wool 89 tn · Gypsum 31 tn	· Cross-laminated timber 938 tn · Timber 70 tn · Windows and doors 56 tn	· Replacing average laminates with market´s greenest laminate 194 tn · Using greener cement mix for floors 17 tn

Table 3.28

Hallway:
material inputs, expected technical service life, and likely end-of-life scenario.

Material inputs	Expected technical service life	Likely end-of-life scenario
65 tn cross-laminated timber	Building's lifetime	Recycling: wood-based board or bioenergy
30 tn timber	Building's lifetime	Recycling: wood-based board or bioenergy
13 tn gypsum	Up to 50 years	Recycling or landfill: Secondary raw material for gypsum boards, other industrial uses or landfill
10 tn acoustic panels	Up to 50 years	Energy recovery
0.3 tn linoleum flooring	Up to 30 years	Energy recovery
0.3 tn paint	20 years	(Will burn in the energy recovery process)
0.2 tn steel	Building's lifetime	Recycling: secondary raw material for new steel products
118 tn total		

Table 3.29

Hallway:
emissions, storages, and further mitigation potential.

Emissions	Storages	Further mitigation potential
38 tonnes	148 tonnes	None identified
• Cross-laminated timber 22 tn • Gypsum 3.7 tn • Timber 3.1 tn • Acoustic boards 2.9 tn	• Cross-laminated timber 100 tn • Timber 46 tn • Acoustic boards 1.3 tn	

Table 3.30

Façades:
material inputs, expected technical service life, and likely end-of-life scenario.

Material inputs	Expected technical service life	Likely end-of-life scenario
57 tn timber	Up to 50 years	Recycling: wood-based board or bioenergy
27 tn cross-laminated timber	Up to 50 years	Recycling: wood-based board or bioenergy
1.2 tn glass	Up to 50 years	Recycling: secondary raw material (e.g. glass wool)
0.9 tn steel	Up to 50 years	Recycling: secondary raw material for steel production
0.3 tn bitumen	35 years	Energy recovery or recycling: secondary raw material for asphalt
0.3 tn paint	20 years	(Will burn in the energy recovery process)
0.2 tn oriented strand boards	35 years	Energy recovery
87 tn total		

Table 3.31

Façades:
emission, storages, and further mitigation potential.

Emissions	Storages	Further mitigation potential
57 tonnes	130 tonnes	None identified
· Metal surfaces 30 tn · Cross-laminated timber 9 tn · Bitumen 8 tn · Timber 6 tn · Glass 1.7 tn	· Timber 88 tn · Cross-laminated timber 42 tn · Oriented strand board 0.6 tn	

Table 3.32

Roofs:
material inputs, expected technical service life, and likely end-of-life scenario.

Material inputs	Expected technical service life	Likely end-of-life scenario
52 tn timber	Building's lifetime	Recycling: wood-based board or bioenergy
11 tn bitumen	35 years	Energy recovery or recycling: secondary raw material for asphalt
8 tn oriented strand boards	35 years	Energy recovery
6.7 tn mineral wool	50 years	Landfill, possibly recycling into new insulation or geopolymers
4.6 tn gypsum	Up to 50 years	Recycling or landfill: secondary raw material for gypsum boards, other industrial uses or landfill
0.2 tn components (hatches)	Up to 50 years	Reuse or recycling into secondary raw materials
0.1 tn steel	Building's lifetime	Recycling: secondary raw material for steel production
83 tn total		

Table 3.33

Roofs:
emissions, storages, and further mitigation potential.

Emissions	Storages	Further mitigation potential
308 tonnes	102 tonnes	9 tonnes
· Bitumen 15 tn · Oriented strand boards 7.5 tn · Mineral wool 6 tn · Timber 5 tn	· Timber 81 tn · Oriented strand boards 21 tn	· Low carbon bitumen 8.8 tn

Table 3.34

Building service installations:
material inputs, expected technical service life, and likely end-of-life scenario.

Material inputs	Expected technical service life	Likely end-of-life scenario
10 tn plastics	25–50 years	Energy recovery Recycling: mechanical recycling into new products
4.9 tn galvanized steel	40 years	Recycling: secondary raw material for steel production
3.6 tn stainless steel	30 years	Recycling: secondary raw material for steel production
3 tn various machines (consisting mostly of metals and plastics)	30–40 years	Recycling into secondary raw materials
2.7 tn copper	25–50 years	Recycling: secondary raw material for copper production
25 tn total		

Table 3.35

**Building service installations:
emissions, storages, and further mitigation potential.**

Emissions	Storages	Further mitigation potential
189 tonnes	None	None identified.
· Plastics 46 tn · Stainless steel 39 tn · Galvanized steel 39 tn · Machines 33 tn · Copper 5 tn	(none)	(none)

MITIGATION POTENTIAL FROM MATERIALS AND SYSTEMS

As we summarize all the theoretical means of lowering the material-related emissions of Puukuokka One, we can find over 560 tonnes of avoidable emissions. Although this figure is theoretical, it exemplifies which interventions could help to build similar building with even smaller carbon footprints

A "greener" cement mix offers the largest potential for reduced emissions. If its workability, cost, and technical properties meet the specified performance criteria, the potential reduction of emissions reduction be as high as 350 tonnes. This represents 17% of all material-related, embodied emissions and 8% of the emissions of the entire building life cycle.

Comparing the environmental impact data of alternative materials could also help. In this case, the example of changing to a lower emission laminate flooring product would have helped to reduce emissions by 194 tonnes and the replacement of a lower impact bituminous material for the roof might have saved a further 9 tonnes. Altogether, a comparison of EPDs could bring 203 tonnes less atmospheric load.

Crushing concrete to form aggregates is another means to reduce the building's carbon footprint, but the figures in the case of Puukuokka One were quite modest: 13 tonnes of potential savings. However, as concrete is crushed and its surface area increases. it will start to carbonate at an accelerated speed. This co-benefit of carbon sequestration would favor the use of crushed concrete aggregate instead of natural gravel or crushed stone.

Again, as discussed in the case study of Common Ground High School, the potential emission reductions will not be enough to make Puukuokka One's material-related emissions zero. To build a truly carbon-neutral building would require a holistic reconsideration of many aspects of the building's design, beyond any material substitutions.

ENERGY

Background to Energy Calculations

In this section of the Puukuokka One case study, we used the calculated amount of annual purchased energy to calculate the carbon footprint attributed to energy use. This information was part of the requirement of a building's energy certification. This method represents an assumption of how the

---

Table 3.36

Mitigation potential from materials and systems.

	Mitigation potential		
Measures	**Avoidable emissions (tn CO$_2$e)**	**Share of embodied emissions (%)**	**Share of life cycle emissions (%)**
Greener cement mix	347	17	8
Low carbon laminate	194	10	5
Concrete rubble	13	0.6	0.3
Low carbon bitumen	9	0.4	0.2
Total	563	28	13

building performs when used as designed, but does not ultimately measure or reflect how the building's users actually consume electricity, heating, or cooling in their daily routines.

The decarbonization of energy raises an interesting aspect of our assessment. As a consequence of international climate efforts—especially the Paris Agreement in 2015—several countries and states have set for themselves goals for lowering the emissions of the energy sector. Some of these goals have been drafted into legislation so it is therefore reasonable to assume that they will become a reality.

For our purposes, we took into account the existing local legislation which requires the elimination of coal as an energy source after 2029. This is part of Finland's commitment to reach carbon neutrality by 2035 and the ban will lower the carbon footprint of both electricity and district heating considerably. Furthermore, we applied a scenario established by the local official building LCA method, which takes into account the forthcoming European development in the decarbonization of energy and the expected price development of the emission trading scheme [15]. In this scheme, the carbon intensity of electricity is expected to drop from 121 gCO_2e/kWh in the 2020s to 0 by 2120. Similarly, the figures for district heating are anticipated to fall from 130 gCO_2e/kWh to 3 gCO_2e/kWh in 100 years.

Results: Energy Efficiency and Related Emissions

As we look at the demand of energy in the building, we can see that heating the domestic hot water consumes most of the energy, altogether 70%. In addition, supplying the apartments with hot water will result in some heat loss from the pipes, which adds to the heat loads of the building. Most of the heat loads, however, come from solar radiation and from that given off by the occupants themselves.

The building loses most of its energy through its windows (55%) and external walls (23%). Heat losses through roof and ground floor slab represent only 11% of all heat losses. Mitigating these emissions would have been possible, if the budget had allowed

for more energy-efficient windows (current U-value 1.0 W/m^2K) or for adding more insulation to the walls (current U-value 0.17 W/m^2K).

The insulating qualities of the massive wood structures allow the temperature of the individual apartments to be controlled independently, without the temperature of one apartment affecting that of the others. The use of massive timber as the structural frame material also made it possible to realize the hallway space in an energy-efficient manner as a semi-conditioned open space. To further minimize the use of heating energy in the complex, the indoor parking garage on the basement level was built as a non-insulated and unheated space.

In order to maintain the desired indoor thermal comfort and as a result of heat losses and loads, the building consumes 546,600 kWh energy per year, or 98 kWh/m^2. District heating accounts for 48% of this total, and electricity 51%. In our calculation, we assumed that the consumption of energy would remain stable over the building's life cycle. Most likely, the consumption of electricity will increase slightly, as we can observe the clear trend of increased consumer electronics use in households. However, the energy efficiency of different appliances is expected to improve at the same time, so the net increase in electricity demand may remain modest.

There are no systems for generating renewable energy in this building. In this aspect, it differs from the Common Ground High School, in which large areas of the roof were covered with solar photovoltaic panels. In the case of Puukuokka, however, a similar solution was not considered relevant. This decision was made in the design phase, when the designers studied the environmental impacts of the local energy companies. As the emissions from the grid energy in the region are clearly lower than the national average, a decision was made to utilize this potential, instead of making investments of money and embodied emissions in renewable energy systems.

ENERGY AND THERMAL EFFICIENCY

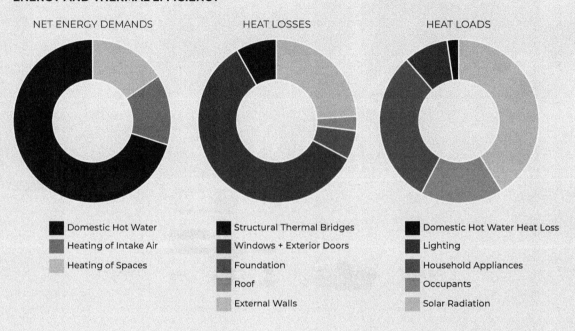

NET ENERGY DEMANDS

HEAT LOSSES

HEAT LOADS

- ■ Domestic Hot Water
- ■ Heating of Intake Air
- ■ Heating of Spaces

- ■ Structural Thermal Bridges
- ■ Windows + Exterior Doors
- ■ Foundation
- ■ Roof
- ■ External Walls

- ■ Domestic Hot Water Heat Loss
- ■ Lighting
- ■ Household Appliances
- ■ Occupants
- ■ Solar Radiation

EMBODIED AND OPERATIONAL EMISSIONS OVER TIME (kgCO$_2$e/m²)

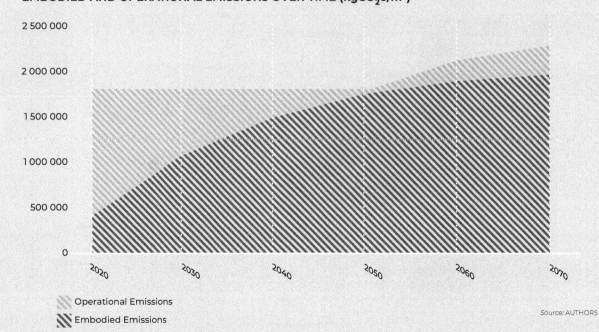

- Operational Emissions
- Embodied Emissions

Source: AUTHORS

The consumed amount of energy leads into operational emissions of 1 978 tonnes of CO_2e during 50 years, or 7.1 $kgCO_2e/m^2$/year. It's worth noting that the emissions from operational energy use drop from 14.5 $kgCO_2e/m^2$/year in the beginning of the building's life cycle in 2015 to only 2.3 $kgCO_2e/m^2$/year near the end of the study period. This is due to the decarbonization of the energy from the grid.

As the operational emissions drop significantly, saving energy through high energy efficiency will remain important in the future as well. This is because electricity, in particular, will be in great demand in tomorrow's carbon-neutral society. If we want to decarbonize cars, airplanes, the production of steel or construction machinery, there will be a massive demand for more electricity. The more that buildings can save electricity and energy—even though this may not have critical climate impacts in the future—the more resources will be available for other sectors of our society. That's why energy efficiency will remain important in the future, even though the climate impacts from the use of energy by buildings will most likely be a lesser concern.

COMPARISON OF THE CASE STUDIES

What Causes the Differences?

Now that we have described some of the details of the case studies, it's informative to discuss the findings in their comparison to each other. Are the values good or bad? Which building performs better? What could we learn—or better yet, adopt into practice—from these studies? Before jumping to these conclusions, let's discuss the differences and similarities of the buildings we've analyzed.

It is important to acknowledge and, more importantly, to understand which parameters or features of policy, regulation, environment, weather, budget or building's occupancy influence its climatic impacts. It can help us to set realistic and achievable ambitions for our projects, and gives us insight as we compare different buildings or regulatory standards. To begin this journey, we've collected some key features of the buildings analyzed. We also offer interpretations of the meaning and relevance of the variables we've found in each of the case studies.

Building Typology

A school and an apartment block are different building types. Therefore, their exact results are not meant to be cross-referenced or directly compared. Apartment buildings have a number of repetitive apartments, which are designed so that the building service shafts and installations are repeated in each floor in a mostly similar manner. The nature of an apartment building is vertical, and there is high degree of repetition of the plan. The school, on the other hand, is horizontal in its layout by nature. Because the building houses a number of functions, and few of them are repetitive, many of the solutions are "unique," and thus there is little

economy of scale. These differences are inherent to the building types and lead to difference assessment results as well.

Physical Features and Structural Solutions

The size and area-to-volume ratio of the building strongly correspond to its material inputs. When comparing the material or energy consumption, we can usually observe that larger buildings perform better, assuming that they are similarly compact.

Puukuokka One is nearly five times larger in its area than the Common Ground High School and its area is spread across with multiple storeys. For this reason, blocks of flats or offices usually have much smaller share of foundation in relation to their floor areas than most public service buildings or single-family homes. And as foundations are built from carbon-intensive materials—concrete, steel, and frost insulations—their relative dominance to material-related emissions is higher in buildings that spread low over larger areas of land.

Location and Weather

The location of the buildings also plays a big role in their emissions. Very few buildings are independent of a municipal energy source. Operational emissions are largely a result of the emissions of the locally or regionally available energy mix. A building designer, at best, can reduce the demand of energy through smart and informed design decisions, and equip the buildings with renewable energy or energy recovery systems. Still, the emissions from the grid energy remain. Furthermore, local or national conditions have a significant influence on the temporal aspect of the operational emissions. In regions where there are policies in place for decarbonizing the grid energy, the operational emissions can be expected to decrease over the chosen study period. This is beyond the control of the building's designer (apart from when considering how to vote in elections).

Understandably, local regulations influence design, and set the baseline against which different solutions are optimized. The average temperatures in New Haven range from -2 Celsius (29 Fahrenheit) to + 22 Celsius (72 Fahrenheit), whereas the same range in Jyväskylä is from -9 Celsius (16 Fahrenheit) to +16 Celsius (61 Fahrenheit). Furthermore, the precipitation is different, and has an impact on the moisture loads on the building, as well as on the thermal comfort of their occupants. These regional differences understandably influence both the consumption of energy and the physical deterioration of the building assembly.

We can readily see the influence of a building's location on its consumption of energy. Common Ground High School uses double the amount of energy (195 kWh/m²/year) in relation to the floor area compared to Puukuokka One (98 kWh/m²/year). Regulations set the minimum levels for energy efficiency, and going beyond the normative minimum is rare in conventional, investment cost-oriented design projects. That is another reason why it is difficult to directly compare the buildings to each other.

There are similarities between the chosen buildings as well. Both have a load-bearing frame made from timber, and both have concrete foundations. Both are equipped with mechanical ventilation and building service systems. The construction methods, however, differ. Whereas both have taken advantage of prefabrication—wood is light and therefore ideal for it—Puukuokka One is made from volumetric units. This has shortened the construction time, without increasing the transportation-related emissions (the factory is less than 100 km from the construction site).

Regulations

One of the differences between the two studied buildings is clearly their energy performance. Although the relative importance of energy efficiency is decreasing in new buildings, its role will remain important. Common Ground High School was designed according to Connecticut High Performance School Regulations [16], which need to be at least 21% better than the existing building code's requirements. The building performed much better, achieving 61% energy savings compared to the baseline code. Puukuokka building, on the other hand, was designed according to local Finnish energy-efficiency standards, which are based on strict European requirements for nearly zero energy buildings [17]. As there are differences between both climatic conditions and regulatory requirements, the outcome of a building optimization process is different. The results of such an optimization can be seen not only in the building system installation, but especially in the assembly of the envelope of the building.

Regulatory differences apply not only to energy efficiency. The fire safety requirements for wood-framed buildings differ considerably from country to country. Furthermore, fire requirements may differ within a country for different building types, such as residential buildings and public buildings. In addition to fire safety, different acoustic requirements may demand different design solutions. It is clear that both fire safety and acoustic comfort have affected the design of the case study buildings. However, as these parameters cannot be normalized, as there is no universal benchmark with which to compare, this difference cannot fully be taken into account in comparing different buildings in different regions.

Table 3.37

How do different variables affect the climate impacts of the studied buildings?

Feature	Common Ground High School	Puukuokka Building One	Influence on climate impacts
Physical features			
Floor area	14,604 sqf 1,357 m²	59,987 sqf 5,573 m²	A compact building is usually more energy- and material-efficient. There are less heat losses or thermal bridges in relation to the floor area. A very compact shape may not be ideal in tropical or hot climates, nor for ensuring natural light for all parts of the building.
Volume	7,374 m³	24,895 m³	
Area-to-volume ratio	0.184	0.224	
Weight	4,750,812 kg/ building	12,709,788 kg/ building	Weight per floor area is a good overall indicator or material efficiency. Light buildings consist of less materials. If these materials are also low in their embodied emissions, the impacts are small. There may be drawbacks regarding acoustic performance or fire safety.
	3,502 kg/m²	2,281 kg/m²	
Number of storeys	2	8	The higher the number of storeys, the smaller the impacts of foundations per floor area. In very high buildings, the pressure on foundations starts growing, with an adverse effect

(Continued)

Table 3.37

How do different variables affect the climate impacts of the studied buildings? (*Continued*)

Feature	Common Ground High School	Puukuokka Building One	Influence on climate impacts
Temperature and weather			
Climate type (Köppen classification)	Humid subtropical (Cfa)	Continental subarctic (Dfc)	Cooler climate increases heating demand. Warmer climate increases cooling demand. Peak high/low values increase peak loads in energy demand for either heating or cooling. This has significance at a regional level.
Average annual temperature	+12°C +54°F	+3°C +38°F	
Average lowest temperature	-2°C +29°F	- 9°C +16°F	
Average highest temperature	+22°C +72°F	+16°C +61°F	
Record temperatures	-21/40°C -5/104°F	-39/+33°C -38/99°F	
Average annual precipitation	1,160 mm 46 in	638 mm 25 in	More humid climate increases weather-related stress on the building envelope
Site			
Soil type	Clay soil	Sandy soil and rock	Softer soil types (clay, silt) require piling or even stabilization. Sandier and rockier sites require less foundation structures. If the bedrock is close to the foundation depth, there may be a need for blasting.
Slope	1:12	1:2	The steeper the slope, the higher the foundation wall
Energy efficiency			
Consumption of energy	195 kWh/m²/year	98 kWh/m²/year	Greater energy efficiency correlates directly with lower operational emissions
Legal requirement of the year of construction	At least 21% better energy performance than in standard buildings	< 150 kWh/m²/year	

COMPARISON OF THE EMISSIONS

Before Use

Both buildings consist of similar set of materials. They have frames made of wood, and foundations of concrete. This results in very similar material-related emissions: 271 kg/m² for Puukuokka and 352 kg/m² for Common Ground High School. The larger size and better area-to-volume ratio of Puukuokka explain the marginal differences.

In both cases, the wooden building components store significant volumes of atmospheric carbon. Common Ground High School has slightly larger storage of carbon (341 kg/m²) compared to Puukuokka (285 kg/m²), due to more wood used per the relative share of the building's material volume. The concrete garage floor of Puukuokka—a necessity for the residents and structurally in accordance with the local fire regulations—produced most of the difference.

In both cases we can observe, how little the transportation or construction work added to the emissions over the study period. That share remains well under 10% in both cases.

Use of Energy During the Operational Stage

The use of energy differentiates the buildings from each other. As described earlier, they consume very different amounts of energy. The reasons for this difference can be found in the local regulations' normative standard, as well as in the typology and area-to-volume ratios of the studied buildings. In the case of Puukuokka, this has led to considerably lower energy consumption. The main reason for the different energy demand is the building's type. Residential blocks of flats do not have as high energy demand in general as schools or other similar public service buildings. Also, because of a better area-to-volume ratio and higher degree of thermal insulation in Puukuokka building;s envelope, the demand for heating energy is lower.

Regarding the emissions caused by the use of energy, there are local differences as well. Electricity, for example, had a lower emission value in Finland (154 g/kWh) than in Connecticut (273 g/kWh) in the year that the buildings were completed. Furthermore, there were regulations in place that further lowered the emissions for Puukuokka, whereas such regulations do not yet exist for the context of Common Ground High School. Although the future evolution of electricity's emissions is speculative, it may lead to very different life cycle emissions, if buildings from different regions or countries are compared. These emissions, however, are beyond the control of the designer. Thus, if a designer would like to achieve the same emission profile as a foreign counterpart, the designer would have to make significant improvements to energy efficiency in regions where the emissions of grid energy are high. And in regions where the decarbonization of grid energy is already well underway, the designer starts with an effective advantage. For these reasons, comparisons are most valuable when one recognizes where the cause of observed differences lies.

Repairs and Replacements

In both buildings, the frequency of material replacement was moderate during the chosen study period of 50 years. The overall impact of replacement and repairs together remained under 10% of overall emissions in both cases. If a longer study period had been chosen, there might have been more surface-material-related differences: in residential buildings, these components are usually replaced upon the exchange of an apartment whereas in schools it is the public budget that more or less determines the cycle of expenditures for replacement and repairs.

After Use

Due to the applied scenarios, the end-of-life stage represented around 5% of life cycle emissions for both buildings. Still, the end-of-life stages of the case study buildings was the most difficult to compare. So many possible scenarios ultimately depended on the waste legislation and waste markets in a distant future, on two different continents. Understandably, these sorts of scenarios are indicative only, and can by no means reflect the actual future outcome. This is the inherent nature of LCA. Still, we think it's better to estimate than not to estimate (if that was the question), as the goal of truly lowering life cycle emissions cannot be achieved unless we do our best to assess the entire arc of a building's formation, use, and, ultimately its material fate and all of the real and theoretical impacts we might incur.

Table 3.38

Comparison of the two case studies.

Emissions		Puukuokka Apartment Block, building 1				Common Ground High School			
A	**Production and Construction**								
A	*Production and construction*	kg/building	kg/m²	kg/m²/a	Share (%)	kg/building	kg/m²	kg/m²/a	Share (%)
A1–3	Production of materials	1,508,456	271	5	35	477,156	352	7	30
A4	Transport to site	146,658	26	1	3	44,903	33	1	3
A5	Construction work	164,181	29	**1**	4	41,267	30	1	3
	Subtotal	1,819,295	326	7	42	563,326	415	8	35
B	*Use*								
B1	Use in building	(not assessed)				(not assessed)			
B2	Maintenance	(not assessed)				(not assessed)			
B3–4	Repairs and replacements	330,324	59	1	8	169,146	125	2	11
B5	Refurbishment	(not assessed)				(not assessed)			
B6	Use of energy (including decarbonization)	1,978,749	355	7	46	794,783	586	12	49
B7	Use of water	(not assessed)				(not assessed)			
	Subtotal	2,309,073	414	8	54	963,929	710	14	60
C	*End-of-life*								
C1	Deconstruction work	43,469	8	0	1	37,669	28	1	2
C2	Transport to waste management	24,513	4	0	1	10,703	14	0	1
C3–4	Waste management and final disposal	86,939	16	0	2	23,065	17	0	1
	Subtotal	154,921	28	1	4	79,517	59	**1**	**5**
	Total	**4,283,289**	**769**	**15**		**1,606,772**	**1,184**	**24**	
	Embodied	2,304,539	414	8	54	811,989	598	12	51
	Operational	1,978,749	355	7	46	794,783	586	12	49

Table 3.38

Comparison of the two case studies. (*Continued*)

Emissions		Puukuokka Apartment Block, building 1				Common Ground High School			
Storages, sinks and climate benefits		kg/building	kg/m²	kg/m²/a	Share (%)	kg/building	kg/m²	kg/m²/a	Share (%)
bio–CO_2	Carbon storages in biobased products	-1,589,913	-285	-6	86	-463,098	-341	-7	89
B1	Carbonization of cement-based products	-5781	-1	0	0	-1,723	-1	0	0
B1	Uptake of carbon into plants and soil	-253,456	-45	-1	14	-55,604	-41	-1	11
D	Net benefits from reuse and recycling	(not assessed)				(not assessed)			
D	Surplus renewable energy	0	0	0	0	0	0	0	0
	Subtotal	-1,849,150	-332	-7	43	-520,424	-384	-8	32
	Carbon balance (emissions - storages)	**2,434,138**	**437**	**9**		**1,086,348**	**801**	**16**	

4 DE-CARBONIZING DESIGN

Emissions / Impacts ↑

low energy efficiency

solar exposure (hot climates)

inefficient planning, overspecification

site selection

new building instead of renovation

energy concept

frame materials

insulation materials

supplementary structures

excavation

tree removals

inefficient planning, spatial inflexibility

Storage / Offsets ↓

(r) reduced
(d) delayed

(d) tree planting

(r) spaces designed for flexible use

(r) use existing soils

(r) appropriate window orientation

(r) compact shape

(r/d) recycled construction materials

(r) access to good public transportation

(r) efficient planning, spatial overlaps

(r) generation of renewable energy onsite

(r) no soil removals

(r) energy storage onsite

(r) passive heating

(r) no stabilization / piling

(r) high energy efficiency goals

(r/d) reused construction materials

(r) renewable energy or energy storage on site

(r) low carbon energy grid

(r) high energy efficiency

(r) renovation instead of new building

(r) passive cooling

PROJECT PREMISE

CONCEPTUAL DESIGN

DEVELOPED DESIGN

Project Stages ⟶

CLIENT / DEVELOPER | DESIGN TEAM

load-bearing structures with short service lives

inadequate weather protection on building site

Max. Divergence

supplementary structures with short service lives

carbon-agnostic product subsitutions

Established Emissions Target

materials & surfaces that require frequent cleaning

Net Zero

(r) design for disassembly

(r) recyclable materials

(r) reflective roof surfaces

(r) energy-efficient building service machinery

(r) digital twin of the building developed for maintenance service provider

(r) full life cycle maintenance manual

(r) air-tightness

(r/d) EPDs compared, best products selected

(r) users / owners briefed on maintenance manual

(r) regular monitoring of structures and surfaces

(r) optimized building automation system

(r) building automation and services monitored and maintained actively

TECHNICAL DOCUMENTATION

BIDDING & NEGOTIATION

CONSTRUCTION ADMINISTRATION

HANDOVER & USE

Potential Divergence from Emissions Target

High Impact

Low Impact

Low Impact

High Impact

Source: AUTHORS

CONTRACTOR

OWNER / USER

CHAPTER FOUR
DE-CARBONIZING DESIGN

As a society, we continue to expect our buildings to be sound, functional, and affordable (and, less tangibly, to provide cultural meaning) but today we must also recognize the potentially existential challenge of climate change, face the significant role that the building sector plays in altering the Earth's physical, chemical, and biological systems, and seek to mitigate, wherever possible, the far-reaching temporally and geographically remote impacts that our decisions may cause. Perhaps the most immediate action we can take, and the one with the greatest potential benefit, is to take control of the complex flows of carbon into and through our buildings.

In earlier chapters of this book, we considered the ways in which carbon is captured in the geologic or biologic formation of raw materials, as well as the fuel that provides energy for building material manufacturing. We examined the ways in which greenhouse gases escape back into the atmosphere as energy is used in the process of compiling and assembling those materials into building components and systems, in continuing emissions generated throughout a building's service life, and finally during a building's demolition or deconstruction. And we observed ways in which both the expansion of constructed landscapes and the accumulation of waste can reduce the Earth's natural capacity to reabsorb and store atmospheric carbon.

We also discussed a number of analytical concepts and assessment tools used to track and quantify the impact of those flows of carbon through the production and operation of the built environment. We can choose to view the sprawling scope of the building life cycle and the array of industrial, economic, regulatory processes it entails as insurmountable challenges. Alternatively, we can understand them instead as an array of opportunities to mitigate the carbon-related impacts of the building sector and as multiple points of entry for our responsible management of the carbon that flows through the buildings we design. We would argue that this is the source of a building designer's agency: the ability to integrate and orchestrate the kinds of analytical principles, tools, and techniques—conducted with a necessarily strategic sense of their underlying systems—that set in motion the flow of materials, energy, and carbon. In introducing the assessment and mitigation of life cycle impacts to the building design process, we do not mean to minimize or preclude the many other concerns of building—many often qualitative—that are so critical to the durability, safety, accessibility, and livability of the built environment. The careful consideration of the flows of material, energy, solid waste, and greenhouse gas emissions should never reduce the safety, durability, accessibility, or economic feasibility of a given building. Rather, we seek to expand those objectives from the individual building to the environmental resources upstream and the landscapes and communities downstream of the building life cycle that may either suffer or benefit from the decisions we make.

A responsive, nimble, inclusive, and—most importantly—achievable design process aimed at the decarbonization of building is the subject of this chapter.

FIGURE 4.1
Source: LEI NUO / UNSPLASH

So Many Things to Consider . . .

Since our species began to construct shelter for its own protection and comfort, the criteria for decision-making in building have adapted and evolved. In our early history, these criteria addressed a range of exigencies: the availability of resources and their proximity to a designated building site; the structural characteristics of a given material and the relative ease with which it might be transported, handled, and worked; and the means by which materials and components can be assembled and aggregated in order to produce durable, useful dwellings. As human populations expanded in size and global reach and human culture gained sophistication, so did its social structures, political institutions, and forms of economic exchange. With that evolution, new building forms and organizations proliferated, along with the demand for a broader range of material and energy resources and more advanced and intensive manufacturing and construction technologies required to extract, process, and assemble those raw materials into safe and functional buildings.

Throughout our history, as architects, engineers, and builders have sought to answer the myriad aesthetic, cultural, technical, and economic expectations of a building design project, their work has been increasingly complicated by the evolution of political and cultural institutions in the increasingly heterogeneous social composition flowing from human migration and resettlement, and the sprawling economies of global consumption.

This represents a fundamental expansion of the building designer's scope of work and shifts the focus of the building design process. We must continue to consider the visible, formal, and tactile attributes of building. But now we must also grasp the invisible, ephemeral, and atmospheric implications of life cycle carbon emissions which are rooted in the provenance of building material and energy and the means of their consumption. With carbon flow as a new, critical criterion during a building's design and construction, we must seek to understand exactly where in that process the responsibility for shaping a building's carbon footprint—and the agency to dramatically reduce it—may lie.

As we've gleaned from our discussion of the building life cycle and its flows of material, energy, and waste, a low-carbon design approach must necessarily and radically expand the boundaries of conventional design consideration: in a carbon-conscious design process, we understand that a building is not a closed system in and of itself; nor can its envelope or even the limits of the project site be considered a reliable boundary of that system. Instead, design considerations expand to encompass all of the energy and material supplied and expended throughout the lifespan of the building. This holistic approach to design avoids the checklist thinking symptomatic of many sustainable certification programs, which often prioritize an adherence to prescribed carbon-reduction methods that may not be uniformly effective nor nimble enough to respond to each project's specific conditions.

This more comprehensive approach relies on adopting two key design strategies: (1) exposing assumptions about the carbon footprints of products, materials, and processes; and (2) iterative testing and assessment during the design process to refine building assemblies and systems in order to identify low-carbon options and their likely performance far into the future. Unlike operational energy modeling—which must make certain assumptions about the anticipated interface between building occupants and the building's energy and environmental systems—calculating a building's projected carbon footprint that arises from its *production stage* can be accomplished with a fairly high degree of accuracy provided that the designer establishes an appropriate analytical scope with effective and meaningful analytical boundaries.

The Building Design Process

Although we argue that those with real agency in decarbonizing the built environment extend beyond the professional boundaries of architectural and engineering practices to include environmental and industrial policy-makers, planners, real estate and building funders and developers, manufacturers, and building contractors and managers, we also recognize that the implementation of decarbonized design strategy falls most heavily on the shoulders of the building design team. The design of a building is an iterative and multi-scaled process of invention and creative problem-solving that transforms an organizational and spatial concept into a functioning, physical structure. Professional responsibility and legal obligation often govern the creative process, organizing and codifying a complex interplay of analysis, assessment, and decision-making into a codified procedure that is linear, sequential, and progressive in order to establish and refine the intent, scope, and extent of a building project.

Throughout this process, the design team, comprised of architects and engineers and often a host of other building consultants, works closely with a client and ultimately a builder to develop and produce an increasingly detailed set of documents—drawings and specifications—intended to communicate not only a design intent, but the physical means of achieving it. Everything from the building's exact position on a site to the color temperature of a lamp falls within the purview and responsibility of the building design team; all of it combines to determine the overall energy consumption and performance of a building and ultimately the carbon saved or emitted in the process.

The depth and breadth of that list of decisions required to execute even a simple building represent a daunting task. And any of those decisions may play some role—and possibly prove critical—in shaping the building's carbon footprint. Until the building is complete, the project team will work together to ensure the compliance of the construction process with the design intent and, when a primary objective is a low carbon building, to assess at each stage whether a decision might either increase or minimize its overall impact.

In an attempt to systematize this decision-making process, the building design and engineering professions, along with commercial manufacturing and construction associations and government agencies, have established an organizational framework and sequence that are strikingly similar in areas around the world. Typically, the design of a building proceeds through a requisite sequence of design phases that evolve in specificity and increase in scale.

As a general summary, this sequence begins with a conceptual design and evolves through increasing elaboration through a schematic phase, then a technical design development phase and culminates in a full set of drawings, specifications, and, increasingly in current practice, a digital Building Information Model (BIM). These are the legal documents through which we convey design intent for construction. At this stage, although the design may be complete, the responsibility of the architecture and engineering team continues to include the identification and selection of a builder, the negotiation of the building costs, and the establishment of a process of information exchange and decision-making that remains in place throughout the construction process until the building is completed.

This process, immaterial at its outset but culminating in an elaborate physical structure and complex operating system, should be understood as an instrument of environmental impacts and outcomes. This process sets in motion a new, but no less critical process that will continue for decades and is not necessarily complete with the end of a building's operational life. It is the specific instrumentality of the design tools and approaches within the industrial, regulatory, and economic context establishing the preconditions of a given building life cycle that will inevitably shape a carbon-conscious design process.

A CONTEXT OF EXTERNALITIES: PRECONDITIONS OF THE DECARBONIZED DESIGN PROCESS

As we've seen in earlier discussions of the building life cycle, many of the decisions and processes embedded in the design and construction of a given building fall outside the professional scope of the design process and therefore may elude the direct agency of the building designer. These preconditions form a set of externalities, embodied impacts, and likely outcomes that the design process can only assess, account for, and, ideally, seek to mitigate wherever possible.

It may be useful to visualize these externalities as occupying a succession of increasingly narrow orbits that surround a building project and the work of the building designer. These concentric rings contain both nested processes with measurable impacts and institutions or individuals with roles, responsibilities, and corresponding agency. These rings of agency and impact radiate inward to shape the building life cycle and, by extension, the design process.

In the broadest orbit, these externalities span across spatial and temporal scales, catalyzed initially in some distant past by the photosynthetic absorption of atmospheric carbon by trees and plants in some historically and geographically remote forest. The growth, death, and cyclical regrowth of that woody matter over the forest life cycle or the slow deposition of its residues in geological strata over millions of years may form the first precondition of our design process. How we choose to understand the land, marine, and soil biomes that store carbohydrates across global landscapes as well as the subterranean deposits of minerals and fossil hydrocarbons that lie beneath them creates a basic list of ingredients of a building. The extraction of material from that landscape and geo-strata will play a significant role in the kinds of fuel consumed and the amounts of carbon emitted during its life cycle.

Within a more recent timescale and slightly closer orbit of a given building life cycle, we may consider our current global and regional exchange of industrial commodities, raw material, and energy extracted from those aforementioned landscapes to create the materials and products we call upon in the technical construction processes we specify and the building solutions they yield. And we can begin to project into some relatively proximate future how the buildings we create might continue to draw upon those material resources during their operational lifespan, through their day-to-day function, their maintenance and potential refurbishment over the course of that useful life, and finally the process of disassembly and material dispersal when our buildings are deemed to no longer serve any valuable purpose.

The instruments of governance of those places, resources, and industrial processes; the specific land-use restrictions and economic policies that may exist to regulate the consumption of land or shape the exchange of commodities across national boundaries; the supply chains that determine the sites where material is industrially refined or the particular mix of industrial fuel consumed in the process; the movement of goods across oceans or mountain ranges; the infrastructures that determine the most expedient corridors and modes of transport. All these combine within another closer orbit with inevitable impact on our design process.

Closer in and still more tangible in our day-to-day activities as design professionals lies an orbit that contains a set of zoning and land use laws. These instruments of local governance establish where buildings are built, their bulk, height, density, and occupancy and they may even drive the development of infrastructures of local and regional transit, energy and potable water supply, and waste management. Alternatively, the policies may derive from or respond to infrastructure that already exists.

Building and life safety regulations have an impact on the form and technical elaboration of the materials and assemblies of a building, establishing minimal dimensions for barrier-free egress, specifying and often limiting a palette of materials rooted in existing commercial standards or building conventions, creating new standards for building system performance or even restricting the use of certain systems, no matter how environmentally beneficial they appear to be. These regulatory systems are codified over long periods of time, responding with appropriate deliberation to changing building sector norms and values.

The most immediate and familiar precondition of the building design process (and one in which the designer may have some more direct role in shaping) is controlled by the client. Whether a future occupant or speculative developer, the individual or entity that commissions a building project holds significant responsibility for determining its carbon footprint. The selection of a building site with its incumbent climatic, physical, regulatory, and infrastructural conditions; the determination of its use, occupancy, and lifespan, and by extension the possible behaviors of an institution, household, or individual who might reside there; and perhaps, most critical, the establishment of a set of overarching and sometimes competing values and objectives that might include immediate financial return, institutional identity, life cycle economy, energy efficiency . . . all will inevitably guide or at least inflect a building's conception and technical elaboration.

Decarbonization: Challenges and Opportunities

One of greatest challenges in the design of a low-carbon building life cycle is that, in practice, all buildings are different. Every building site, lodged within its particular climate zone, may have a unique micro-climate inflected by solar exposure or an array of physical features such as building context, topography, forest and plant cover, and soil conditions. Dense urban and remote rural sites alike may have significant challenges with equipment access, material handling during construction, refurbishment, and ultimately decommissioning. One construction project might be well served by maritime transport; another by rail or highway. In some cases, optimal material sources may lie within a relatively local radius to a building site but be separated by a mountain range, dramatically increasing fuel consumption in highway transport and making far more distant sources—ironically—more carbon-efficient. Regional or national energy suppliers may generate the energy buildings consume using more or less decarbonized sources. Land-use regulations and governance, planning and zoning laws, and open space conservation restrictions may differ from locality to locality. Regional building methods, even within countries with fairly uniform building regulatory requirements and ready access to an array of commercially standardized building materials and systems, may vary, due to architectural and building tradition, local cultural affinities for a given material or building form, or a well-established and therefore reliable material or product supply chain. Clients apply different value systems for the buildings they commission, and as such they also use different criteria to evaluate particular design solutions. Occupant or user behavior may distort the best predictions of a given building's performance, despite the designer's best

intentions. ("There are no net-zero houses; only net-zero families" is an insight that could be scaled up to describe societies and human settlement more generally.) All these varying factors call upon the designer to develop a nuanced approach to carbon management in the design process.

Points of Inflection and Influence in the Building Life Cycle

Given the extent and systemic complexity of the building life cycle, it can seem initially daunting to seek to influence its carbon flows. At each juncture in the multi-step sequence of a building's design and construction the team must recognize the specific agency of different project participants and seek to identify critical points of inflection where carbon impacts may be mitigated or even possibly eliminated altogether.

At one end of the spectrum—what we've referred to previously as "upstream" in the flow of building material and energy—low-carbon buildings rely on renewable or recycled materials and consume dramatically fewer finite resources, preserving land and habitats that might otherwise have been affected by extractive industrial activity or converted to less ecologically valuable uses. If low-carbon buildings are constructed in mid-rise, urban neighborhoods rather than in distant, suburban greenfield sites, development and infrastructure are more efficiently concentrated while landscapes are preserved as productive sites for sourcing biogenic material and sequestering carbon.

At the other end of the supply chain, low-carbon buildings produce a number of "downstream" benefits. By specifying materials and production methods with reduced carbon demands, designers are able to lower the building's embodied energy and greenhouse gas emissions. By improving the efficiency of mechanical and electrical systems and bolstering the insulative capacity of the building envelope, designers can lower a building's lifetime operational energy demands. By configuring construction assemblies for easy access and disassembly, and carefully considering the relative life cycles of materials and systems, designers can optimize the energy required for building repair and maintenance.

Finally, low-carbon design seeks not only to reduce the emission of carbon during the construction and operation of a building but also posits possible scenarios for the end of a building's life in order to extend the initial investment and amortize the impacts caused by the extraction and processing of material resources. Rather than consigning the large volumes of material contained in a given building to landfill, a forward-thinking, low-carbon building can serve as a future material source for ongoing cycles of manufacture and construction. By engaging circular economic strategies that seek to draw upon and ultimately return material to a closed circuit of reusable waste and by specifying renewable, bio-based materials that may promote the protection, restoration, and expansion of global biomes, a building designer can begin to radically reduce the global impact of her or his own activity. The corollary challenge is that in doing so, the designer also accepts greater responsibility in the design process. This in turn requires more work to engage that broader set of concerns, to employ a new set of evaluative design tools and criteria, and ultimately successfully manage all of it. It is the management of that expanded scope that we will here attempt to address.

THE DECARBONIZED DESIGN PROCESS

A Note of Caution: Benefits and Pitfalls of Checklist Thinking

Sustainable building rating systems (such as LEED and BREEAM) have played an undeniable role in increasing professional and public awareness, building consensus among project team members, providing indicators, setting targets and establishing benchmarks for building performance and, ultimately reducing building sector impacts [1]. Today, many sustainable certification schemes include LCA as a requirement. They can also be helpful in describing qualitative goals that may be difficult or impossible to quantify, such as a participatory design process, design attributes that address the context of a site's building context or landforms, and promote even more forward-

looking objectives such as design for disassembly. But these elective green-building scorecard and branding schemes may also present a significant challenge to building designers who seek specific and reliable quantitative information to aid their decision-making process at a sufficiently granular level or to utilize tools that are responsive and detailed enough to assist them in weighing up the relative impacts of alternative design options. And, as noted in earlier chapters of this book, the assumptions underlying the evaluative criteria used and the credits assigned can remain unclear. It is for this reason that a more nuanced and project-specific method of carbon accounting and impact assessment must be integrated into the earliest phases of the building design process. Ultimately, by incorporating and weighing up a number of strategies and systems of analysis during the design process, designers may avoid the checklist thinking that a simplistic understanding of certification standards suggests.

A Low-Carbon Concord

The decarbonized design process—one that seeks to reduce the consumption of material and energy and minimize the emission of carbon throughout the building life cycle—starts with a fundamental concord. For a building design team, then, this is formed in a consensus with a clear set of strategies shared by all parties involved in a building's conception and execution to minimize the greenhouse gas emissions and waste associated with its production, operation, and ultimately, the end of its life. This entails a set of specific requirements—established by authorities, funders, clients, or end-users—and achievable objectives, along with measurable benchmarks that allow for the assessment of progress through the course of the implementation of the building's design. It also calls for a legible set of guidelines and standards for future users who will maintain, repair, adapt, and finally dismantle it. Underlying that concord, and the objectives and means of measurement and compliance that spring from it, is a new set of shared criteria for decision-making and an expanded process of analysis and design sector that can effectively address our role in a contemporary and global environmental crisis.

Some Basic Rules of Engagement

We might visualize the low carbon building design process as a kind of triangle, of which its three points represent overarching and strategic means by the building development, design, and construction to reduce a building's life cycle emissions. If we can employ any of these basic strategies to mitigate potential impacts and do so as comprehensively as possible, we will progressively decarbonize our design process, and, by extension, the buildings we design. And if we can advance on two or three fronts at the same time, the climate benefits are multiplied.

Premise

The *premise* of a building project, different from a program or brief (which we'll discuss later in this section) is the fundamental reason for the building's existence. It's risky perhaps, to make value judgments about a project's efficacy, but we feel strongly that in a world threatened by excessive consumption and all the land, material, energy, and industrial activity that it entails, existential considerations about the necessity of initiating a building project are one of the more powerful means we have to limit carbon emissions. Beyond the black-and-white decision whether a project should or shouldn't take place, how we choose to manifest the project will influence the degree to which we can truly decarbonize our building, regardless of its architectural excellence, its functionality, or the degree to which it may be enjoyed by its users. The same residential program, for instance, can be developed as a multi-story apartment block in the inner ring of a city, a series of row houses, or as a suburban subdivision. Depending on the building typology we choose, we will consume different amounts of material and energy for the same usable floor area over the life cycle of the building. Similarly, if we refurbish an unused and abandoned factory building for office space instead of constructing a new office building, not only do we convey a message of resourcefulness but also we allow for remarkable reductions in overall environmental impact and possibly spare land for ecosystem services. To consider whether or not to build an expansive vacation home on an undisturbed site in the countryside may be open to philosophical debate, but the associated industrial processes and environmental loads— the material we consume, the energy demands we incur, and the land we disturb—will have an indisputably significant carbon footprint. These are challenging and profoundly philosophical, political, and cultural conversations, but they are ones that a society seeking systemic decarbonization should be having about the buildings we consider making.

Sufficiency

We'll be repeatedly addressing the implications of size and different means of its reduction in later sections of this chapter but size matters. As we'll see, this can be accomplished through careful assessment of programmatic need (do we really need a media room?) spatially (all volumes are not the same) and through the careful selection of material and its technical application, but all reductions in size will inevitably reduce the energy and materials we consume over the life cycle of a building. This is a question of sufficiency: how much, in environmental terms, can we *afford* to build? This is not necessarily a fashionable topic, and in some contexts the increase of floor area per occupant is indeed necessary, in order to achieve other important aspects of sustainable development. But as architects and building designers, we should primarily focus on increasing the *quality* of floor area or a building's volume, and be critical regarding the quantity.

Efficiency

Once we've determined that a building has a low-carbon premise and we have done everything we can imagine to minimize its necessary size without creating organizational or spatial dysfunction, we can begin the iterative process of capturing potential efficiencies. By optimizing spatial, material, and energy efficiency, we begin to activate the third component of decarbonized design agency by inducing fewer life cycle emissions to produce the same level of functional service and architectural quality. It is important to note that we should not rush into comparing different means of increasing the efficiency of the building before we have carefully considered the premise and its sufficiency to deliver our low-carbon goals. Systemic inefficiency, the focus of past sustainable design discourse, may only be the proverbial tip of an enormous iceberg of impacts that lurk below the surface of our work. If we fail to answer the fundamental questions of material and spatial sufficiency and assess the validity of a project's premise, then in the bigger picture of climate change, our continual refinement of building efficiency is effectively meaningless.

PHASES OF DECARBONIZED BUILDING DESIGN

As noted earlier in this chapter, contemporary professional building design around the world, despite varying terminology and means of categorization, is managed through a fairly consistent set of procedures that follow a similar flow of increasing conceptual reinforcement and technical elaboration. For the purposes of this discussion, and in order to ensure that the design process we describe is recognizable to a broad readership, we've divided that general process into phases easily recognized by their attendant scope of design activity. Although readers may not recognize the specific headings we use, we expect that they'll be familiar with the benchmarks in the flow of design as well as the specific opportunities for decarbonized decision-making that we intend to describe.

THE PRE-DESIGN OR PROJECT PREPARATION PHASE: LAYING THE GROUNDWORK FOR DECARBONIZED BUILDING DESIGN

From the earliest stages of a project's conception, before the first lines of a building's contours are drawn or its materials and systems are assigned, the client and the design team will make critical decisions with significant implications for a project's carbon footprint. Building designers often have specific expertise in matters of zoning and building regulation in specific jurisdictions, knowledge of regional energy infrastructures and their associated balance of renewable or fossil energy, or unique insights into the particularities of the local real estate market. They may feel comfortable in advising a client on a range of externalities that could possibly affect the emission of greenhouse gas over a building's lifetime. For the purposes of this chapter and the scope of this book, however, we ascribe the greatest source of a building designer's agency at the project's initial preparation phase to two of its fundamental preconditions: the way in which a building is to be used, and the piece of ground that it will occupy.

The earliest phase of a project's development offers the project team critical opportunities to chart a decarbonized course of decision-making that will affect the life cycle impacts of a building. Project preparation or pre-design entails a series of analyses and decisions by which a client or development team cements important parameters that may affect, to varying degrees, the options the design team has to reduce a building's carbon footprint. This is where the consideration of the *premise* and *sufficiency* of the design can be most influential. These parameters are fundamental to the design process but often take place without the consultation of the design team members or without the life cycle assessment tools they might bring to those decisions. They include the development of a program of use and occupancy, goals for spatial sufficiency and efficiency, the selection of a site, a review of regulatory constraints that may bear upon the design, the creation of a financial budget and the identification of funding streams and the determination of the expected lifespan of the building. The decisions made by a client or developer in this earliest project stage (often pre-dating the engagement of the design team) may deeply inflect all subsequent low-carbon design strategies, making them either more feasible or more difficult to achieve. Ideally, in the case of a decarbonized building design, the team would establish a "carbon budget" based on relevant building precedents and performance benchmarks which may give rise to a set of strategies and realistic targets for the life cycle reduction of the building's greenhouse gas emissions. Such objectives, established early enough in the conceptualization of a project, will inevitably provide valuable criteria for a number of critical decisions with regard to a building's life cycle impacts before we draw the first line in the design process.

Context Is Everything: the Carbon Implications of Jurisdiction, Region, and Climate

Although selecting the city or region in which to build is not usually an option in most projects for a host of reasons, an awareness of the municipal and regional context will definitely affect the strategies available to the building designer to mitigate impacts. The stresses on buildings that local weather patterns and the broader climate context may create, the restrictions that a municipal or regional regulatory framework might impose, and the flow of energy and material that regional supply systems, regional energy policy and infrastructure, or waste management system may either restrict or enhance, will inevitably shape the scenarios we set for our assessments and most often determine the design tools and building technologies we use to optimize building life cycle performance.

Climate Forces and Energy Systems

The host of passive environmental strategies that may serve to reduce energy consumption are by now familiar to most building designers, but their effectiveness is highly dependent on the climate in which they are implemented. Exterior shading systems, such as roof overhangs or louvers are particularly effective in more arid regions with relatively low humidity and sustained periods of sunlight, whereas the promotion of air movement through stack ventilation may be worth considering in hot humid climates. A cold climate may demand a compact building volume with a low exterior surface area to floor area ratio, where less material is required to produce a thermally insulated and airtight envelope, while a hot climate may seek to dissipate heat through larger surface areas of the building envelope. Anticipating the use of solar photovoltaic arrays for on-site energy generation in a region with relatively few sunny days may so reduce the system's effectiveness that it makes it uneconomical in terms of life cycle costs and makes it difficult to offset the embodied production stage emissions from a life cycle impact perspective.

When we consider more active energy systems for buildings, we inevitably face the externalities of regional energy supply, and the mix of fuels or renewable sources used to generate that energy. A regional energy grid fed by solar, hydroelectric, or wind power, may be so decarbonized that it offsets other building strategies whose material and energy inputs in the production stage result in significant embodied emissions. On the back end of the building life cycle, a region or even a municipality with increasingly refined and systematized waste management policies and practices may dramatically expand end-of-waste opportunities at the end of a material or a building's service life. In such a case, the technical design and material specification of a building for disassembly and reuse, will contribute to the overall reduction of the building's carbon footprint.

Regional Supply Chains

The availability of certain materials may also limit our options in shaping a low-carbon building strategy. A richly forested region with a robust supply chain and sophisticated manufacturing capabilities will make the utilization of mass timber structural products an effective means to store carbon and offset life cycle impacts. Likewise, in areas where value chains and enabling regulations for reusing and recycling building materials exist, the potential for a circular economy can bring significant carbon reductions. But the regional context may work the other way, too. For instance, the remote impacts created by poor, unregulated, and extractive logging practices will inevitably make the specification of regionally harvested wood products a calculated risk to the environment. Likewise, in a region with limited renewable or recycled resources, transcontinental or transoceanic transport may far offset the environmental benefits captured in bio-based material carbon storage or the circular economy.

Regulatory Frameworks

Although it's not often the case, local planning and zoning statutes, energy codes, regional or national building and life safety regulations, or explicit stipulations of certain architectural forms, details, and material expression may all influence the dominance of different life cycle stages by setting either restrictions or incentives. This may be due to restrictions on building height or lot coverage or required setbacks, limits on (or requirements for) the use of certain kinds of materials or their degree of exposure within different construction types or use groups. The effect may be to limit scenarios for alternative materials for either exterior finishes or primary structure, various building forms that might better optimize performance, or positions on a site that might take better advantage of available ecosystem services.

Even zoning restrictions that require excessive front yard zoning setbacks or vehicular parking requirements may require more area of paving for street or road access or create the need for parking garages, all with a range of potential impacts associated with material consumption and the conversion of biomass into constructed impervious surface areas. These issues may seem of secondary concern to a development team focused on immediate returns on investment, the logistical feasibility of construction, or the long-term utility of the proposed building. But as we consider all the ramifications of a possible site, the way in which it drives the consumption of land area, biomass, material, and energy may determine its carbon as well as its physical footprint.

In addition to the constraints they may impose, there are also opportunities to be exploited in the regulatory frameworks that govern building, so it's important that the designers avail themselves of the potential benefits that they may gain from environmentally targeted policies and programs. Certain forward-thinking municipalities or jurisdictions may offer different forms of regulation or other incentives for low-carbon building practices. Examples include caps on the life cycle emissions of buildings, tax rebates for renewable energy generation or increased bulk or floor area allowances for buildings that implement high performance exterior assemblies, renewable materials, and on-site energy generation. "Pay-as-you-throw" waste metering policies may incentivize a developer or building manager to adopt carbon-positive strategies that reduce the flows of waste from the production through the end-of life stages of a building. In the future, as the cost of emitting carbon rises, buildings that can demonstrate the capacity

to store biogenic carbon may be able to sell carbon offsets in regional cap and trade markets.

It's broadly understood in the building sector that externalities, such as climatic forces, product and energy markets, and regulatory frameworks, may all have an impact on building budgets. That they might also play a role in shaping a building's carbon footprint is less understood and more difficult to quantify. But as preconditions to nearly every building project, our acknowledgment of their capacity to drive a host of potential impacts may prove a powerful tool in advocating for and ultimately implementing low-carbon design strategies.

SELECTING A LOW-CARBON SITE

If we zoom in from our regional map to the scale of something closer to a district or block plan, the increased resolution exposes new scales of information and another set of existing conditions that may factor heavily into our decarbonized design process.

Land Use

In the best case we would not need to convert natural areas into human developments. We could, instead, utilize and densify existing built-up areas by refurbishing existing buildings or by increasing the height of existing structures. If we can manage this, then the precious carbon dynamics of natural ecosystems would not be risked, and we would also allow animals and plants more room for coping with the changing climate. So, if any possibilities can be found for not converting natural land into built-up area, those strategies should be explored first before considering converting natural landscapes. Old industrial areas, unused railroad deposits, or any other built areas that have ceased to operate effectively should be the primary direction of new construction. This is often easier said than done. Still, within cities there are plenty of opportunities for building next to or on top of the existing buildings, increasing the capacity of developed parcels to support additional development. While densifying the urban fabric, however, we should avoid pushing the valuable urban ecosystem services—provided to us free of charge—to the margins of the built environment.

Soil Type

One of the most influential factors defining the embodied emissions of a building lies underground, invisible. A soft or wet soil—typically clay in former fields or coastal areas—usually requires both cement stabilization and piling. Both of these groundworks are very material-intensive, and (still mostly) rely on the use of Portland cement. If a building is built on a site that requires both of these, it means the amount of embodied emissions that go below the ground can be as much as for the rest of the building above the ground [2]. From a carbon perspective, building on soft ground may mean doubling the embodied emissions of a building. Therefore, such sites should be avoided, whenever possible. This is often easier said than done, as in growing urban areas the best sites are already occupied. If one needs to build on a soft soil, substitutes for cement in stabilization should be a minimum requirement.

Orientation: Sun and Shading

An attribute of a potential site with which practitioners of sustainable building design are probably most familiar is its orientation. A site's solar exposure, depending on the climate characteristics of a particular location, may have significant ramifications for use-stage energy consumption and associated emissions. In a colder climate, in which significantly more energy is spent heating the building over the course of the year than cooling it, a site sunlit throughout the day may present strategies to exploit the amount of solar radiation that reaches its different surfaces or *insolation*, to aid in the passive warming of interior spaces. Alternatively, in a climate zone in which a large number of annual cooling days drives energy consumption and associated emissions, a building may benefit from the shade provided by adjacent buildings or from mature trees standing on site. From the standpoint of renewable energy, however, those same shading structures may obviate our effective implementation of onsite photovoltaic or solar thermal energy generation.

We can map the insolation of a site—with and without a facsimile of our proposed building—to determine throughout the day and over the course of the year which portions of it will see the most solar heat gain. This will provide clues as to how to best locate and orient the building generally, where to create outdoor spaces for winter warmth and summer shading and thereby encourage their seasonal use by occupants, and to how manage the design of ground and building surfaces that will see the greatest solar exposure and heat gain. Each has implications for the technical requirements of the building's envelope and mechanical systems and for the comfort and utility of its spaces. Both might potentially drive impact in either the consumption of material in the production stage or occupant behavior in the use stage of the building life cycle.

Prevailing Winds and Ventilation

Exposure to prevailing wind has similar implications for building energy efficiency and its use-stage greenhouse gas emissions. If a site is unsheltered by surrounding buildings or large trees, a wind rose will tell us a great deal about the strength and direction of seasonal prevailing winds and hint at passive cooling and ventilation techniques that we might utilize to increase the comfort of interior spaces and reduce the likelihood that a user will, by reflex, turn on or turn up the building's air-conditioning system.

Access and Accessibility

The access to a site—its relative distance to different modes of freight and human transportation and the more immediate ways onto the site for both construction equipment and future occupants—will carry with it environmental implications and, more specifically, emissions impacts that fall both within and outside the typical system boundaries of life cycle assessment. Access to the site for construction and ongoing maintenance and repair will affect the construction, use, and end-of-life stages of the building life cycle, each requiring different types of vehicles and equipment for material delivery and handling. These factors are quantifiable within the methodological frameworks of life cycle assessment. More challenging to quantify are the impacts implied by the site's proximity to mass transit hubs, its safe accessibility by foot or by bicycle, and the building's potential to inflect future transit patterns. Despite these unknowns, we would see varying use-stage impacts were we to calculate different scenarios for the daily commute of each of the occupants over the lifespan of the building.

Ecosystem Services

With a slightly closer magnification which includes only the boundaries of our site and the surfaces or physical structures immediately adjacent to it, we start to recognize a site of existing conditions that we will alter, either favorably or deleteriously, depending on those conditions. On a so-called greenfield site, on which there has been no former disturbance by either past building or prior land conversion, we will observe some amount of biomass in both the form of plants and in the site's soils. If these are mature plants in the late stages of generational succession, as in a forest, for example, the process of construction of a building and its associated site structures will create indisputable disturbance by reducing the carbon storage capacity of both above-ground plant biomass and the organic matter held in the soil, by altering its biodiversity and hydrologic function. These existing conditions imply a range of ecosystem services: storm water absorption and filtration, photosynthetic oxygen formation and CO_2 uptake, the role of insect pollinators and animal seed-bearers in promoting generations of plant growth. Once lost, all these ecological benefits, but specifically the natural banks of carbon, are replaced only through extensive planting, species reintroduction, and site and soil remediation efforts, each with their own attendant financial costs and emissions' impacts. This is an important consideration in site selection: building on a greenfield site will place a significant carbon debit on the balance sheet at the outset of a project.

Topography

Another important criterion for selecting a site for a new building is its topographical character. It's a good rule of thumb to avoid steeply sloping sites wherever possible for the simple reason that building on them will entail significantly more energy and material consumption. In many jurisdictions, construction on steep sites, usually defined by a maximum allowable gradient, is heavily regulated and for good reasons. Excavation and soil stabilization requirements demand more equipment and energy and create a larger footprint of physical disturbance in order to balance cuts and fills; foundations require more structural material to resist sliding on unstable soil or surcharges from uphill retainage. In altering the natural hydrology of the site, we incur the impact of replacing it with engineered storm water infrastructure that collects and redirects sheet flow. By stripping adjacent surface soils of even a thin plant and root layer, we reduce the natural surface's resistance to scouring and erosion. The construction of site structures that will make a building on a sloping site accessible and occupiable—exterior steps, ramps, and retaining walls with guards and handrails, for example—imply the further investment in and consumption of material and energy with all their systemic life cycle impacts. Of course, it's sometimes unavoidable to build on slopes. It's important to recognize, as with construction on greenfield sites with relatively healthy ecosystems in place, we face an uphill climb with respect to reducing our carbon footprint. And although the same pun doesn't apply, the same can be said for the implications of building near or in close proximity to wetland or flood-prone landscapes.

Building Context

When we select a brownfield site (one that's already been disturbed through past conversion from a formerly "natural" state by any number of human activities— for agricultural, industrial, or infrastructural uses, for the dumping of waste, or for the construction of prior buildings), our strategy shifts from one of minimizing impact to natural systems to one of potentially restoring them, or at least remediating any conditions that are toxic or otherwise hazardous to both people and/or the environment. If we choose to build on a site from which significant amounts of biomass have already been removed or destroyed, landforms have been altered, soils have been degraded by intensive agricultural activity or heavy traffic or rendered impervious by paving, or perhaps occupied by an existing building structure, the low-carbon design approach would be to ameliorate deleterious environmental conditions, build productive organic soil, restore biological health where possible, and reuse existing construction materials or building structures where possible and feasible. And promisingly—also perhaps surprisingly—the capacity of urban soils to sequester carbon may exceed that of natural soils [3]. In doing so, we tap into previous building and land-use life cycles, engaging the circular economy through our willingness to appropriate sites and structures consigned to the status of waste and endowing those materials and landscapes with newfound value as reusable and remediable resources that serve, rather than burden, the health of the global environment.

PROGRAMMING A LOW-CARBON BUILDING

It goes without saying that the need for a building—its program of use and the identification of the users it will serve—is an existential prerequisite to its design. Put another way, without the demand for a building, there would be no need for us to design it. In this earliest phase of the building's conception, however, the rigorous review and careful refinement of the program of spaces, systems, and occupancies, and the daily and yearly cycles of occupancy may prove to be one of the most powerful tools we can employ to reduce its life cycle impacts. The consideration of *sufficiency* in this programming endows a client or development team with enormous agency in controlling the flow of carbon through the buildings they commission.

At the outset of any building design process, a designer receives from a client (or, on occasion, develops for the client) a programmatic prescription for the building. This may take the form, at the very least, of a list that identifies required spaces and their associated uses or functions. It also may describe critical adjacencies between particular spaces that will increase overall functionality. Sometimes specific dimensions are assigned, and, on occasion, a client may go so far as to define performance characteristics of each space, such as allowable ranges of interior temperature variation,

required light levels or degrees of acoustical separation. No matter how general or specific that initial prescription, it is the designer's task to organize and refine the program using any number of criteria which may range from the utilitarian to the typological or the cultural. For the low-carbon building, the designer and client must scrutinize the daily schedule or seasonal calendar of building use, to identify programmatic opportunities that reduce spatial redundancy, optimize overlaps in use, and allow spaces and systems to do multiple duties and serve multiple purposes. In this way, *they may avoid the misapplication and over-specification of critical resources where no real need may exist.*

Perhaps one of the most familiar examples of misused resources is the car parking lot of a shopping mall designed with the maximum capacity to serve the parking requirements of a holiday rush of shoppers. For nearly the entire year, that land area, and the huge investment in paving material and lighting infrastructure, lie unused. The sight of empty acres of asphalt may be one of the more disheartening results of a society accustomed to the luxuries of not only consumer products but the luxuries of cheap material and energy extracted from virgin sources. But if we consider how we use space ourselves, as institutions or as individuals in our homes, we may recognize the tendency to over-program, to consume space in redundant ways, or to fail to timeshare spaces when a regularly repeating schedule of use might allow it. To carry the metaphor a bit further, how might we schedule the use of that parking lot for programs other than storing automobiles when demand is low? In the same regard, how might we create more flexibility in our patterns of use, seek greater efficiencies in our associated consumption of space, and reduce the life cycle emissions incurred in the material formation of those spaces? If we can show in the initial programming process that we need build and operate only 90% of the building we initially envisioned—or that we can schedule and accommodate more uses than we had originally planned for, we will simultaneously increase the social or economic value of the project while reducing the impacts of its production, operation, and ultimately its disassembly and removal.

ANTICIPATING THE LIFESPAN OF A BUILDING

The aspect of time in low-carbon building extends to periods far greater than daily, weekly, or even annual use cycles. One of the most significant ways for the building client or developer to control impacts is to identify clearly at the outset of a project how long they intend the building to last. The life expectancy of a building's use can help the design team calibrate their specification of material and the detailing of connections to that building life cycle. It's important to state here that the objective of a long service life for all buildings is fundamental to decarbonized design and to the reduction of material consumption and waste associated with the conventional economics of building devaluation and disposability. Decarbonized project planning seeks to extend the life of a building for as long as possible in order to amortize not only the initial costs of material and land, but also the emissions incurred in the first stages of the building life cycle. We'll discuss concepts of durability and reversibility later in this chapter but it's important that we focus here on conceptual distinctions between the *design*, *technical*, *functional*, and *economic* service lives of our building in order to better strategize the organization of its spaces and assemblies and the application of material within them.

A *design life* is a temporal goal for a building, usually established by its user or owner, and plays a crucial role in determining its overall climate impacts. The ideal, of course, is that the actual service life of a building would exceed its proposed design life, thereby further safeguarding and extending the value of the resources poured into the building whatever the "currency" by which we measure those expenditures— money, time, material, energy, or carbon emissions. No designer can actually guarantee that a well-designed building might live beyond its design life, because the way in which the building is used and maintained will have significant ramifications for its lifespan. But by applying service life planning, the likeliness of this grows considerably, which will inevitably pay off by decreasing the need for premature component repair or replacement.

At this point it probably goes without saying that a material or component's durability will avoid future emissions from the production and transport of new materials as well as from waste management of the obsolete and discarded ones. Although there are many materials that will last for centuries in some form or another, it's rarely possible or even practical to assign materials throughout a building's assemblies and systems with technical service lives of hundreds of years. If we're to automatically assume that a building must "last forever"—no matter how desirable product durability may be within a circular economic framework—the design team may fall into the trap of over-specifying materials, producing irreversible connection details, and failing to sync up the differing life cycles of materials within the building assembly.

It's also important to recognize that a (theoretically) long *technical* service life doesn't often guarantee an equally long *functional* or *economic* service life. In offices, restaurants, shops, or hotels, for example, many changes take place due to the need to adjust or refresh the surfaces, fixtures, and fittings of a space—whether because a new tenant needs to renovate or adapt a space to meet a particular need, function, or aesthetic goal or simply because a particular tile pattern is out of fashion. For these reasons, it may be rational to allow some layers of the building to have shorter (technical) service life than, for example, the load-bearing frame or the foundations. As Stewart Brand so elegantly observed in his now famous "shearing diagram" of the building life cycle, each material layer that comprises the assemblies and systems of a building has different performance requirements and replacement cycles. Usually, the costliest part of the building and the least accessible for repair and replacement is the primary structure, so these components need to be extremely durable, protected by secondary and tertiary layers of the assembly—substrates, membranes, finishes, and cladding—and with a single life cycle that should be synchronized with the design life of the building. More exposed and easily accessed layers and systems (such as fittings and finishes) within the building have shorter life cycles. Exterior and interior surfaces, partition walls, suspended ceilings, and most building service systems have a life expectancy of a few decades at best, due to exposure, wear and tear, as well as to the number and complexity of component parts and connections. Since we can be fairly confident that these building products and parts won't last as long as a building's primary structure, a forward-thinking, low-carbon design strategy would carefully consider and plan for the *second* service lives of their materials and components. Coordinating and calibrating those life cycles within the building assembly may reduce unnecessary material consumption through dyssynchronous cycles of repair and replacement and all the emissions embodied in those processes.[1]

THE CONCEPTUAL OR SCHEMATIC DESIGN PHASE

The conceptual or schematic design phase is the point in the process at which decarbonized design agency shifts from national, regional, and municipal governments and policy-makers or real estate developers and building clients to the building design team. In this phase, we initiate the design process proper, positioning the building in the site, sizing and organizing the spaces of both site and building, and testing the complex interrelationships and adjacencies of their respective uses and functions. Although this early phase of design lacks the technical specificity of later phases and we may adjust or rework our initial suppositions through successive iteration as more information is brought to bear on the process, the concept phase often proves to be a critical point of inflection in the decarbonized design process, the point at which the bulk of decisions made will play an outsize role in determining our building's carbon footprint [1]. This is the phase of design in which we establish not only the building's basic position, orientation, and organization but also its formal and spatial character and the system (if not detail) of its structure, enclosure, fenestration, and services as well as its material palette. Unless we dramatically alter the design in a later phase, even a schematic quantity survey and assessment of the materials posited in this phase would give us a good sense of the embodied impacts our building is likely to incur.

Right-Sizing the Building

Let's consider size. How much space—in terms of either floor area or building volume—do we really need to meet the functional needs called for in a client's design brief? Is there a way to make smart design choices, that can offer same (or better) level of experience and satisfaction, but use less space? Although we have already addressed the topics of sufficiency and efficiency and the temporal overlap of different uses in our earlier discussion of the client's preparation of the design brief, it is during the schematic design phase that more nuanced opportunities will be uncovered through the analysis of the way in which occupants use a building's spaces, and the iterative testing of spatial alternatives. The reflexive and lazy response of adding more space (and thereby additional building, material, and energy) to meet increased functional demand is one we should avoid, especially in a low-carbon design process in which we seek to extract as much benefit—measured in a building's architectural quality and the satisfaction of its occupants—from as few resources (energy, material, land) as possible. It is the designer's responsibility to show where a client may not only settle for but *thrive with* less.

[1]Factors that influence the service life include the qualities of the component, design and construction work, environmental factors inside and outside of the building, use patterns, and maintenance. Service life planning as a process is standardized (ISO 15686 suite). Methods for estimating the duration of a product's service life include experimental methods, testing, and calculations. For some structural parts of a building—such as certain concrete, steel and timber structures—it is possible to estimate a service life mathematically. Similar methods, however, are not available for many components or materials, which leads to the use of statistical data on reference service lives of components in comparable use conditions. As service life planning requires skills and experience, it can be one of the factors included in a multi-objective building optimization process.

Low-Carbon Siting

As discussed earlier, the selection of a site will establish a number of preconditions for the organization of a building's spaces and the utilization of its existing municipal utilities and ecosystem services. Once we've identified the site, however, and are working within its boundaries, we may be saddled with constraints that limit design options, but we also have infinitely more agency and wider range of tools with which to determine its life cycle impacts.

If we're designing a new building, the initial and perhaps most basic constraint we'll face at the outset of the design process is the area available for positioning the building within the site. A site constrained in a particular dimension by the size or shape of its lot or otherwise subject to regulatory or logistical or environmental restrictions may severely curtail the options for its size and bulk. But this is where careful design study within the parameters of those site conditions and the requirements of the building program is most effective. To those programmatic objectives which determine the size and adjacencies of the building's spaces, we should add site-design criteria that may affect the building's carbon footprint. The amount of ecological disturbance we generate through the transformation and occupation of the site might be measured by the amount of soil we have to displace or the array of plants we need to remove to specifically position a building. The amount of material we are forced to consume during the production stage of the life cycle may be driven by steep slopes or soils with poor bearing capacity and the extensiveness or intensiveness of building foundations and the associated filling and grading that are required to stabilize our building. With proper analysis, we may gain the benefit of existing site ecosystem services and the pleasant micro-climatic experiences they might provide, such as shading or windbreaks from existing trees or, at a more technical level, the natural hydrological function of the site's topography and soil types, and their capacity to absorb and filter storm water without the need for extensive hard-piping and civil infrastructure and their extensive energy or material inputs. Alternatively, the orientation of our building may force us to remove soil or existing vegetation and lose their stored carbon, as well as their capacity to photosynthesize and capture more carbon over

their lifetime. Or the building's orientation may expose it to harsh climatic conditions, such as high winds, driven rain, or heat gain from solar radiation, all of which may inevitably create life cycle demands for operational energy or shorten the service life of the materials and components we specify. Of course, we may exploit those same forces to passive thermal or ventilation advantage, but we will always be accounting for and ideally balancing those potential impacts or benefits by the specific positioning and orientation of our building.

Shape Matters

The way in which we choose to develop the form and volume of a new building can have significant implications for its life cycle impacts. Even without today's sophisticated digital modeling software, we can translate a project brief's prescription for a given floor area into an array of volumetric geometries. As we've just noted, site dimensions and zoning restrictions may heavily influence a building's footprint, bulk, and height. Despite those typical preconditions, we still have a good deal of leeway in our elaboration of our building's geometry, to optimize its performance and reduce its greenhouse gas emissions in the production and use life cycle stages.

Volumetric Efficiency

There are two significant means in the earliest phases of design to reduce material and energy consumption. The first is to minimize the ratio of the usable floor area to the surface area of the building envelope. An efficient building volume with a more concentrated footprint will reduce the extent of foundations. A smaller area of exterior enclosure will require less material, expose less area to thermal stresses and potential heat loss or gain and reduce material on surfaces prone to weathering, which will in turn reduce the number of replacement cycles for cladding and roofing material. There are, of course, challenges with minimizing surface area to floor area ratios that may create collateral impacts. If an efficient, condensed building volume creates deep multi-story floor plates, it may also create spaces that have limited access to daylight and natural ventilation which may require a compensating increase in electrical and mechanical system loads and these may offset the benefits of the material and thermal efficiency of the building. And there may be solutions in which added volume and increased surface area to floor area ratios can easily be justified in terms of spatial comfort and pleasure, but also by improving natural daylight or promoting passive ventilation. We can assess and compare these trade-offs with quick calculations using the *streamlined LCA* techniques described in Chapter 2.

Volumetric Simplicity

In addition to increasing the volumetric efficiency of a building, we can also simplify its volume. It goes without saying that there are many important criteria for elaborating building form and shape, not the least of which are the cultural and typological associations that are such a critical part of the architectural discipline. But we also know that with each change in the surface plane and make-up of a building assembly, we create additional joints in the building envelope and potentially incur attendant impacts. These added points of connection may entail additional material and structural detailing (flashings, transfer beams, or connectors) with implications for production stage emissions. Transitions may create more vulnerabilities to weather which may increase cycles of repair and replacement and their embodied emissions or increase the risk of thermal, vapor, air, or water leakage which inevitably affect energy performance and increase demand in the use stage. Excessive shifts in building shape and form may produce anomalous material shapes and fastening requirements that may reduce the reusability of the material at the end of the building's life. The more complex the building volume, the more likely it is to produce impact in at least one of the stages of the building life cycle. The balance of those potential life cycle benefits and impacts is fundamental to the assessments described in Chapter 2. Those assessments, in turn, must be weighed against whatever architectural values—spatial experience, heritage, spectacle—we consider critical to a given design.

Optimizing Daylight

One of the most effective means to mitigate carbon flows through energy consumption (and to create convivial and comfortable working and living conditions) is to use natural daylight as a substitute for electrical illumination. It would be wrong to assume that naturally lit buildings rely on large expanses of glass with all their attendant sources of impact such as high production stage emissions and

thermal inefficiency, and potential for solar heat gain. Effective daylighting instead relies not on the *area* of glazed apertures but their relative placement to each other and to adjacent reflective surfaces, such as walls, ceilings, and floors. Well-balanced daylighting strategies reduce glare and associated fatigue for building occupants while minimizing the material and energy impacts incurred in both the manufacture of window glass, frames, seals, and flashings, and in the energy demands for operational, lighting, heating, and cooling. We can employ the organization, enclosure, and fenestration of a building in the earliest stages of the design process to improve its spatial and experiential quality and reduce its carbon footprint.

Operational Energy Consumption (and Generation)

As discussed in the previous section on the project preparation phase, the degree of decarbonization of the energy networks that supply our building may fall outside of our purview and control as building designers. If our energy supply is dependent on the combustion of fossil hydrocarbons—coal or gas—then we should seek efficiencies in the areas of building design that affect operational energy consumption. If we are fortunate that our energy infrastructure is already largely decarbonized or in transition to non-fossil sources, then we can shift our focus to mitigating production stage and end-of-life impacts by reducing initial material demands, specifying durable materials, and designing building assemblies for feasible disassembly and material reuse.

We've touched throughout this book on different approaches to reducing emissions associated with operational energy consumption, but it's worth restating here the opportunities during the schematic design phase to stem the flow of carbon through our building by the decisions we make. At a basic level, energy consumption will depend heavily on the size and shape of the building as well as the solar orientation of its façades. The size, orientation, and shading of glazed apertures to minimize thermal loss and insolation and to optimize daylighting offer us additional opportunities to reduce operational energy use in this early design phase. A next level of consideration and assessment is the design and specification of a well-insulated building envelope to reduce heating and cooling loads in concert with other passive heating and natural ventilation strategies. Schematizing at this early stage an efficient, well-integrated, and accessible service infrastructure that accommodates electrical wiring, ducting, piping, etc. will ease repair, replacement, and renovation, but will also lead to a better balanced and functioning overall system with potentially significant operational energy benefits. Finally, where possible, we should seek opportunities to generate or store the energy to meet at least some of our demands on site: solar photovoltaic arrays optimally oriented; solar thermal manifolds and an insulated storage system that will supplement and, if efficiently deployed, potentially replace electrical hot water heating; ground- or water-source heat pumps that exploit the subsoils, geo-strata or even bodies of water for thermal mass— coupled with solar PVs to provide pump energy, such systems can entirely replace oil and gas boilers to meet the heating and cooling demands of our building; in rare cases, we may employ localized wind turbines although their performance is highly dependent on building location and micro-climatic wind patterns. We can also look for possibilities for exploiting soil and rock for seasonal thermal storages under the building. Through relatively simple technologies, we can utilize the layers of clay or bedrock for pumping extra heat (harvested from the building's or the parking lot's surfaces or from ventilation) into the ground during summer and extracting it back into the building in winter.

As noted in Chapter 2, we should assess any of these use-stage energy and emissions reduction strategies with an understanding of the potential production of end-of-life stage they may entail.

Tectonics and Materiality

During the conceptual or schematic design phase, we assign a tectonic character and materiality to our building. Although we'll discuss in the technical design phases of this chapter the different classes of building material in their various applications within the building system and their global warming potential, it's important to begin to strategize on how our conception of building form and materiality might entail significant material and energy inputs in the production and use stages of the building life cycle. If we seek an aesthetic and experiential transparency or translucency, we may

drive the production of significant areas of glass plastic sheet, metal substructure, and chemically synthesized sealants. A massive masonry building may require significantly larger foundations which will expand our building's carbon footprint. Alternatively, a timber building may carry with it a large carbon storage capacity, but if source forests are poorly managed, the off-site impacts of forest loss or degradation that are encouraged by our use of wood products from over-harvested or otherwise exploited forest land, may offset and outweigh the benefits of wood's carbon storage capacity [4].

A highly articulated building surface, regardless of material selection, may create vulnerabilities with respect to weathering and wear, placing more requirements on use-stage repair replacement, all with implications for life cycle carbon emissions. It would be a mistake to suggest that a low-carbon building is agnostic to material choice. However, it is inevitable that for a host of reasons we may need to choose materials that carry with them large embodied emissions. Our strategy, then, should be to use those materials as efficiently and sparingly as possible and to seek points of inflection within the building life cycle where we may take advantage of those material properties. Might those sheets of glass be repurposed for future building, or those large extents of reinforced concrete foundations be crushed and used for the base of roadbeds, or as aggregate for future, low-carbon, concrete applications? One of the most fundamental premises of a life cycle approach to design is that we use the span of time and processes we apply to building to seek to balance impact where avoiding it altogether is impossible.

Inspiring and Promoting Good Behavior

It would be a significant oversight if we were to fail to mention one of the most important criteria for the decarbonization of building during the schematic design phase: its ability to make legible the carbon-conscious features of its design so as to facilitate a change in our behavior as building users and occupants. This is obviously extremely difficult to quantify in advance of the building's operation and occupancy, but we should apply our own experience to our judgment of how best to promote better habits among the building inhabitation. Such a list of goals might include the encouragement of those behaviors that reduce energy consumption through targeted planning, improved spatial quality, and, as we'll discuss in the next section, savvy technical detailing; stairs and ramps situated as the vertical circulation of first choice instead of elevators and escalators; pleasant, weather-protected and plant-filled outdoor gathering and resting spaces that are readily accessible to interior rooms so as to encourage relaxation and recreation in fresh air; where exterior space is constrained, safe, easily understood and easily operated natural ventilation systems with sufficiently appreciable effect that they encourage occupants to control the temperature of their rooms and spaces rather than demanding more heating or air conditioning or mechanical ventilation; well-balanced and sufficient daylight to recondition our reflex to turn on light switches; and—initiated beyond the boundaries of the building site but extending into it—pedestrian routes and capacious bicycle access and storage that reduce people's need or desire to drive. Although these examples have developed over decades as part of a checklist of sustainable design practices that have yielded reductions in greenhouse gas emissions from energy consumption, some may entail systemic change to environmental policy, urban governance, and building practice. Nevertheless, all are catalysts for the decarbonization of human behavior, and each is a tool that lies within easy reach in the earliest phases of the decarbonized design process.

THE DESIGN DEVELOPMENT PHASE

The design development phase marks an upward shift in the scales at which we study the design of the building and an increase in the specificity and precision that we ascribe to its materiality, the methods of its assembly, and the coordinated and complementary function of its thermal envelope and the mechanical, electrical, and plumbing systems. At this next stage of advancement in our design process, we carefully record our design decisions, orchestrate their structural and functional interdependency, and nest them within the design's evolving documentation. Accordingly, for the decarbonized design process, we also weigh up the physical, spatial, and technical solutions of our design for the production stage impacts they imply, the energy and water consumption they will likely incur over the building's service life, and the degree to which they promote the reuse, or recycling

of material and reduce the generation of waste at its life's end. The design development phase is one in which we consolidate and refine and, hopefully, capitalize upon the groundwork for decarbonization that we've laid in earlier design phases.

A carbon-conscious design process focuses on three primary means of reducing or eliminating the carbon that flows through the typical building life cycle: (1) the selection of materials with low production stage emissions or with significant capacity to store photosynthesized carbon or to sequester mineralized carbon; (2) engineering the building envelope and its environmental control systems so as to reduce energy consumption and associated emissions throughout the building's service life; and (3) the optimization of the building's physical assemblies so as to promote ease of assembly and disassembly both during and at the end of its long life of use and increase the likelihood that the constituent materials of the building can be diverted from the waste stream and instead reused or recycled.

Decarbonizing Building Material

As noted in our discussion of the earlier phases of the decarbonized design process, the size and shape of a building will largely define its life cycle demands for construction material. An optimized building form may begin to offset the impacts we incur if, by necessity, we're forced to use materials with a large carbon footprint.

In the conceptual or schematic design phase we've already developed, along with the form of the building, a strong notion of the materials we intend to use in its structure and finishes, assigning material in a general *tectonic* sense. It's in the more advanced phases of design development and technical elaboration that we identify specific material products, their weights, sizes, and shapes, and we detail the means by which they are fastened together to form the overall building assembly. In this stage of material selection and application, we would be wise to utilize the kinds of third-party environmental product declarations (EPDs) discussed in Chapter 2. But it's also important to apply a set of working principles to guide us in our selection process in order to narrow down our options and focus our decarbonization efforts all along the building life cycle.

Decarbonizing the Production Stage: Material Priorities

With the built environment responsible for over a third of all global material consumption, it is incumbent upon the building designer to be circumspect about the environmental consequences of material selection and strategic about the use of materials to minimize atmospheric emissions and solid waste. In order to decarbonize our material palette, a simple hierarchy should guide us in our specification of any given material or product. Inspired by the *waste hierarchy* discussed in Chapter 2, we can classify and order them as follows:

Materials that absorb and store carbon:
The sheer volume and weight of material entailed in the remediation, renovation, and new construction of buildings and their sites make it absolutely critical that we use every opportunity to include carbon-storing and carbon-absorbing materials in our building assemblies: plant-based materials comprised in large part of naturally photosynthesized carbon; site plantings and soils with the ongoing capacity to absorb and photosynthesize atmospheric carbon; non-bio-based materials that sequester atmospheric carbon through the mineralization of CO_2.

The use of bio-based materials may carry with them source impacts so we should ensure that cycles of growth and harvest are managed sustainably and protect the biodiversity and ecological balance of their source sites. We should also pay close attention to their processing emissions as energy-intensive manufacturing and transport may largely or even entirely offset potential carbon storage benefits. We should also make every attempt to ensure when detailing their incorporation into our building's assemblies that those carbon-positive materials can be readily recovered in the end-of-life stage and reused in a second or third life cycle as part of another building or some other consumer product. Otherwise, we fail to capitalize on the potential long-term benefit of those constructed carbon banks.

There are a number of technologies currently in the research and testing phase of their development. Industrial carbon capture, enhanced photosynthesis, or biochar, represent compelling if as yet logistically challenging or biologically risky means to draw down anthropogenic carbon emissions. Each has, for the moment, limited applicability to the immediate work of designing and constructing buildings.

Reused materials:
We should try to utilize reused products wherever possible. In doing so, we can avoid replicating most of the emissions already embodied in a vast bank of consumer and construction material already in circulation. By virtue of our demand for that reused material, we incentivize the building sector to move toward more circular economic practices. Care should be taken, however, with the specification of reused materials to ensure that they are properly vetted and prepared for use, uncontaminated by toxins or other safety hazards, with their original material properties sufficiently intact.

Products that are recycled or high in recycled content:
Although the recycling process entails more inputs of manufacturing activity and energy than basic reuse, there are significant impact reductions in comparison to a newly manufactured material drawn from virgin sources. Again, as with bio-based materials, we need to keep in mind the processing emissions of recycled material, rather than take the fact of their being recycled at face value.

Virgin materials from non-renewable sources:
Any such materials should be used sparingly as they incur impacts at the beginning and end of the building life cycle. Often these materials, although perhaps highly effective and durable during the building life cycle, are associated with intensive extraction and manufacture and cannot be naturally reabsorbed by the planet's soils and waters.

Chemically harmful materials:

The lowest material class and one we should seek to avoid at all costs are products that contain harmful substances or whose manufacturing processes require them. There are many such products on the market, permitted despite increasing environmental and public health concerns, because of the relatively low quantities of toxins they contain. It's important to note that a product recycled from a previous product that contained a harmful substance is little better than its predecessor, and by using the recycled content we may have avoided production stage emissions, but we have simply transferred another set of potential impacts into another life cycle of building. In this case, we should probably demote that recycled material to this lowest use category. In the formation of our building material palette, we always seek to work within the upper categories of this material hierarchy.

MATERIAL CLASSES AND THEIR CARBON CONSEQUENCES

In the contemporary global building economy, an astounding array of material options for structure, finish, insulation, and weatherproofing lie ready to hand for the building designer's selection and application. Some of these products are straightforward and familiar; others are formed from highly innovative and complex material and chemical composites that combine several classes and forms of material through processes of mechanical adhesion or industrial chemical synthesis. We apply all these materials to our building assemblies for reasons that range from a particular cultural or aesthetic association and preference to the technical attributes we associate with their physical properties; density, thermal and electrical conductivity, strength and stiffness, hardness, durability, ductility, elasticity, workability . . . the list of those material characteristics that we so prize in the formation of building is long and complicated. Only recently have we begun to consider the inherent

environmental implications of a material: the impacts to source landscapes; the energy, emissions, and waste associated with its manufacture, and the likelihood that it might be reused or reprocessed rather than discarded. As we transition from the early phases of design ideation into the technically specific phases of its implementation, we may consider some of the inherent characteristics of the materials in our design palette that will either mitigate or exacerbate the flows of carbon at the beginning and end of the building life cycle.

Stone

Stone, the construction material, and rock, the geological source of that material, underpin the history of building. Though stone (the proper name for the vestiges of glacial or alluvial action or processed units of rock we use in building) is less commonly used today for primary structure. From a life cycle standpoint, the lithosphere is the substrate from which we extract ores, minerals, and fossil hydrocarbons. For the purposes of building, stone is a material whose weight, hardness, and compressive strength are its primary structural properties. These have significant implications for its performance and life cycle impacts. When detailed for stability, it is an extremely durable material, but construction logistics may produce unintended impacts. Due to its density and resulting weight and its lack of tensile strength (both as a material and as part of an unreinforced system), larger foundations and reinforcement may be required to support it, especially when sited in unstable soils. This requirement, in turn, may generate collateral impacts in the form of additional material consumption or land disturbance. When quarried, processed, and shipped, there may be significant production-stage impacts. However, when drawn from the immediate surroundings of its intended site and sized to be handled with light equipment and machinery within a carefully controlled area, construction impacts can be avoided. Stone is readily found naturally in various global landscapes in the form of geological formations, ledge outcroppings, glacial talus and scree, alluvial gravels, and industrial tailings, but great care should be taken in the process of its removal as these natural formation and industrial vestiges may provide plant and animal habitat. Stone is a valuable circular economic resource, reusable in many forms and applications.

Brick and Ceramics

The manufacture and use of brick represent a notable chapter in the history of human inhabitation, settlement, and industry, produced from the gathering and sintering (chemical bonding under high heat) of minerals drawn from the riverine soils and rocky terrains of a variety of the Earth's landscapes. It also forms the artifacts of buildings and material still recognizable in human settlements around the world. The industrial process of brick-making has become more efficient in recent years but still requires significant energy inputs that can generate toxic emissions.

Brick, however, is an obvious choice for circular economic construction because it is produced in units and its assemblies can be dismantled and the units reused (with little processing requirements) in a variety of applications beyond conventional masonry construction: assembled in gabion matts and baskets; used as filler or aggregate for lightweight or stabilized soils; added to reduce the required volume of cement in reinforced concrete; applied as riprap for retainage, reinforcement, and the reduction of storm water scouring. It is hygroscopic (water-absorbing) so may enhance plant growth and can be returned safely to soil at the end of its final life cycle.

Cement and Concrete

Cement and its composite formulation as concrete remain a necessary and ubiquitous part of the contemporary construction palette due to its strength, formal plasticity, and impact and wear resistance, but its use should be limited as much as possible due to its overall environmental footprint: impacts associated with mineral extraction processes, the high fossil energy inputs required in the production of Portland cement, the consumption of resource-critical materials that are its constituent components—potable

water and sharp sand—and the extremely high GHG emissions associated with its production and transport. Although cement mineralizes atmospheric CO_2 with exposure to air as it ages, the benefit of that carbon storage is far offset by its life cycle emissions. It is nonetheless invaluable for structural foundations for large structures though its volume should be reduced as much as possible. Where appropriate and necessary, cements with high fly ash content and recycled aggregate should replace Portland cement. For smaller, lighter structures, geo-piles, rock and soil anchors or other forms of masonry foundation should be considered as an alternative.

As a matter of construction logistics, the significant cured weight of concrete or, alternatively, the short duration of its initial hydration (curing) time can create significant technical challenges for building in remote locations or in extremely tall buildings of the contemporary cityscape.

As a circular economic material, concrete is difficult to reuse unless carefully implemented as precast elements with generic structural applications (cement masonry units, slabs, planks, columns, etc.). Demolition of site-cast reinforced concrete is energy-intensive due to its being interwoven with steel reinforcing. At the end of a concrete structure's functional life, it can be crushed and its steel reinforcing separated for recycling. Reusing the mineral portion of those residues for aggregates, gravels, or riprap is the best circular economic practice for concrete waste, as it replaces materials mined from virgin rock and alluvial soils.

Most forward-thinking cement companies have already made significant reductions in production phase emissions. These include the development and implementation of alternative hydraulic binders to Portland cement and the replacement in experimental cases of solar manufacturing energy for more conventional hydrocarbon fuel sources. In additional research, still at the experimental level, the cement industry is seeking to enhance the capacity of concrete to sequester atmospheric carbon.

Metals

Due to their properties of strength, workability, and durability, metals of various types and alloys have been a part of building for millennia, but the industrial revolution and attendant availability of industrial fuels with high energy densities-coal, oil, gas—have made the use of both ferrous and non-ferrous metals ubiquitous as the structure and surfaces of contemporary building. Various metal alloys serve a range of applications with widely varying material characteristics: ductility, malleability, elasticity, resistance to oxidation and wear. In recent decades, the structural steel industry has made significant reductions in manufacturing energy and raw material requirements through the shift from basic oxygen to electric arc furnaces and the use of recycled feedstocks.

Many contemporary metallurgists as well as environmentalists, however, are concerned about the high volume of the flow of metals in the building sector, due to the energy intensiveness of both initial processing and recycling. Alloys of unknown metallurgical make-up make diverting metals within the waste stream challenging. Bespoke applications of steel for structural connectors, for example, may mean that a certain percentage of the material in a building may not be able to be directly reused, but instead must be re-melted with high energy inputs. In the form of sheets, or as commercial structural sections with relatively little post-processing, steel can be reused quite easily. Copper and aluminum are used primarily as weathering surfaces or as electrical wiring, but sources of ore are depleted and recycling is energy- and emissions-intensive. In general, the application of metals in any construction assembly should be optimized for cost, functionality, and environmental impact.

Glass

Rare in its transparency but ubiquitous in its application to all kinds of contemporary building apertures and envelopes, glass has a limited lifespan due to its breakage capacity, its reduced transparency due to abrasion and chemical degradation by acidic environments, or because the secondary structural and sealant systems, the frames, mullions, sashes, gaskets, films that are typical components of window and glazing assemblies, fail around them. Glass panels can be reused if unbroken and, depending on their initial formulation and treatment (laminating, tempering, annealing) may be able to be cut down into smaller components. The alternative end-of-life scenario for glass is recycling. This typically entails melting it, and in order to achieve the high temperatures required, we consume energy and generate emissions.

Plastics

Most plastic polymers currently in use in construction applications (thin membranes, extruded sheets and sections, castings, and foams) originate as fossil hydrocarbons. They are synthesized using extremely complex and intensive chemical industrial processes with significant energy inputs and associated emissions. They do not biodegrade and therefore form the largest and most environmentally durable portion of the human consumer waste stream, all with significant impacts to planetary health. Plastic recycling is energy-intensive throughout the recycling process (sorting and distribution, material handling and transport, shredding, melting, and reforming).

Plastic, in all its forms, permeates contemporary buildings as membranes, insulation, adhesives, caulks and seals, piping, wire insulation, and more remotely but still instrumental to the building process, in all the forms of packing we use to organize and protect our building materials for transport. Most of these eventually leave the building site as some form of undifferentiated waste. In order to decarbonize our building assemblies, we should avoid the use of plastic of fossil origin except where we are reusing it directly in innovative assemblies comprised of material drawn directly from the consumer product waste stream, or composed of 100% recycled content, thereby helping to remove plastics—for at least the next product life cycle, from the flow of waste and, inevitably, from the Earth's soils and waters. Due to the physical durability and potential toxicity of certain plastics, as well as their production and end-of-life emissions, we should be careful to consult environmental product declarations and product red lists to determine their environmental efficacy. Exciting research and development in bioplastics promise a whole new class of low-carbon alternatives.

For the most part, however, these products have not yet penetrated the building products market.

Wood

Despite its ubiquity in low-rise free-standing buildings and as interior finishes, wood has been under-utilized during the twentieth century due to fears—both legitimate and misplaced—of regional deforestation and its poor performance over time due to its material degradability, combustibility, and weakness. Wood, however, when properly applied and detailed, has the durability of steel and concrete and a higher strength to weight ratio than either. As a material class of biological origin and a complex carbohydrate, it is unique in both its renewability and its capacity to sequester or store atmospheric carbon. Various species already available commercially or part of an emerging class of building products, have a wide range of material properties and characteristics. When applied conventionally in building—in the form of small sticks of limited cross-sectional dimension using a large number of fasteners—wood has a propensity to fail over time due to weather exposure, decay, and decomposition, or subjection to fire. When applied in more monolithic forms, as large solid timber or adhesive laminated cross-sections, wood's structural performance in fire conditions is even comparable to masonry or concrete, and its durability vis-à-vis weather exposure and biological decay can readily be predicted and the cross-section calibrated to the intended life span of a structure. New non-toxic cellular modifications to wood fiber—such as torrefaction and acetylation—can dramatically extend the life span of weather-exposed wood. When harvested using sustainable silvicultural practices and sourced from regional forests and product manufacturers, timber as construction material is very low in its life cycle carbon emissions and high in its carbon storage. In large, monolithic sections, vulnerable points of connection are reduced in number and a massive timber component is highly amenable to reuse in building, reprocessing for other consumer products, or if barring those options, carbonized as biochar, burned for energy as biomass or safely reintroduced into the soil biome. The contemporary harvested wood product industry has found a range of uses for mill residues like flake, strand, and particles in both primary and secondary engineered structural components that include boards, beams, and posts. What cannot be incorporated into the product stream has served as a manufacturing energy source.

Plastic resins used in a range of structural adhesives such as epoxies and polyurethanes have made it possible to create engineered timber components of significant size and structural capacity—glue-laminated timber, laminated veneer and cross-laminated timber panels—but the amount of glue required in the manufacture of some engineered wood members, the emissions associated with the production of those resins, and their introduction into the construction waste stream may begin to offset some of the carbon benefits of using wood. As an alternative, mechanical lamination techniques utilizing wooden dowels or readily-recyclable and machinable aluminum nails may replace adhesives with high emissions coefficients.

In light of the broad set of ecosystem services that forests provide, as well as the significant carbon absorption and storage capacity of both the above-ground and below-ground woody matter contained in forest ecosystems, it is absolutely critical that we are careful to avoid timber species and products extracted from over-harvested, poorly managed, or biologically vulnerable forests. As the critical importance of forest ecosystems as carbon sinks is becoming better understood by emerging research [4], we should aspire to develop design solutions for wood buildings that leverage this valuable natural asset to maximize the substitution potential compared to alternative solutions.

Our design choices—whether for primary structural applications or durable finishes—must specify only those harvested wood products drawn from renewable and sustainably harvested forests, with carefully designed and vetted, long-term management plans that select for successional regeneration and biodiversity. As with the toxicity of chemically synthesized material classes, it is incumbent upon us to verify that we are not producing upstream or downstream environmental impact. Using industry EPDs, consumer red-lists, and forest product certifications we can specify, at the very least, products of certified origin and, ideally, track the chain of custody of the wood products we apply in our buildings from stump to mill. In this way, our best efforts to store carbon in our buildings will work synergistically and sustainably with the critical ecosystemic resource that our global forests represent.

Other Bio-Based Materials

Building materials and products derived from non-timber plant cellulose are becoming more readily available as we impose increasing environmental constraint and economic penalty on our consumption of virgin, non-renewable building material and seek more biological renewability and technical circularity in the future building economy. The use of post-agricultural waste—plant husks and stalks—as well as rapidly renewable grasses, straw, and reeds can be used as the tensile component of composite boards, agro-masonry units, and panels, or as raw material for thermal and acoustical insulation—makes the prospect of carbon storage in building components other than primary timber structures an increasingly realistic alternative to products formed almost entirely from mineral- and petroleum-based materials.

The promise of synthetic biology, in which building materials are "grown" as a by-product of natural bacteriological or fungal formation represents a new frontier in building material production. Mushroom, or mycelium, the vegetative component of living fungus has been demonstrated to form structural masonry units, albeit in fairly small-scale applications. In a similar vein, utilizing a process that mimics the formation of coral or the shells of marine organisms like mollusks, certain bacteria can be mixed with sand to create cementious material for bricks [5, 6].

Soils

Except in more traditional examples or bespoke cases of contemporary building experimentation, we rarely think of soil as a construction material. But the planet's soils are where our story of human building activity begins and ends. A range of soil types, too numerous to list here, represents a matrix of fine organic and mineral matter that serves alternately as biome and building structure. As builders, we draw from soil—directly or indirectly and over a range of time scales—nearly all the substances with which we build. As a traditional material, soil has been mounded, compacted, wetted, molded, heated, and dried to produce the monolithic platforms on which our buildings stand or the masonry units which we stack as walls or form as vaults. We move vast amounts of soil to reshape landscapes and create new, smaller habitats for the plant material we specify on our building sites.

In the effort to decarbonize building, soil plays two important roles. As a consumable *resource*, soil can be formed into a range of new or rediscovered building materials—adobe bricks or rammed earth are perhaps the most familiar of these. Where these materials can substitute for more conventional components of the building assembly with significantly higher production stage emissions and unlikely end-of-life reuse scenarios, soil-based building products can serve to reduce a building's carbon footprint. We must take care, however, not to abuse global landscapes and ecosystems through extractive industrial processes as we search for suitably workable soils.

As a *biome,* soil is invaluable. Unfortunately, during the Anthropocene, it has been the vast repository of the waste of much of human activity, which includes the residues of construction and demolition. Our human tendency to contaminate global soils or entomb them in impervious materials—asphalt and concrete that cover over vast areas of otherwise biologically productive surfaces of the Earth—represents a steady and destructive slide, one that has resulted in the accelerated warming of our planet and the extinction of plant and animal species.

Regenerative carbon-conscious design seeks to build *soils* as well as buildings. By designing sites as biomass-rich ecosystems, by planning and promoting the selective diversion of production and operational waste streams to capture nutrient-rich compostable materials, and by specifying and detailing construction materials that can safely be returned to the land at the end of the building (or other product) life cycle, we can potentially enrich, rather than continue to degrade live-giving soils.

THE DECARBONIZED BUILDING ASSEMBLY

It's obvious that such a basic overview of the kinds of materials we use in building can never completely represent the complexity of the building assembly or the ever-changing composition of the building products on the market, nor can it reflect the past and future carbon impacts incurred by each material we specify. But as we methodically assemble our buildings during the technical development phase of the design process, we can begin to assess the relative weights and volumes of the materials we assign to our building assemblies and we can seek low-carbon alternatives to those products with significant environmental impacts and quantify those we are unable to avoid. In this critical design phase, in which the implementation of architectural ideas meets the intense demands of structural and thermal performance, weatherproofing, airtightness, durability, and serviceability, not to mention the general safety and comfort of the building's users, it can seem overwhelming to try to avoid all of the evident and latent ramifications for the environment of each of the materials that comprise the building assembly. This is especially so given our professional reliance on product testing and warranties. But the embodied impacts we avoid through careful, circumspect material selections and the potential pressure that places on product manufacturers and suppliers to reduce those impacts in order to protect their market share, are all seeded in the technical elaboration of the enclosures and assemblies in this important phase of the design process.

Decarbonizing the Use Stage: Energy Consumption, Airtightness, and Thermal Performance

The reduction of energy consumption during the use stage of the building life cycle has been a primary focus of the sustainable building movement over the past half-century. The fruits of these efforts have been manifest and multi-fold, with a proliferation of research and testing on building systems and assemblies and a host of new high-performance products brought to market. The result has been a significant increase in the efficiency of heating, cooling, and ventilation systems, more stringent thermal insulation and airtightness standards embedded in the code, and a generally better understanding by architects and builders of building envelope detailing to avoid air leakage, vapor migration, and thermal conduction through building assemblies.

These increases in building energy performance and efficiency have brought correlated reductions in the greenhouse gas emissions associated with the use-stage of the building life cycle. In some cases, these benefits have come at the expense of increased toxicity and carbon-related impacts in the production and end-of-life stages of the building life cycle, such as in the proliferation of highly effective but environmentally deleterious forms of foam plastic insulation, or with the increased complexity and material intensiveness of the contemporary high performance building envelope. Because the building sector has compiled such a trove of written resources on the subject of operational energy in buildings, let it suffice here for us to restate the importance of designing the building envelope for enhanced thermal performance—observing, of course, prior recommendations about the materials we apply to it—so as to minimize emissions and energy consumption throughout that protracted period of a lifespan of operation and use. During the technical development phase of the design process, we must prioritize, optimize, and organize durable, low-energy technological solutions—appliances and equipment—that are designed to function in a coordinated and synergistic way with available ecosystem services, that acknowledge and exploit the thermodynamic properties of material and shapes of interior space. We understand such a design approach to be transcalar and comprehensive. They include appropriating general and micro-climatic conditions of the region and site as valuable constants in our equations of energy efficiency; detailing our building apertures to optimize interior daylight and minimize solar heat gain and thermal heat loss while promoting, where useful and relevant, passive heating and cooling; in the broadest sense, conceiving of our building's tectonic expression, and at the smallest scale, detailing its building envelope to ensure airtightness at all joints and eliminate all thermal bridging between its interior and exterior spaces and surfaces, and, wherever possible, using the building's site, surfaces, systems, and sheer mass, to generate, recover, and distribute energy.

The actual way in which those designed systems will be used by the building's future inhabitants or maintenance, repair, and renovations will be conducted by some future building manager is a challenge to predict. It is nearly impossible to anticipate how the behavior of a building's users will comport with the goals and methods of the design team. But if the principles and details of the building assembly and systems are either clearly legible in the building itself, or well documented in the as-built drawings or models and well described in a building's systems manual, then the design team has done everything possible to convey the environmental values, principles, and objectives of the building design as well as the specific design and engineering solutions that underpin them. We'll address the post-occupancy phase of the building process in a subsequent section of this chapter.

It's critical that we recognize the technical development phase of the design process as the point at which we consolidate and implement all of the carbon-conscious design decisions we've made in the earlier phases of design. This is especially important with respect to energy efficiency. The fact that we may have elected in the concept design phase to generate renewable energy onsite, for example, does not relieve us of the responsibility to produce a well-insulated, airtight, and thermally broken assembly. For the decarbonized building project, every effort to reduce emissions or energy consumption must be substantiated and reinforced through decisions made in subsequent phases of design.

Detailing for Disassembly in the Building's End-of-Life Stage

Just as it is difficult to predict some future inhabitant's or building owner's patterns of use with respect to the energy consumption of operating a building, it is unlikely that we can predict the waste management policies and practices that will be in place in a distant future when our building is to be demolished or dismantled. If, however, we can strategize to facilitate the careful disassembly of our building at the end of its operational life and deploy materials in ways that make them easier to process for reuse or recycling, then we increase the likelihood that that material can be diverted from future waste streams. This requires that we examine the durability and life cycle prospects of the materials we select; that we deploy them according

to the likely frequency of their cycles of repair or replacement within the layers of the building assembly; that we engineer the reversibility of the building assembly process through the connection and fastening methods we specify; that we observe basic principles of optimization, repeatability, and minimize inconsistency and particularity in the dimensioning and shaping of the material we employ. Guided by these basic principles, we lay the groundwork for material reuse and potentially avoid many of the production stage emissions that would be required for another future building or some other set of consumer products.

Detailing for Disassembly: Considerations for Material Reuse

Many of the technical design strategies we might use to ease future disassembly of the buildings we design are the same as those utilized in the prefabricated building industry. Though some of these techniques may be less familiar or seem time-consuming or exceedingly costly to builders of conventional buildings, they are fundamental to the economies of industrialized building where the optimization of any given set of materials and building operations is designed to reduce material waste and processing inefficiencies or where prefabricated assemblies must be put together in the factory, disassembled and then shipped to the building site for reassembly. In some cases, where access for repair or clearances for maintenance is constrained, a design solution may also employ similar techniques to ensure that a building can be feasibly serviced.

Reversibility

The first and perhaps most obvious principle in the design of buildings for future disassembly is that what we put together, we must be able to take apart. In designing not just the physical object, but the process of its assembly, the building designer is effectively rehearsing both its actual assembly as well as its potential disassembly at some future date. If we fasten materials indiscriminately using nails and construction adhesives, or if the order of assembly operations is unclear and one layer of that assembly inadvertently interweaves with another, we make it all the more likely that the building will be razed using crude methods of demolition. If, on the other hand, the assembly process uses fasteners that are reversible, such as screws and bolts, long-lasting adhesives are used sparingly, and the layers of assembly are clear and discrete, then we have set the stage for future disassembly. In contemporary timber construction, a revolution in screw technology has all but obviated the more bespoke and artisan joinery systems of traditional timber joinery, eliminating, perhaps some of the romance of old-school craftsmanship but making the construction and, ultimately, dismantling of new timber building structures relatively easy and requiring little skilled labor. The rivet of nineteenth-century steel construction has been largely replaced by specialized bolts. Pre-cast and post-tensioned concrete structures make the reuse of pre-cast structural members feasible in the future whereas site-cast concrete ensures that only concrete rubble can leave the site at the end of the building life cycle.

As industrialized prefabrication of building components and modules becomes increasingly the norm, the principle of reversibility and the building techniques that underpin it will become increasingly common. To that context we may add new or expanded markets for specific components drawn from disassembled buildings and new systems for cataloguing reusable materials and components as they become available. Instead of trading in scrap for recycling, we may create a building sector that increasingly trades in previously used constructive elements. This will inevitably open up an entirely new set of responsibilities and opportunities for the building designer.

Optimization and Repeatability

Complex, irregular, and bespoke material shapes and dimensions—although of potential interest and value from an entirely aesthetic standpoint—may be feasible in an age of digitally controlled mass customization but they make material reuse extremely difficult. As with the industrialized building process, material components that are optimized both in their efficient use of a raw material or manufactured product and then deployed repetitively to offer some economies of scale are inevitably more cost-effective. These same principles can guide us in the technical development phase of the design process as we organize the application of materials and products within the building assembly. As a corollary to that principle, if we can harvest from buildings at the end-of-life stage of their life cycle materials that are both

undamaged by the removal process and repetitive in their dimension and shape, there will inevitably be a greater bandwidth of possible applications for their reuse in buildings or other manufactured products. In the preparation of material for reuse at this critical moment in the building life cycle, as with the initial processing of raw material into products, optimization and standardization of material, equipment, and tooling, and the processing steps required inevitably make production more efficient and therefore economical (as well as less energy- and emissions-intensive) and ultimately more marketable. In a sense, in designing buildings for disassembly rather than indiscriminate demolition, we are predicting what kinds of products and product lines our building assemblies might ultimately yield.

As we've seen in our discussion in Chapter 2 of the "end-of-waste criteria" for reused material re-entering the manufactured product stream, one of the criteria is that the processed waste material can be used in exactly the same way as the non-waste material produced from virgin resources. This criterion suggests, for example, that a piece of plywood sheathing harvested from a dismantled building must have at least the same structural properties, if not the same dimensions, as a newly manufactured sheet of plywood. To achieve such a status, that panel of plywood would need to have been attached to the structure with removable fasteners, which is to say that its connections must be reversible. In addition, if all the sheets readily harvested from the building were of equal dimensions, we expand opportunities for their potential reuse and make their resale more feasible and likely. Irregular components are less broadly applicable and therefore less marketable for reuse. This holds significant implications for the way we choose to deploy material within the building assembly during the technical development phase of the design process.

The Ramifications of Size

In our discussion of the different phases of the design process, we've raised the issue of dimension repeatedly. At the initiation of a building project and in the earliest stages of its conception, as we begin to assess the spatial and dimensional implications of a project brief, we challenge ourselves to consider whether we can accomplish what we need with less than the specified volume or floor area, whether spaces are redundant or necessary at all. In this case, size is to some degree a predictor of efficiency, with implications for both production and use-stage greenhouse gas emissions. Within the obvious downward limits of spatial functionality or structural performance, smaller, in many cases, may be better.

As we move into the more advanced technical phases of design, the question of size and sufficiency becomes more complicated. This requires that we assess the optimal range of potential criteria with respect to life cycle impacts: the reduction of extraction impacts and material processing emissions in the production stage; the performance and durability of a building component throughout the use stage, and the way that material may be discarded as waste or prepared for reuse as a new industrial material. For example, a large panel of cross-laminated timber may contain more material than a similar dimensioned panel constructed from light wood framing and plywood sheathing and its weight may require larger material handling equipment with construction stage emissions but in the end-of-life stage, that large panel may have significantly broader applications for reuse than the small sticks and thinner wood sheathing. A large steel member with minimal end detailing may be reused more feasibly than the short cords of a truss with their specific end connections. While the large recovered steel member might conceivably go directly to a secondary materials market, the truss components might be fated for a lower rung in the waste hierarchy such as recycling, which might incur greater emissions in the process of re-melting. We might choose a triple rather than a double pane insulated glazing unit because of its superior thermal resistance but learn that the increased processing emissions generated in the addition of the extra sheet of glass and the added structure necessary to carry its added weight, offset the life cycle benefit of the superior energy performance. In these cases, larger may be better. This is what makes the technical detailing phase so challenging if we consider the potential decarbonization of the building assembly. The difficulty of predicting outcomes so far in the future, within a range of possible political and economic contexts and their

associated environmental practices, makes our assessment an educated guess at best. What may seem like a hard and fast rule at one scale of design consideration may fail to serve us in a later stage. The best we can do is make our choices based on the kinds of localized LCA scenarios and standards we've described in Chapter 2, which at least rely on established standards and agreed-upon assumptions about future waste management policies and practices.

Material Homogeneity

A critical attribute of a potentially reusable building material is its purity and homogeneity. Different materials combined as a product through intensive chemical or mechanical bonding processes may obscure its material properties for future users, may make either make recycling challenging or obviate it all together, and, of course, this neglects the principle of reversibility. This has been a real challenge in the material recovery industry. Plastic sheet laminated with adhesive over a fiberboard substrate makes the reuse of the panel or the recovery and recycling of either its plastic or wood fiber nearly impossible. Certain metal alloys designed to perform in highly specific applications make the end-of-life discernment of their metallurgical make-up a matter of forensic analysis rather than visual assessment and thereby practically ensure that the material will be downcycled, if recycled at all. This means some future reuser won't be able to offset the alloy's initial extraction and processing emissions by applying it to another building or product life cycle. As with highly processed food with multiple additives designed to optimize a product's shelf life or make its color more appetizing, material composites or alloys may provide more specific solutions to a building application, but that same specificity may also make it harder to sort or, in a more sophisticated reuse or recycling scenario, entail more cost and time to successfully analyze, and in the end, prove rather unhealthy. All of these challenges increase the likelihood that materials will inevitably enter the waste stream. Our focus during the technical detailing of the building systems and assemblies should be to make the building perform efficiently and effectively but also to make it easier and more obvious for a future waste manager to divert the materials that comprise it back to the manufacturing sector as a virgin industrial resource.

THE LATER DESIGN PHASES: CONTRACT DOCUMENTATION, BIDDING AND NEGOTIATION, AND CONSTRUCTION ADMINISTRATION

Once we've reached the point at which we begin the comprehensive process of drawing the building in its final dimension and geometry and specifying its material, products, and systems for use as both a guide to its construction and a contractual document that binds a project team to a building design, nearly all of the decisions within the control of the design and engineering team that will affect the building's carbon footprint have been made. From this point forward, our responsibility to the decarbonized design process, as with our professional obligation, is to protect those decisions and ensure that we've clearly conveyed them through our documents, through the process of negotiating the building contract and assessing and applying potential cost-saving measures, and by overseeing the construction process and assuring compliance with the decarbonized design documents.

The contract documentation phase is one in which we finalize all technical decisions, coordinate assemblies and systems, and specify materials, products, and equipment. The accuracy of dimensioning and the precision of specification are critical to any robust building process and even more so with a building that aspires to minimize the environmental impacts of its life cycle impacts. As insurance in this process, we need to clearly communicate the decarbonization criteria for our material selections and the reasons for the means and methods their assembly entails.

The bidding and negotiation phase of a building project is the point at which we convey the totality of design decisions and the technical details and specifications through which they are conveyed to potential builders and then shepherd them through the process of finalizing a contract with a builder. Negotiations between the design team, the client, and a builder almost invariably include at least some efforts at reducing costs, often through suggestions for material and product substitutions as well as

alternative details, means, and methods. It is at this point in the process that many of the design solutions relating specifically to the decarbonization of the construction process and resulting building are most vulnerable to cost pressures. We should be ready with a range of potential material and systems substitutions that will satisfy our decarbonization goals while providing our client and builder with cost and performance options. At the very least, we should be armed with a clear set of criteria for assessing proposed changes. This is also the moment of opportunity, in which we firmly establish those decarbonized building objectives with the negotiating parties and we reaffirm our low-carbon concord.

The construction administration phase is—to use a perhaps conflicted metaphor—where the rubber meets the road. During the long and arduous building process, the decarbonized design team works to assure compliance with the contract documents. The designer working alongside a builder in the field will inevitably be faced with unforeseen discoveries—especially in building renovations—in which the knowledge of potential life cycle sources of greenhouse gas emissions will greatly enhance the agility with which we make important decisions when response times are limited and far-reaching environmental impacts may be hard to determine. In these cases, we can only use our informed intuition and educated best guesses at potential implications of a field decision for the project's overall carbon footprint.

A number of volumes could be written about the range of possible conditions that might arise in which a set of carbon-conscious decisions might be compromised during the process of their implementation. Let it suffice to point out here that in these phases of the design process, the members of the building design team are most expert in tracking the flows of carbon through that particular building's life cycle. It's likely that we know best where a client or builder might find further opportunities to reduce emissions, where different life cycle scenarios for a substituted material or alternative detail may or may not create roughly equivalent footprints, and which are the decisions that we should most fiercely protect if we're to meet the low carbon objectives of our design and preserve the carbon efficacy of our building.

What Happens After Construction? (One More Design Phase to Consider)

The post-construction or post-occupancy phase of a building project is not typically—professionally, contractually, or really even reasonably—a part of the conventional building design process. This phase begins when the design team verifies the builder's contractual compliance with the design documents and thereby closes out the building contract. In some cases, the design team's responsibilities may include a process of building commissioning and/or post-occupancy assessment that observes whether occupants are using that building systems as intended or measures the actual performance of its systems and assemblies. Most of the time, with the handover of the building from the builder to the client, the designer relinquishes direct control of the building's future. The subsequent *building use phase* and, ultimately, its *end-of-life phase*, may represent a time-frame that is decades-long and will most likely entail the largest share of a building's life cycle emissions. Building designers can only seek to predict and thereby prepare for the eventualities that may occur during so protracted a period of time. It is true, that once a set design of design decisions has been fully documented and faithfully implemented during the construction process, the design team has very little capacity to change the behavior of the building's users, to specify and ensure appropriate procedures for the building's maintenance, repair or renovation, or to direct the building's ultimate disassembly and the diversion of its constituent parts way from the waste stream and into more productive use as resources for circular economic manufacture.

But we mention late life cycle phases here as a reminder that in considering possible futures of the building *during* the design process, a design team can embed the logics of a low-carbon life cycle into the building's organization of space and material. In addition to our efforts to manifest directly our low carbon strategies in the spaces and assemblies of the building themselves, we have an opportunity to convey those inherent low-carbon logics either directly through tools such as users' manuals or as-built building information models, that focus on the production or recovery and distribution of energy, automated controls for the buildings environmental systems, and, to harken back to the adage—"if you can't measure it, you can't manage it," metering systems that clearly show to users and managers their role in reducing their building's energy use. By transmitting the principles and means of low carbon occupancy and operation to those with the agency to take most advantage of them, the design team may continue to play a role in the decarbonization of the building life cycle long after the design work is completed.

PRINCIPLES OF DECARBONIZED DESIGN

In organizing our approach to stemming the flows of carbon through the life cycles of the buildings we design, we need to search for meaningful guidance in the form of reliable information and effective strategies that can guide our work. Although there's an increasing abundance of information-rich databases that catalog material impacts, environmental product declarations, and digital assessment tools, it's also the case that a particularly intrepid researcher with a great deal of free time can unearth a host of conflicting and contested information about the correct approach to reducing environmental impacts. The problem is not that the sources of that information and those guidelines are intentionally misleading, but that the contexts for their underlying assessments may be targeted to too specific an economy, a region, a culture, a climate zone or a moment in time. How then to proceed, if the value and veracity of information are so fluid, and conditions on the planet are changing at so surprising a rate? The methodical process of life cycle assessment described in earlier sections of this series is a relatively simple undertaking. However, it's also important that we are guided in that process of quantification and analysis—as in the process of building design that frames that assessment—by a set of guiding principles and criteria that reinforce our intuition and refine our ability to effectively orchestrate our decisions.

Although all building projects differ, with different occupancies and programmatic requirements, varying cultural, economic, political, regulatory, physical, and climatic contexts—and even projected lifespans— we should keep in mind some overarching principles for the design of low carbon buildings. These decarbonized design strategies can be applied—keeping an ever-watchful eye out for potential unintended consequences—throughout the design process, at varying scales of consideration, and with potential benefits to be found throughout the building life cycle. The following principles should guide us as we seek to decarbonize the buildings we design.

1. Simplify

The first principle is to simplify :*Systemic simplification* serves as an overarching and trans-scalar concept in decarbonized design and building, with implications for the entire design process and every stage of the building life cycle that the design will set in motion. In the decarbonized design process, the goal of simplicity should guide the development and elaboration of a building, from its tectonic, spatial, and formal conception to the degree of complexity and the corresponding density of detail entailed in its execution—the technical intensiveness of its enclosure, structure, and systems; the number and interrelationship of different materials and products; their method of connection and the sheer number of joints or parts required.

Production and construction stage simplifications. In the production stage of the building life cycle, designers can promote simplicity through the specification of materials and products that require fewer and less energy- and technology-intensive steps in manufacturing. During the construction phase, the simplification of building forms, systems, and details speeds construction schedules,

shortens transport distances for personnel and material, and reduces the associated energy expenditures and waste generation associated with both factory-fabrication and the on-site assembly and installation process.

Operational and end-of-life phase simplifications. The simplification of a building's spaces, surfaces, systems, and detail makes it easier to operate and maintain, repair, and refurbish, making it less energy- and waste-intensive over its operational lifespan. By simplifying its assemblies and making their means of attachment more legible, the building designer can ease the ultimate dismantling of a building at the end of its life, making the redistribution and reuse of material an easier, more obvious, and potentially economically attractive alternative to landfilling. Simplification promotes the "end of waste" status that is fundamental to a circular economy and the reduction of life cycle carbon emissions.

2. Reduce Weight

A corollary to simplification is weight reduction, which effectively means use less matter—less and lighter material—to produce a building. Needless to say, a building design still needs to answer all of its programmatic, functional, and structural requirements, and it should ensure appropriate levels of durability and environmental performance, but a basic weight reduction strategy may yield significant efficiencies in the material and energy consumed and all the emissions associated with their extraction, processing, and transport. There may even be structural savings in the decrease of material required to support an otherwise heavier structure. It goes without saying that heavy, dense materials play a critical role in building, but their indiscriminate use might well be avoided in a low carbon design strategy.

3. Minimize Disturbance

A third principle calls on us to minimize disturbance. Change can be good or necessary, but the more upheaval that takes place in the process of making that change, the more likely it is to consume greater amounts of energy and material, emitting more CO_2 in the process. First, consider any existing physical structures—whether they are geological, biological, or man-made in origin— not as impediments to be dug up or demolished to make room for your new building, but as potential resources that have already been created through the extensive investment of some form of material and energy. These may include a site's existing biomass in the form of surface plantings or the woody matter embedded in its soils (and by extension the carbon stored there); or existing buildings that might find a new and imaginative role as part of the new building design. These resources should be protected and strengthened wherever sensible and feasible. It's worth noting that by minimizing disturbance, we may actually contribute to the previous strategy—the overall reduction in the weight of material we consume.

4. Optimize Ecosystem Services

A fourth principle seeks not only to minimize disturbance to existing ecosystems but to optimize the services they provide. At whatever scale we choose to consider them, functioning ecosystems are valuable resources. Their photosynthesis of oxygen, their filtration of storm water through their soils, or the summer shading a deciduous tree may provide—should be understood as potentially synergistic with the building services we expend so much energy and material to produce and operate. Ecosystems, both distant and remote ones, should be protected and reinforced, their services optimized in functional tandem with the services our building is expected to provide.

Such a strategy might include the careful maintenance of uncompacted planted soils to help absorb storm water and reduce runoff; the protection of large trees to provide natural exterior shading that reduces solar heat gain—in lieu of increased cooling loads or the complexities of constructing and maintaining mechanical shading devices; or offsetting life cycle CO_2 emissions by sequestering carbon in the building's timber structure, sourced from some sustainably harvested regional forest. By optimizing ecosystem services, we inevitably supplement the first three principles we've enumerated: simplification, reducing weight (and corresponding material and energy consumption), and minimizing disturbance.

5. Reuse

Human-made structures, like the ecosystems already in place (whether functioning roadways or deciduous trees) should be understood as providing potential services to a building (in the form of access or shade, to extend the examples). Those services may be optimized to work in synergy with your building, and potentially serve to supplement the first two strategies of reducing material and energy consumption and protecting existing physical resources and their embodied "investments."

6. Design for Durability and Then Reversibility

Another principle is to design for *durability* and then *reversibility*. Durability is one of the critical concepts in circular economic design. It seeks to extend the lifespan of any material we introduce into a manufactured product, thereby increasing its exergy—or the ultimate effectiveness of the energy embodied in its production. This is a principle which works to counteract our current culture and economic system of disposability. Durability entails lasting cultural meaning and value—a challenging task for a designer—but also continuing functional utility and flexibility, and, of course, material resistance to wear.

Because buildings are complex material systems exposed to harsh conditions of environmental stress and continuous, heavy use, their most exposed surfaces inevitably break down, leading to secondary and tertiary failures of the overall building system. When these systems begin to fail, they need to be easily replaced. A building is also subject to programmatic or cultural obsolescence, when an occupant or a community can no longer find a suitable use for it and it is thus devalued. By anticipating this moment in either a material or building life cycle, a designer can ensure, by observing and designing with the principle of "reversibility" in mind, that the building can be readily dismantled, with as little damage as possible to its components and materials so as to facilitate their preparation for use as new "raw materials" for manufacture.

The principle of reversibility is also relevant at the outset of the building life cycle, during the processing of raw materials and the manufacture of products. More technologically intensive products—complex chemical compounds, polymers, alloys, composites, and bonded materials—may be more durable than their conventional and industrially simpler alternatives, but they tend to have larger carbon footprints. More to the point, they're significantly less "reversible," making their reuse and recycling a challenge. Examples of these abound in contemporary building, from reinforced concrete to stainless steel to blown-in foam insulation.

The concepts of durability and reversibility may seem to conflict in principle, but in terms of circular economic design and construction, the two objectives are synergistic.

7. Keep Track of Time and Distance

Throughout this book, our examination of carbon flows through the built environment has sought to widen the analytical *system boundaries* of both buildings and the building process. To do so, we recognize that while a building, by itself, may be a clear physical demarcation of property, of community identity or individual privacy, it is not a closed system of energy and material exchange. In order to understand the extents and scope, we've employed two means of measurement: time and distance.

With the temporal scale we've measured how long it takes to form different classes of carbon-based materials. As a simplification we might say that the longer it takes to generate raw materials naturally and the more intensive technological steps are required for their processing, the more energy will be required and finally more CO_2 emissions be generated. For instance, mining raw materials from deep geologic strata increases both production costs

and corresponding environmental loads. Utilizing renewable or recycled materials, these loads can in most cases be avoided.

This principle of tracking time refers to the systemic relationships among different materials within a building, their relative life cycles, and the implications of those nested relationships for the building's durability. This is best captured in a well-known diagram by the writer Stewart Brand, which describes a hierarchy of material durability within a building assembly [7]. It suggests that it is most effective to position the least easily placed components—building structure for example—in the least accessible areas of that building assembly. Correspondingly, the most exposed materials in building—surface finishes, furnishings—are easily accessed and should therefore be allowed shorter cycles of replacement.

On the one hand, this might seem to promote disposability. Seen another way, this principle suggests that the life cycles of different materials can be positioned strategically to facilitate both only replacement and planned reuse, while the heavier, and more emissions-intensive materials and systems—such as that structural frame—can serve more durably over the full extent of the building's service life.

Another form of time management critical to the decarbonization of building is the consideration of life cycle impacts relative to broader planetary changes, most notably the rapid global warming that has occurred since the industrial revolution. Today, the strategic, temporal management of building life cycle emissions—discussed in Chapter 2—allows a building to minimize production phase emissions at a time in our atmospheric history when they may create the most deleterious impacts. Needless to say, reducing all stages of emissions in the building life cycle is important, but it may be the case that the production phase emissions entailed in some high-performance building component, will create a CO_2 spike at the beginning of the building life cycle that can only be "recovered" over decades of efficient operation.

The laws of physics inevitably bear heavily on the building process. The history of building is one in which transformations in energy source, edible carbohydrate and protein, wood for combustion, coal, oil, gas, and, by extension, most electricity, have changed the way in which our species constructed its built environment. The advent of ever denser and more transportable fossil fuels enabled materials to be lifted, loaded, and carried over ever greater distances from their source landscapes to their building sites. Today, our dynamic, fossil hydrocarbon-fueled economy, with its global network of marine, air, and land transport, allow us to move the heaviest materials over mountains and across oceans at relatively small financial cost. But those quantifiable costs ignore significant externalities such as associated carbon emissions that can be accounted for. As with the tracking of time, it's helpful to map the implications of design decisions in terms of spatial and geographic dimension. Just as we might think about how difficult it is to lift a heavy material or appliance up a set of stairs, we might also consider the distance the dimensional and geographic scale of the construction process expended to move material is directly related to the mode of transport, the fuel used by a given transport system, and it's likely that a building that draws its material resources from geographically remote landscapes will consume more energy and expend more CO_2 in the transport of those materials, than a building that sources its materials locally.

If we combine these two scales of measurement—distance and time—and consider their implications for the industrially generated flows of carbon, then we can reasonably assume that the shorter the building supply chain—or in an advanced circular economy, the tighter the circuits of waste and supply—the lower the carbon impacts.

8. Share
As they say, "sharing is good," and this is also the case in decarbonized building. Sharing spaces, through the careful scheduling of their use in the earliest phases of design and thereby avoiding redundant underutilized constructed building volume; sharing

precious land by building more densely, thereby reducing sprawl and the potential destruction of valuable biomass; sharing infrastructure and building enclosures in dense multi-family housing configurations or more hybridized forms of building occupancy—all seek to use less space more effectively and efficiently. Of course, this will have the benefit of lowering initial resource consumption and make the operation of the built environment easier and its inhabitation more convivial.

9. Store Carbon
Carbon sequestration is conceptually and theoretically simple but challenging to implement at any meaningful scale. By building densely using bio-based building assemblies wherever possible in order to meet the rapidly rising demand for building and infrastructure of our rapidly growing and urbanizing global population, we begin to garner the natural photosynthetic properties of plants, utilizing the vast "material manufacturing" power of global forests and other forms of biomass, and finally taking advantage of what was once considered too low a density energy form to be exploited for industry: sunlight.

Carbon storage in dense urban aggregations of mid-rise building serves as a force multiplier in carbon mitigation: incentivizing both forest restoration and afforestation, creating new forest growth that absorbs more atmospheric, avoiding through bio-genic substitution for steel and concrete, and storing carbon in a building landscape that will be built anyway. Of course, this strategy will demand rapid transition in building economies accompanied by robust silvicultural and sustainable forestry management to ensure that we don't simply treat forests as we did geological substrata, with extractive disregard for the impacts we create.

10. Decouple
We'll address our final guiding principle, decoupling, as an economic concept in the final chapter of this book. We've used the term in Chapter 1 to refer at the global scale to the disentanglement of the growth and urbanization

of world populations from the consumption of our planet's finite resources and the corresponding emission and accumulation of anthropogenic waste in its oceans, soils, and air. But at the more granular scale of the design process, within the realm of the immediate and effective agency of the building designer, decoupling refers to our disabusing ourselves of the assumption that there is an inherent and inextricable relationship between excessive material and energy consumption and architectural value, i.e., beauty, utility, and durability. This may be the most effective reversal of contemporary practice that we can undertake as building designers: to make excellent buildings that meet the growing needs of individuals, communities, and global populations, while protecting the vanishing resources and increasingly vulnerable ecosystems that make our planet habitable.

UNDERSTANDING DESIGN AGENCY: SHIFTING ROLES AND RESPONSIBILITIES

Across this geographically and temporally sprawling system of consumption and impact associated with the building life cycle, we can see that the responsibility for the management of carbon flows and greenhouse gas emissions fall to a cross-section of human institutions and sectors of political, economic, and social activity. Although much of that responsibility falls outside of the design process proper, it is clear that the building designer has varying degrees of agency in minimizing the harmful impacts by (and then, recursively, back onto) the building sector. In fact, a core concept of life cycle thinking is not only its description and assessment, but ultimately a determination of the varying roles of participants and their specific agency in reducing impacts throughout that life cycle.

In a sense, the acknowledgment of design agency and the assignment of responsibility for mitigating carbon impacts in the building life cycle are a process akin to one studied in Chapter 2: the establishment of useful and effective system boundaries in life cycle assessment. In order to set useful boundaries for such an analysis, it is critical to understand the broad, systemic inputs and outputs (in this case, one of global carbon storage and emission) and their sensitivity to different forces, factors, and influences.

The design process and, more specifically, the agency of the designer should be understood in similar conceptual terms: as part of a larger system in which the roles played by different nested institutions of governance, industry, commerce, and professional practice standards exert lesser or greater degrees of influence on the conduct of the building life cycle and its ultimate impact on the environment. In that context, the building designer's agency might be thought to fall into certain realms of influence with varying degrees of agency: as a citizen, with a political voice in shaping policies that promote environmental protection; as a consumer, with notable leverage in specifying products and processes with the least impact and engaging industries committed to providing transparent information about those products; as a decision-maker, with responsibility for steering the complex processes of building design and construction and anticipating and accommodating a building's lifespan of operation, maintenance, and ultimately removal, reuse or disposal, long after the conventional design process has come to an end.

While it is without question the case that forces beyond the purview and direct control of the designer and construction process will inevitably contribute to the building carbon footprint of the building life cycle, it is also true that the design team will make the bulk of decisions that will either exacerbate or mitigate a building's carbon emissions. By providing the project team— from client to building crew—with the right information at critical junctures in the design and construction process, the building designer can create a comprehensive strategy for controlling—and more importantly, reducing—the flows of carbon through the built environment.

Therein lies the unique role and pivotal position of the building designer. Ultimately, whatever the preconditions of a design, and no matter how unpredictable the future of any building, it falls to the design team to identify and execute a strategy for the organization of material and energy resources as they shepherd a client's initial vision from nascent idea to fully resolved building, setting clear carbon benchmarks throughout the design and construction project against which any design decision can be evaluated. An overall design and construction strategy for limiting the carbon impacts throughout the building life cycle, supported by well-informed decisions throughout the design and construction process, give the design and construction team unique agency and influence.

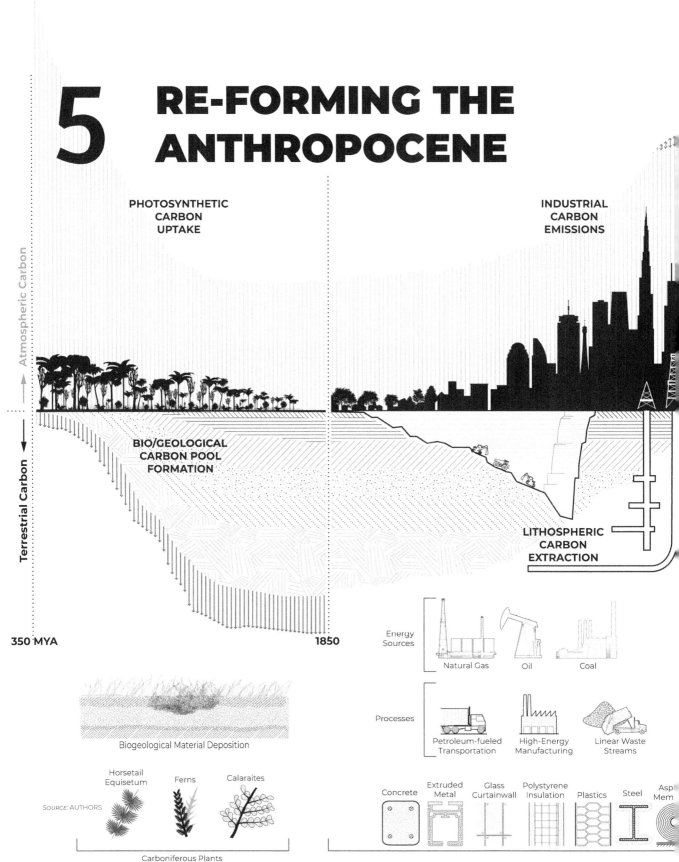

5 RE-FORMING THE ANTHROPOCENE

PHOTOSYNTHETIC CARBON UPTAKE

INDUSTRIAL CARBON EMISSIONS

Atmospheric Carbon

Terrestrial Carbon

BIO/GEOLOGICAL CARBON POOL FORMATION

LITHOSPHERIC CARBON EXTRACTION

350 MYA

1850

Biogeological Material Deposition

Horsetail Equisetum

Ferns

Calaraites

SOURCE: AUTHORS

Carboniferous Plants

Energy Sources

Natural Gas

Oil

Coal

Processes

Petroleum-fueled Transportation

High-Energy Manufacturing

Linear Waste Streams

Concrete

Extruded Metal

Glass Curtainwall

Polystyrene Insulation

Plastics

Steel

Asp Mem

Extractive Mineral-based Materials

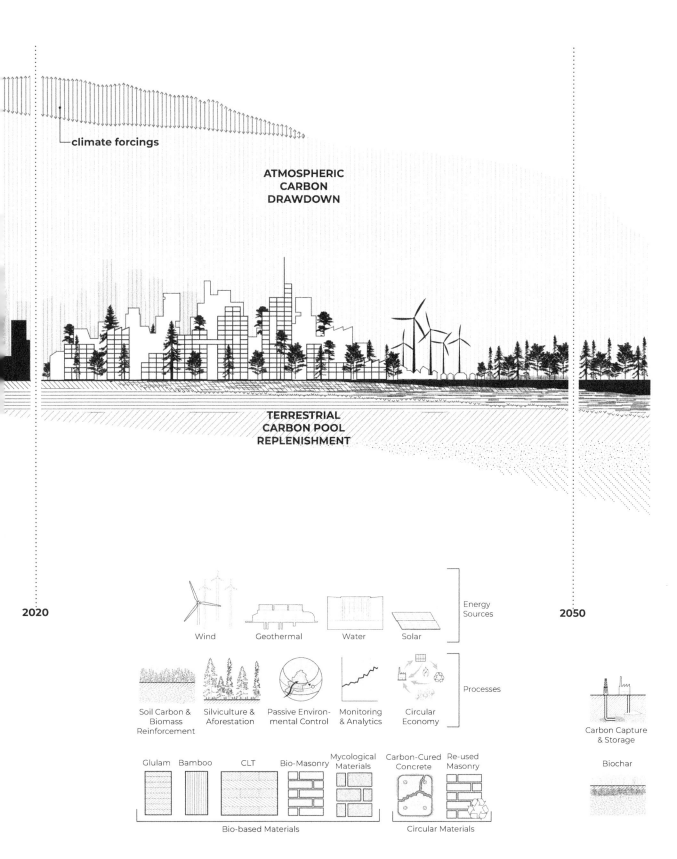

climate forcings

**ATMOSPHERIC
CARBON
DRAWDOWN**

**TERRESTRIAL
CARBON POOL
REPLENISHMENT**

2020

2050

Wind   Geothermal   Water   Solar

Energy
Sources

Soil Carbon &
Biomass
Reinforcement

Silviculture &
Aforestation

Passive Environ-
mental Control

Monitoring
& Analytics

Circular
Economy

Processes

Carbon Capture
& Storage

Glulam   Bamboo   CLT   Bio-Masonry   Mycological
Materials

Carbon-Cured
Concrete

Re-used
Masonry

Bio-based Materials

Circular Materials

Biochar

CHAPTER FIVE
RE-FORMING THE ANTHROPOCENE

BEYOND SUSTAINABLE

Making More than Measurements
Over billions of years, through steady accretion and occasional upheaval and involution, the crust of our planet has developed into a lithospheric repository. It has recorded its geological, biological, and climatic history and archived it in legible strata of rock, soil, fossilized plant matter, and dust. That lithospheric repository is now changing. A new layer of human activity is being added to the planetary record. We might say that humanity itself has become a geologic force.

Our planet's biological, chemical, and physical systems have begun to shift under the burden that our industrial and commercial activities have heaped on them. As our atmosphere continues to carbonize and we seek with increasing urgency to understand our role in creating those impacts and our agency in mitigating them, we face, as architects, engineers, and builders, fundamental—perhaps existential—questions about the nature and objectives of our work. The overarching question—what would a decarbonized building actually look and feel like?—might be distilled into a more targeted set of questions worthy of our consideration throughout the building conception, design, and construction process.

How would we design a building that captures and stores more carbon than it emits?

Where would its materials come from?

Through what methods would they be processed?

How would these materials be assembled in response to the constituent demands of a building—providing shelter from weather; insulating from excessive cold or heat; buffering swings in humidity; resisting the large mechanical forces as well as the small chemical reactions that will enable it to withstand the stress and deterioration caused by gravity, weather, and wear?

Where would we get the energy or even the water that we need to operate the building or, for that matter, to process its material and manufacture the components of its system?

And when the building becomes obsolete and no longer feasible to use, how will we dispose of it?

Where will all its materials ultimately go?

These are questions that are at once prosaic and profound. As we've seen, they carry with them broad political, economic, social, and environmental implications. They also entail decisions we make every day in the design studio and the building site. In so deeply permeating every process entailed in the formation of the built environment, we can expect that there will be costs. But none of those costs will be as great as the price we—and our children—will ultimately be forced to pay for our own inaction.

FIGURE 5.1
Source: DANIEL OLAH / UNSPLASH

THINKING OUTSIDE THE BUILDING'S LIFE CYCLE

From Problems to Solutions

In this book we've described our current carbon problem, presented a methodology for quantifying the flow of carbon in the built environment, exemplified these flows through two building case studies, and suggested design strategies that aim to reduce carbon emissions from buildings to the lowest levels possible. The topics are interdependent, offering different lenses through which to view the same issue: the potential decarbonization of building and buildings. Life cycle assessment, for example, has little meaning as a purely analytical exercise that lacks a systemic overview of the challenges we face, especially if we're unable to draw from it critical lessons with the power to inflect our future decisions. In the same way, a design process, no matter how putatively principled and carbon-conscious its motivations, may produce negligible benefits without quantification and verification.

The life cycle approach to building design that we've outlined in this book is really only the starting point for an accountable architecture, a mode of building design and construction that quantifies its potential impacts for the purpose of reducing destructiveness and waste. Our ambitions for the building can be greater than record-keeping and thriftiness. We can aim higher, for a regenerative architecture of the built environment, expanding the scope of our disciplinary concerns to include measures that may restore, strengthen, and work in synergy with the terrestrial, marine, and atmospheric systems from which we benefit.

Life cycle thinking helps to frame the consequences of our design choices within the system boundary and temporal scale of a building. This physical scope and timeframe are inextricably linked to the human activities associated with the built environment: a building's construction, inhabitation, maintenance, and ultimate demolition. Each of these stages commands specific flows of energy and materials that are part of a much larger, eternal flow of energy and materials. Humanity's brief marshalling of these flows into and out of the built environment merely modifies their inevitable march toward entropy, momentarily redirecting the flow of energy and materials from their natural paths. When borrowing these planetary flows for our use, we should be sure to rebalance them once we've met our temporary needs for shelter and comfort.

Through science, technology and, mostly, by dint of the sheer magnitude and weight of our physical presence, humanity has become a force capable of leaving permanent geological traces on our planet. At the moment, these traces are mostly deleterious: plastics that saturate our oceans, emissions that foul our atmosphere, chemicals and radiation that damage the DNA of living organisms.

This is the Anthropocene. Since the disturbance to the Earth's equilibrium is by our hand, it's fair to say that it's also our responsibility to at least attempt to restore the planet's physical and chemical balance, to reform the *way* we build as well as the buildings themselves. If our activities have the capacity to irrevocably alter the planet, would it be possible, through the same technological ingenuity that created the problems we face, that we might *benefit* the global environment? And what would be the shape and magnitude of the change required—to our modes of thought as well as to the value chains of the construction sector and the political economic systems that frame them—in order for this to take place?

Making Our Building Economy Circular

The circular economy is an industrial system that is restorative or regenerative by intention and design [1], a system that acknowledges the embedded impacts of industrial material extraction, product manufacture, and waste generation and so seeks to maximize the durability of products, materials, and services through multiple life cycles of use. By reintroducing what we've historically considered as waste back into the manufacturing process as a material resource, we effectively reduce our impact at both the cradle and the grave of the product life cycle, amortizing those environmental costs through greater utility and thereby increasing the value of the products we make. The circular economy's inherent principles promote the design of a consumer product not just as an object or system, but as an entire product life cycle with potential future useful life cycles, to maximize those life cycles, to facilitate the future reuse or recycling of materials as products reach the end of their service life and to reapply them across diverse industries and value chains [2].

Recent research has shown that the extensive reuse (and to a less effective degree, recycling) of construction materials will produce significant reductions in emissions in the building sector. In several case studies, emissions reductions at the product level exceeded 50% and, in rarer cases reached 90% [3]. (We've recognized the same potential in the case studies in Chapter 3.)

Although industrial processing emissions would remain, in a theoretically perfect circular economy, the concept of material waste disappears, along with its detrimental environmental effects. Although such an entirely hermetic metabolic system may be practically impossible to achieve, it's helpful to understand its primary cycles of material flow—one, a technical cycle comprised of circulating industrial material, initially extracted from finite sources; the other a biological and renewable cycle that incentivizes the regeneration of the Earth's ecosystems—and to imagine how and where they might intersect to produce all the material we need for building. Such an economy would future-proof building against landfill and fuel cycles of successive material reuse until some future point at which the material residues that remain can be introduced safely, without detriment, back into the Earth's soils, waters, and atmosphere.

What if instead of thinking of a building as the mere assembly of products and materials, we understood it as a vessel for material investment—a material and product bank, with initial deposits and, ultimately, withdrawals?

How might we strategize over the long term, to plan to reinvest those resources we withdraw to make our building in some other future building or product?

And how might that anticipation of the cyclical reinvestment of material inflect our design decisions?

What would be the arc of the entire construction process and what would be the shape and materiality of our buildings?

We've discussed the principles of design for disassembly earlier in this book, but if we were to actively promote the reuse of building material at the end of a building's life cycle, rather than simply facilitate its dismantling, how would we break the links of contemporary supply chains and re-forge them into new loops of use and reuse? As we slide toward climate catastrophe (and the possible collapse of modern society as we know it), the critical objective of closing those loops of the building sector as tightly as possible represents at once a monumental task and a game-changing opportunity. But it starts with a building, conceived and developed as an accelerator of circular material flows. The benefits that follow from such an approach—reductions in consumption and waste and the elimination of their share of impacts to land, water, and air—serve as a kind of environmental force multiplier to the benefit of human health and well-being that building already aims to offer.

Neutralizing Anthropogenic Carbon

A global balance between the material and energy we consume and the greenhouse gases we emit means that our carbon emissions can never exceed the capacity of biological, geological, or technological carbon sinks to absorb and store them. This will inevitably entail a system-wide shift in policy, industrial process, commercial transaction, and human behavior across all sectors of our economy and society. In acknowledgment of these systemic implications, a number of countries, regions, and cities have adopted the goal of carbon neutrality. We might set this same target for the building sector and, by extension, the buildings we design. The World Green Building Council, in collaboration with several leading large construction companies, and city and national governments, promotes economic mechanisms and construction methods that will achieve carbon neutrality in the building sector by 2050. For our existing building stock, this "Net Zero Carbon Commitment" [4] will require significant increases in energy efficiency along with the decarbonization of our energy system. For new buildings which we will inevitably need

CARBON FLOWS
IN SOURCES OF PRIMARY ENERGY

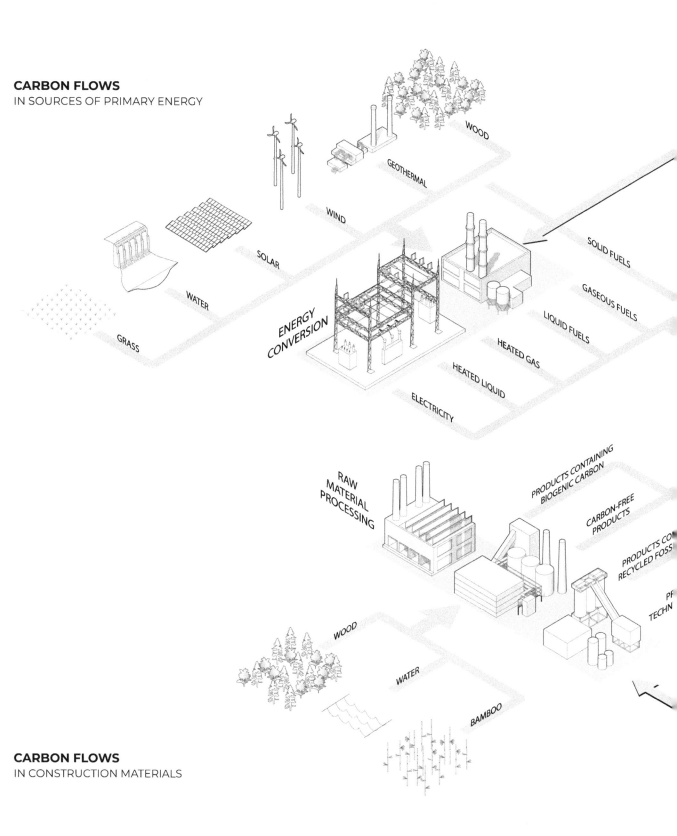

WOOD

GEOTHERMAL

WIND

SOLAR

WATER

GRASS

ENERGY CONVERSION

SOLID FUELS

GASEOUS FUELS

LIQUID FUELS

HEATED GAS

HEATED LIQUID

ELECTRICITY

RAW MATERIAL PROCESSING

PRODUCTS CONTAINING BIOGENIC CARBON

CARBON-FREE PRODUCTS

PRODUCTS CO RECYCLED FOSS

PF TECHN

WOOD

WATER

BAMBOO

CARBON FLOWS
IN CONSTRUCTION MATERIALS

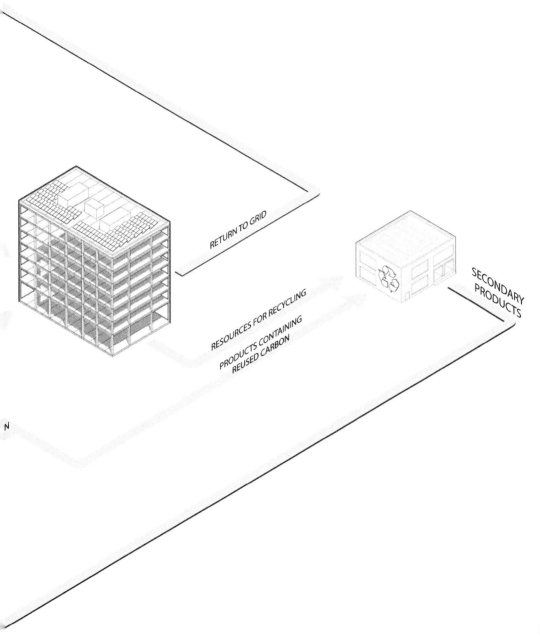

RETURN TO GRID

RESOURCES FOR RECYCLING

PRODUCTS CONTAINING
REUSED CARBON

SECONDARY
PRODUCTS

N

CARBON FLOWS
IN WASTE STREAMS

FIGURE 5.2 CIRCULAR
CARBON FLOWS IN THE BUILT
ENVIRONMENT.
SOURCE: AUTHORS

to meet the demands of a growing and urbanizing global population, we'll need to address emissions throughout the building life cycle, both embodied and operational.

Within the system bounded by all activities and material and energy transactions that occur over the life of our building, we would begin, in concert with our clients and our design team, by addressing the fundamental efficacy of each building we propose. We would carefully examine the building's *premise*, considering whether its synthesis of location, site, and program makes the goal of decarbonization possible. At the outset, we would seek to adjust each of those preconditions to the utmost degree possible in order to optimize the building's life cycle (and even successive cycles of material and land-use) that we will initiate through our work.

We would also assess our project's *sufficiency*. How much space, material, energy, and land do we really need to achieve our goals? What alternative scenarios might we consider that would have the benefit of reducing our demands on resources?

Finally, as our work gets underway, we would target every possible means of creating material and energy *efficiency* through the rigor of our design process and the selection and specification of materials whose producers also seek impact reduction. That effort to find efficiencies would reach far into the future, minimizing the necessary inputs of energy and material during the building's use stage and, further, anticipating and detailing the building's assemblies for all the possible ways in which its constituent materials and systems might be dismantled and redeployed for reuse or recycling.

"First Do No Harm" and Then . . .

If we're to successfully neutralize our carbon emissions across all sectors of human activity as well as in the individual buildings we design, then it's not enough to zero-out the accounting of our individual building's life cycle emissions. We might also find ways to offset the emissions from other sectors that will inevitably struggle to reduce their own. The concept of emissions offsets, fundamental

to any carbon cap and trade scheme, provides a significant opportunity for building designers and owners alike who manage a relatively significant share of material and energy and whose ongoing and outsized demand has the capacity to shape their sources and means of supply. For a building design and ownership team working under a regime of carbon neutrality, the trade of offsets cuts both ways. Obviously, if we're unable to reduce our own emissions, then we would seek to compensate for them by purchasing offsets from those entities whose activities or holdings demonstrably reduce emissions, such as the renewable energy industry or forest landowners. On the other hand, we can potentially offer offsets if we're able to engage our buildings as active instruments of decarbonization—for example, producing so much on-site energy that we're able to compensate for not only our own but others' energy consumption, or by storing such significant amounts of carbon in our site or building assemblies. This may offer financial as well as environmental benefit. Markets for carbon compensations are gaining a foothold in various economies and various mechanisms for carbon accounting and monetization are gaining in both refinement and comprehensiveness, making it easier for us to compare them. Buildings or aggregations of buildings districts, neighborhoods, cities themselves––may begin to exploit the carbon efficacy of their own constructed environments to compensate for, and thereby be compensated by, others.

Carbon Uptake for Carbon Drawdown

Current estimates suggest that in order to photosynthetically re-absorb the excess carbon that humanity currently emits, the planet would need an additional forest area of just under a billion hectares, a scale of afforestation that would entail an area nearly the size of Europe. At odds with the hope of such an undertaking are the countervailing forces of forest land conversion—urban and suburban expansion to house a growing population, agricultural expansion to feed it, resource-extractive and land-destructive practices of the mining and logging industries that serve all of it, and climate change itself, have served instead to reduce forests in health and reach, and weakened them as carbon sinks. In fact, cities and city building present an ongoing existential threat to the world's natural land-based carbon sinks.

What if, instead of that antagonistic relationship, cities worked synergistically with sustainably managed forests to amplify the forest's capacity to store carbon and thereby incentivize the investment in forest restoration, expansion, and general health? In Chapter 4, we discussed both existing and emerging means to sequester and store more carbon in the built environment. Through the protection of existing plants and soils on our building sites and the planting of new biomass, we promote the capacity of once-disturbed landscapes to absorb carbon storing biomass on our building sites. The carbonation of cements, part of the natural aging process of the exposed surfaces of concrete and mortar joints, will play an additional role as an agent of carbon sequestration. The use of plants, such as trees and other biofibers as building material—chemically half carbon by weight––represents the most significant medium of carbon storage. A five-storey building whose primary structure is comprised of engineered timber has the capacity to store more carbon than the above- and below-ground woody matter in an area of temperate rainforest the same size as that building's footprint [5].

This does not reflect the dynamic richness and all the associated benefits of the forest biome as a carbon sink, one far superior in comparison to the more static means of carbon storage we might achieve in building structures. Nor should this simplified comparison suggest a zero-sum game in which we trade one for the other. But we are implying a synergistic system and synchronized cycle of forest growth and mortality and building material demand. Put in metaphorical terms, what if we were to *grow* cities, using *photosynthesis* instead of fossil hydrocarbon combustion or even photovoltaic energy, as an energy system for the manufacture of building material? Managed properly, this relatively fast cycle of material formation would mean that the constituent layers of our building assemblies were largely biological instead of geological or geochemical in origin, a by-product of the carbon

cycle rather than a disturbance to it. As we continue to make demands on our planet's natural resources, it becomes inevitable that we also seek to densify the carbon sequestration and storage potential of all the environments that we manage. The built environment, rather than acting as a source of greenhouse gas emissions, may begin to be understood as a tool to mitigate them, with cities serving the circular economy as material banks and the overloaded carbon cycle as a carbon bank.

A recent study has suggested that the rapid adoption of bio-based building in concert with regenerative forestry practices has the capacity to store and avoid emissions of other material classes in quantities amounting to billions of tons of carbon removed from the atmosphere [5]. Among the many invaluable ecosystem services provided by global forests—oxygen production, water filtration, vapor transpiration, bio-diverse animal and plant habitat, foods—the growth of structural biomass may be the most pertinent to the building sector within the temporal context of rapid climate change and a rapidly closing window for climate action. As the availability of global carbon offsets become more constrained—and costly—the production and enhancement of the built environment as large, dense, and human-made carbon sinks become increasingly important.

If building for a rapidly growing global population is inevitable and therefore effectively a "sunk" material and energy cost, why wouldn't we attempt to make those materials do more than simply resist gravity and weather? The instrumentality of building as an environmentally beneficial force rather than a source of deleterious impact is perhaps the most ambitious but promising carbon mitigation tool we can apply to the problem of rapid climate change and environmental degradation.

Making a Carbon Handprint

A footprint is a metaphor that describes the environmental load we place on the planet with each industrial process we initiate. Although we've broached the topic of environmental impact generally and in its many forms, the focus of this book has been our carbon footprint and its dire implications for our atmospheric equilibrium and our rapidly changing climate. Depending on the breadth of our knowledge, the depth of our consideration, and the degree to which we bring these concerns to bear on the design process, our footprint may be large or small. But it remains a footprint, something we leave behind that will irrevocably alter, if only to a small extent, the future livability of the planet.

Although it may be impossible to build in a manner that leaves no negative environmental or social footprints, a potentially enormous opportunity beckons for designers and producers of the built environment. What if we could ameliorate ecological or social disturbance and restore and strengthen functioning ecosystems through the management of our material and energy demands? Our carbon *handprint* is another metaphor, one we use to describe such benefits that would not occur naturally without our intervention. What if, instead of simply accounting for and reducing our emissions, we sought every possible opportunity by which our design decisions might actively heal environmental affliction? In terms of carbon impacts, this would suggest that in addition to designing physical artifacts such as buildings and cities, we also design the flow of carbon through them.

Carbon handprinting has proven in a number of commercial sectors to be an effective means of acknowledging our impacts and seeking to counteract them [6]. It has offered companies and institutions a sense of agency and empowerment within the framework of climate action, encouraging them to improve their environmental performance. It has also offered funders and investors a mechanism for financing a sustainable growth. Where it fails to yield measurable benefit and more specifically, a radical reduction in the consumption of finite resources and the generation of waste, then it will fall short as a guiding principle.

Regenerative Building

As an extension of the carbon handprint metaphor, we propose a proactive and *regenerative* approach to building. As we noted in the introduction of this book, building designers (along with all those who work along the building supply chain) are both makers and consumers. We produce large and materially intensive artifacts that ideally serve the needs of individuals and the smooth functioning of our society and economy. In doing so, we become professional resource consumers, drawing on and managing material and energy supplies at a rate and with an intensity that dwarf our habits of consumption as individuals going about our private lives. This is our source of opportunity as well as responsibility. Our knowledge of and interaction with these complex systems give us a special agency to think strategically, with environmental benevolence rather than negligence. How far we're able, as individual practitioners and as a collective discipline, to project good intentions into meaningful actions remains an unanswered question but represents a critical goal.

Throughout this and previous chapters, we've noted examples of what we might describe as regenerative building, design strategies that engage broader ecological, material, and thermodynamic systems than those bounded by the activities, exchanges of raw material and waste, and the resulting performance of a single building life cycle. A building that produces more renewable electricity on-site than it uses can then share its surplus with other buildings, thereby lowering the overall demands for electricity from the grid. A building that incorporates reused building parts or industrial residues that would otherwise have been processed as waste avoids associated emissions and land impacts. A building site plan that incorporates, expands, and deepens existing plant biomass may extend the resulting ecosystem services to its neighbors. A building waste and water management system that reabsorbs and processes its effluent and waste on site inevitably reduces loads on overburdened infrastructure and landscapes, and, if properly designed, may serve to build healthy soil, improve hydrologic function, and strengthen site biomes. A building that stores as much carbon as possible in the materials that make up its assemblies plays a role in rebalancing the carbon cycle. With proper planning and detailing, a building's carbon-laden materials can be redeployed in new durable products or buildings at the end of its life, avoiding the loss of those carbon stores to aerobic decay and emission in a landfill.

In an economic sense, a regenerative approach to building would remap supply chains into supply circuits, in which building waste forms the energy and material feedstocks of industry. Ecologically speaking, such an approach to design and construction would entail their conceptual and material integration into a regional metabolism, in which flows of waste never overwhelm the Earth's physical, biological, and chemical systems or our own species' activities to absorb them. Instead of relying on the most highly industrially refined and uniform materials, building design would be an agile process that optimizes material resources that are readily available.

A regenerative approach to architectural design and building construction represents our willingness as a discipline to catalyze and hasten through our decisions and decision-making power what might otherwise take place as a slow but inevitable evolution of industries faced with increasing resource scarcity, a lack of raw material and the land area on which to dump its waste.

As discussed in preceding chapters, our design and building techniques will need to acknowledge, quantify, and then reduce environmental impacts across the building life cycle first. But we also need to actively promote metabolic, non-mechanistic approaches to the production of the built environment. By engaging renewable material supply chains and energy systems, by tapping industrial waste streams as sources of raw material, by detailing building assemblies for durability, reparability and, ultimately, ease of disassembly, regenerative techniques in building would attempt to avoid the conventions of our current linear, extractive systems of resource consumption and the extensive, often unseen ecological impacts created by the building sector. By engaging ecological processes as a natural cyclical system of growth and mortality, we reintegrate our building process as well as our buildings into a potentially homeostatic global balance. By gaming the climatic forces of our building sites—temperature, humidity, air flow, and pressure—through the manipulation of building form, the configuration of interior pace and aperture, and the deployment of materials that line architectural surfaces, we perform a kind

of thermo- and hydro-dynamic ju-jitsu, flipping climate forces into energy to operate our buildings. In its essence, regenerative building design embraces the constraints, conditions, processes, and impacts that we have to this point been allowed to ignore as economic and environmental externalities.

RE-FORMING THE ANTHROPOCENE

What does this carbon outlook and the responsibilities it entails actually mean for building designers? How will we effect such a necessarily rapid yet fundamental transition from an increasingly outmoded and linear building economy to a decarbonized and more ecologically integrated one? What realignments of the policy, planning, design, property development and construction professions will such a shift require? The methods we employ and the objectives we set for the work ahead will be underpinned by the quantitative techniques, economic theories, political strategies, and societal and environmental aspirations that we've named and briefly described in this book and chapter. Life cycle thinking, carbon neutrality and (potentially) positivity, carbon handprinting, circular economic and regenerative building will all expand and intersect as concepts and methods as the next turbulent decades unfold. All share similar goals, although their focus, their systems of analysis, and their evaluative criteria may differ. They provide a kind of conceptual kit of parts for a new framework for action in the building sector that will allow us to withstand and overcome the dire challenges we face.

We have argued that to be effective agents of environmental stabilization and restoration, we need to start by rebalancing our atmosphere. We must *instrumentalize* building as a tool to *mitigate* climate change rather than deploying it simply as a means to adapt to it. This would represent a paradigmatic shift for our discipline and profession, its ambitions, modes of thought, systems of education, configurations of practice and process, and all the intensive industrial processes it puts into motion. Although there's no way of knowing how well our global efforts to halt climate change and fairly balance our finite resources will succeed, the buildings we make (or remake) now will see at least decades, if not centuries, that their designers will not.

Building design—the conception, visualization, and production of the built environment—is a disciplinary activity which operates at and around the center of the global environmental disturbance that has become the most significant planetary marker of our species. That's not to say that building designers and producers have been the primary motive force in each of the incremental conceptual shifts that have culminated in our current modes of industrial and commercial activity. But by intention or neglect, architects, engineers, and builders, have sat at the right hand of those drivers of environmental change and through our work have facilitated the enormous transactions of material and energy that have given physical shape and shelter to the habits of extraction and consumption in the global marketplace.

So, we have a special opportunity and responsibility to chart the course of this next stage of building in the Anthropocene. Based on our experience as architects, researchers, teachers, and policy-makers, we've come to the conclusion that building designers need a new set of priorities: the urgent *decoupling* of building's functional and aesthetic quality and value from its environmental impacts, the radical *simplification* of buildings and the materials, means, and methods we use to build and operate them in order to align their complexity with our ability to manage them and their flows of carbon; and perhaps most important, a systemic and carbon-conscious approach to design, which is to say, *a new role for architecture and architects*.

Decoupling

We need to decouple what we deem to be quality in the built environment from its environmental impact. Decoupling is a term usually referred to in resource efficiency and circular economics. In economic terms, it refers to the separation of gross domestic product (GDP) growth from resource consumption.

Decoupling can be either relative (in which case, resource use grows slower than GDP) or absolute (in which case, resource use decreases while GDP increases). We also suggested at the outset of this book that we must decouple inevitable population growth and the associated rise in the consumption of resources from its current level of environmental impact. We must do so also with the languages, technical systems, and cultural expectations of our architecture.

In architecture, however, decoupling might best be defined as minimizing the correlation of architectural quality—functionality; stability and durability; beauty (or its equivalent cultural value)—to its resulting environmental impact. In current building design and construction practice, we often fail to acknowledge our assumptions of infinite resource availability and its relationship to what we consider to be the necessary attributes of a building. Although as architects, engineers, and builders, we're trained to prioritize form and function, we now have an urgent responsibility to decouple those goals from the potential increase in material consumption and waste that they may incur.

There are two degrees of decoupling we should consider with respect to building: relative and absolute. *Relative decoupling* has been our basic approach to sustainability thus far. It seeks to reduce the ecological intensity of our buildings in comparison to other buildings or alternative methods of developing our building in comparison to alternatives, measured within the same system boundary. This has generated some improvement, or in the case of carbon emissions, impact reduction as value of buildings has increased.

Absolute decoupling seeks to zero out impacts associated with a building's life cycle and, where our buildings actually store more carbon than they emit, compensate for the failure by other buildings and sectors to neutralize their emissions. In this case, the value of buildings can increase while their emissions diminish.

For building, the relative decoupling of architectural quality from its demands and ecological impacts will certainly improve its environmental performance and offers a fair characterization of our approach to building sustainability. While improvement is better than business as usual, it won't meet the challenges we created for our planet.

Climate scientist Johan Rockström and his colleagues have proposed a pathway for "rapid decarbonization" [7]. They've pointed out the "alarming inconsistencies between science-based targets and national commitments." They suggest that global greenhouse gas emissions should be halved every decade and carbon neutrality achieved by 2050 in order to avoid the deepest economic and environmental costs and political and social turmoil caused by the planet's warming.

As our case studies have shown, even energy and materially efficient buildings, when we measure the entirety of their impacts from cradle to grave, still fall short of true carbon neutrality. If our planet is to be carbon-neutral by this century's midpoint, we'll need to halve the life cycle emissions of our buildings every decade. What would a building that emitted half the carbon of the case study buildings look like? And then if we were to halve those buildings emissions again? And again?

As a starting point, let's reflect on buildings like the ones in the case studies of Chapter 3: ecologically well-intended, their impacts comprehensively examined. Now imagine that a building designed 10 years from now would need to be built with materials that have an embodied carbon footprint that's half the size of the case study buildings, and with its energy-related emissions halved as well. The challenge seems daunting for even a small freestanding building on a site with ready access to natural material resources and abundant solar exposure. However, if we broaden our view to the entire taxonomic landscape of building types and occupancies for both existing and new buildings and for physical infrastructure, then we have an acutely clearer picture of what we need to undertake as a discipline. To put the previous question more

broadly: what would the absolute decoupling of a building's quality and performance actually mean for the building design process, the construction sector, and moreover, society's expectations of its built environment?

If we cannot lower emissions from the construction sector according to the "rapid decarbonization" plan, two theoretical options remain. In one scenario, another industrial sector will push its emissions so far below zero that it compensates for the shortcomings of the construction sector. Given recent progress, or the notable lack of it, this prospect seems unlikely. The remaining option would be for the construction sector to launch a massive, sectoral cap and trade system, with carbon-positive building material producers, energy suppliers, and building managers neutralizing the emissions that cannot be avoided. Such a concerted effort would inevitably and necessarily up-end the conventional transactional relationships between designers and product suppliers and between architects, clients, and building contractors. Building sector carbon neutrality so achieved is theoretically possible, but it would lean heavily on both natural and anthropogenic carbon sinks. Natural sinks, such as soils and forests, are under a continuous, significant stress due to growing global population and consequent land-use changes. Anthropogenic solutions, such as carbon capture and storage, are still expensive and unproven at scale.

If absolute decoupling, despite its profound challenges, is the conceptual regime by which we decarbonize our work and contribute to keeping our planet livable, then building designers will need to reflect on their potential role as ecological *de-couplers*.

Simplification
We need to simplify the processes and end-products of construction across all scales.

As building designers, we are consumers of material and energy by proxy, orchestrating on behalf of future users a complex sequence of industrial processes with geographic dimension extending far beyond the boundaries of our buildings and sites. We should seek to retract the reach of our demands or minimize the steps entailed in producing the buildings we design. We need to be able to actually "see"—which is to say, measure and manage—each of their procedural inputs and outputs.

Our work has temporal implications that touch individuals and communities far into the future. We need to simplify our products and systems to at least a level at which the users, builders, design practitioners can manage them in the future. It's important to understand that many of the raw materials of today's building products, machines or their fuels, lubricants, and coolants, may no longer be available in the future—not at least affordably. Therefore, future-proofing the buildings that we design today is much easier, if we can keep them simple.

Rarely do we understand the provenance of a product we specify beyond the location of the end-suppliers from whom a builder ultimately purchases it. Few practitioners have the time or the patience to trace the myriad individual steps in the process of making a product they specify, or the resources and information to map the distances covered to bring those products to our buildings (and then take them away again at the end of their service lives). This is not a concern purely about distances covered or the number of steps entailed in moving a raw material from source to site (although an honest accounting of both would stand in as a pretty good indicator of impact). Instead, we should manage through our decision-making process, the means and modes of transport and material handling, the routes traveled, and topographies traversed. Were each manufacturer's environmental product declaration to include a cradle-to-gate map of their product's journey to the construction site or a manufacturing diagram of the specific sequence in the processing of the product, the tools, machines, or equipment used to fashion raw material into a building component, we would have a better (and perhaps more visceral) view of environmental impact than what might be provided by a pie chart, bar graph or table. These provide valuable information while

serving as mediating devices that soften the impact. Like the geographic and temporal immediacy of the "farm-to-table" model of food consumption, we might consider—as one architect pithily put it—a "forest-to-frame" mentality in the way we consume building material.

We don't need to *imagine* how difficult it will be to dismantle today's buildings at some point in the future because we recognize from our experience with the ways we build them their inherent and often irreversible complexity. The inextricably laminated, interwoven, materially composite nature of their make-up arises in large part in how they are made. We reflexively reach for those building products that irreversibly bind paper to gypsum, weave plastic and copper wire and complex forms of sheet metal ducting through the cavities of walls and floors, mix metals to produce alloys with highly specific performance characteristics, glue plastic to wood fiber substrates and cut them into an array of irregular shapes and often nail, glue, or caulk them into underlying structural assemblies.

As noted in Chapter 4, the products that we use for construction originate from a variety of raw materials, combined in chemical and mechanical compounds that are durable but, in practice, often impossible to dismantle. In many cases, despite the emergence of product and environmental impact data that are slowly becoming prerequisites to market entry, it's often surprisingly hard to find out exactly which chemicals or additives have been used in a building product. There are well over 100,000 chemicals on the market (of which only a small fraction have been adequately tested for health and environmental impacts [8]), and we lack a real understanding of their influence on the quality of the indoor air we breathe or the impact of their toxicity on ecological systems or the fluidity of their circulation through the atmosphere, soils, and water once they've been discarded during building repair or demolition. Limiting our building's material ingredients to only those whose provenance and future impacts we can account for while minimizing the complexity of our building assemblies will better assure that we've minimized their future impacts, creating cost-savings during their repair and facilitating their separation and reuse at the end of their initial life cycle.

This will serve to promote a potentially circular economy. Just as a significant barrier to the recycling of household waste plastics or metals has been their cross-contamination, building products of a materially composite nature or structural configurations that are by design irreversible increase the likelihood that material or chemical streams will be mixed up during demolitions, making their reuse or recycling less feasible and therefore more unlikely. We should make our buildings in such a way that their methodical disassembly, across their chemical, material, structural, and infrastructural scales, will make their recycling at some point in the future faster and more profitable.

As our weather changes due to the atmospheric turmoil caused by rising global temperatures, our building system responses to the changes will need to be agile and flexible to address new climatic stresses. Increased precipitation and moisture content have been noted to change the building physical performance of heavily insulated structures [9]. The diffusion of moisture through a structure changes in the interfaces of different layers of materials. Thus, decreasing the number of layers may reduce these changes and risks associated to them.

Building environmental systems and services are essential for a contemporary building and we don't mean to demonize those technologies that keep our buildings warm (or cool) and ambient moisture levels appropriately steady. We need though to acknowledge the ever-increasing complexity of building mechanical systems that take an increasing share of a building's financial and environmental budget. Even operationally efficient passive house construction—which should in theory be "passive" throughout its entire life cycle––has come to entail systemic intensity in the design of its assemblies and mechanical equipment. But it would also

only be fair to note that we should seek to reassess our own expectations of comfort, to accept less stringent tolerances for temperature ranges across a given room and swings over the course of the day which will allow us to simplify our design of our building's environmental services.

A critique of the complexity of contemporary building mechanical, plumbing, and electrical systems is probably the point at which we should state emphatically that we are not arguing for some kind of twenty-first-century Luddism, Romantic escapism, or dystopic paranoia about the accumulation of chemicals in our environment. Architects, engineers, and builders are often (and for good reason) avid technologists who try to understand the best of historical and contemporary material and manufacturing technology as a means to make their buildings feel and perform better. In arguing for simplification, we are calling for the implementation of more straightforward, transparent, and environmentally convivial technologies. We want to avoid the compounding complexity that serves only a brief and immediate moment in a building's lifespan. In order for them to operate effectively and to treat the environment kindly, we want our buildings to be responsive, not just to initial budgets and first users but to decades or even centuries of functionality, utility, and pleasure. Simplification will make our buildings less destructive and also more resilient.

It would be an oversight if we failed to acknowledge the many external economic, legal, and logistical forces and factors in professional design and building practice that reinforce our reflexive specification of available products and acceptance of systemic complexity in the make-up of our buildings. The value of ease, familiarity, and security are significant incentives in an inherently complex and challenging undertaking that the conception, technical elaboration, and construction of a building represent. Product uniformity, facilitated by ready-to-hand specifications and performance warranties are familiar to those who will estimate the costs and execute the details of the buildings we design, and makes our work easier. But through active design imagination and scrupulous assessment, we can counter the entropic tendency to allow our buildings to become systemically unwieldy and inflexible, not to mention ecologically detrimental.

We acknowledge that the existing complexity of even the simplest components of the contemporary construction economy serves as a strong disincentive to the prospect of so granular an analysis and so elemental a reform of our building culture and practice. But building designers work at a granular level, first conceptually and then physically to assemble buildings, brick by brick, panel by panel, screw by screw, to try to bring all of it into a well-functioning, durable, and culturally meaningful whole. We recognize this systemic complexity because of our intimate relationship to the objects we craft. This gives us the power and agency to craft the conceptual means and demand the material and technical methods of their simplification.

A New Role for Architecture

We need to take ourselves out of the cultural and economic margins of building production and redefine our roles and responsibilities that match the scope and depth of our agency. We call for a new and expanded role for architecture.

In acknowledging the sprawling impacts to our lives and to the planet that the activities of the building sector have created and continue to engender, we should also recognize the sector's unique capacity to make significant change, to work to re-equilibrate our atmospheric chemistry, to support and promote biodiversity, to absolve the Earth's surface of expanses of waste, to minimize the consumption of increasingly precious resources, and to offset the ongoing impacts by other sectors more resistant to reform. As a discipline committed to the conception, technical elaboration, and physical implementation of buildings and places intended to improve human experience and public well-being, building designers have both a special obligation and an enormous opportunity to heal our planet as well as shape a truly sustainable future for human settlement.

Although we've directed our approach and its recommendations to building designers in particular—architects, engineers, and students of those disciplines—we mean to invite a much broader range of actors who hold a stake and a share of responsibility for the way in which we build, to work to decarbonize our materials, means, and methods and, by extension, the buildings and infrastructure they form. Builders and building occupants; clients and real estate developers; local and regional planning, zoning, and building officials; regional or national policy-makers—those whose remit requires that they make decisions with the potential to inflect the way we conceive of, produce, and operate any part of the built environment—will all play a role in exacerbating or, alternatively, staunching the flows of carbon through the many building life cycles we will initiate in coming decades. If, by your decisions, you help to shape the way we procure and distribute energy, the means by which we transport goods or people, the methods manufacturers will use to process building materials and the sources their industrial supply chains draw upon, the ways in which we use or convert land and, in doing so, shift its ecological balance, then you, too, are inescapably the architects of our building future. This is not an *architecture* circumscribed by the narrow concerns of our current professional design discipline, but defined more broadly, one that seeks to assess and potentially reform the complex system of human settlement that is our species' mark on the planet.

In the face of rapidly increasing demand for global building construction, stringent dietary restriction alone won't prevent the ongoing geologic accretion of manufacturing residues and consumer waste, the chemical alteration of our water and air, and/or the incremental destruction of the planet's once-rich array of organisms. No matter how efficiently architects and engineers design the built environment, we still face the issue of numbers. The sheer number of human beings and those animals that we raise for our food represent 90% of all vertebrates [10]. According to projections, there may be 11 billion of us on this planet by the end of the century [11]. Who will decide how much energy we all can use? Who will set the limits for the raw material we consume as we build and live in our homes? And what sort of consumption patterns do the cities and buildings we design encourage or discourage? Facilitating a systemic transition to a carbon-neutral future will entail not just the careful assessment of the buildings we design, but what the built environment enables or disables for the rest of society and the broader global environment.

In spite of our past modes of thought and patterns of behavior, building designers face great opportunities as well as daunting challenges. New design approaches and building practices can systematically avoid the exploitation of increasingly critical resources and the destruction of source landscapes and habitats. We can track the flows of material and atmospheric carbon in an effort to recapture and store fugitive fossil carbon in our forests and in the dense bio-based building assemblies of our cities. We can promote energy sources for manufacturing and building operations that are infinitely renewable. We can mine consumer waste and industrial residues as the new "raw" material of building. These, among others, are the circular economic and regenerative materials, means, and methods we will employ as we design, build, and sustain a healthy and more durable future. What will it take?

Stepping Out of the Margins
We have variously described architecture's potential role in mitigating climate change. We have argued that in the face of the huge challenges ahead of us, our agency as both drivers of consumption and orchestrators of material, energy, and human activity (all at significant scale) offer as yet untapped opportunity to ameliorate our current environmental crisis. At the same time, we are witnesses to the increasing marginalization of architectural concerns—we might even go so far as to say the profession itself—by an array of economic and cultural forces too widespread to enumerate and

too philosophically and economically complex to elaborate upon here in any detail. As buildings have become more commodified and the building process has evolved into increasingly uniform exercises in cost-optimization, and litigation avoidance, building design, engineering, and construction have become accordingly institutionalized, siloed, and risk-averse. Although formal and stylistic innovation flourishes, construction methodologies and building innovation have flattened into a consistently narrow set of conventions—better armored against liability and more easily insured — in all but the most bespoke margins of small building practice, academic experimentation, and in the very most expensive buildings which are available and accessible to an exceedingly miniscule slice of global society. This is not to suggest that we abrogate our responsibility to make our buildings efficient and cost-effective. We need to do all that we can to provide affordable as well as convivial and well-built spaces in which people can comfortably and joyfully live and work. But cost efficiency today is the result of our degree of compliance with systems of cost estimation and building valuation, uninflected by the as-yet largely externalized costs of environmental impact. And we currently measure building cost in familiar currency—whether in dollars, euros, or renminbi. As greenhouse gas emissions continue to rise and their costs begin to be internalized by global economies, we'll inevitably translate the basis of our econometric analysis into a new monetary instrument: carbon. In a sense, the way in which our design processes and building methods will be shaped by that new bottom line has been the subject and focus of this book.

We need to break down those disciplinary and professional silos and reinvigorate the building design process with circular economic and regenerative construction priorities and foster the low-impact material, organizational, and technical innovations that would flow from that realignment of design intent and material demand. We should focus innovation—immediately and until we've rectified our current atmospheric imbalance—on our sector's rapid drawdown of greenhouse gas emissions, the contraction and containment of the physical and environmental footprint of the built environment, the restoration of biologically regenerative ecosystems, and the development of potential synergies between the biological and technical cycles of production to optimize the uptake and storage of carbon dioxide.

We'll need the support and collaboration of the biological, physical, chemical sciences, industry, and ecology as well as industrial ecology, and land-use governance. Such an interdisciplinary model of building design may seem potentially unwieldy and unresponsive, but building designers are already the passive recipients of solutions and mandates handed down from the aforementioned disciplines, so we need to refashion those relationships into strategic partnerships. If we're successful in the next few decades in drawing down our sector's carbon emissions––ideally so successful that we compensate for those sectors that are unable to reduce their impacts—we'll inevitably find that our environmental priorities have shifted, with the avoidance of other environmental impacts forming a new focus of our efforts to achieve global equilibrium. By that time, we'll have reshaped our practice and culture to address more than short-term economic constraint.

This is the point in this discussion when we should make clear that these recommendations are not founded on some nostalgic desire to recover the centrality of the master builder—if such a thing ever existed. Instead, we seek to organize and effectively orchestrate the instruments at our disposal, an instrumentation that is as potentially vast and harmonious as the reach of the building sector's impacts are deleterious and dissonant.

How we refocus societal and sectoral priorities that sponsor the transformation of the political economies of building is a question too profound and comprehensive to take on in this book. For our purposes, however, the reshaping of building design practice—its inspirations, motivations, and techniques—will be challenging to effect in our professional offices. It will take place incrementally and through activism and directed effort. But

the supply of young brainpower to those design practices is a potential source of meaningful and effective generational change for the profession. As with the life cycle material flows that form our buildings, it starts in the cradle.

A New Role for Design and Building Education

Imagine if you were a physician trained in cosmetic surgery or psychiatry suddenly dropped into an emergency room receiving incoming patients from some catastrophic accident or raging pandemic. You would make do and undoubtedly save lives in the process but the scope of your former clinical knowledge and experience would be severely tested. Needless to say, the trauma specialists would be in a better position to effectively address the inflow of injured patients. At the risk of overextending the metaphor (and recognizing that the concerns of body-image and emotional health are fundamental to human well-being), we are facing eco-systemic trauma and its dire consequences for life on the planet.

How do we train the next generation of building designers? It is this new generation of designers and builders, in fact, who will likely reformulate design and construction practice to neutralize the building sector's carbon emissions. If they're successful, they can go on to tackle all the other challenges of building safely, beautifully, and equitably for all the members of our rapidly expanding human community.

First, we need to stop teaching "sustainable" technologies and start teaching the science that will make our new technologies support sustenance. We're currently conveying an outdated message to a critical generation of practitioners that ecological and environmental stewardship is merely a well-intended, value-added proposition for buildings rather than an existential responsibility. As we've seen, our current technological fixes for the impacts we engender—consider photovoltaic semiconductors, plastic foam-based super-insulation, "high performance" mechanical systems, complex enclosure assemblies like solar buffer walls, carbon capture—are each fraught with their own systemic environmental implications, consequences that we've barely begun to uncover, let alone effectively address. Impact reduction as a checklist of tasks, rather than a set of principles, is akin to teaching an assembly line worker how to operate a single machine. In fact, the very concept of "sustainable technology" is as oxymoronic as "sustainable growth." At this point, the concept of sustainability itself, and all the building sustainability techniques that it has promulgated, seem an increasingly quaint notion. As teachers, we need to put teeth into the problem of climate change for all the design agents of global material and energy transaction. Survivability, if not for the human species but for those facing the next mass extinction, should be our new curricular keyword.

The components of our professional design curriculum are vestiges of the nineteenth-century educational models of the Beaux Arts and the Polytechnic. Studio, theory, structures, visualization and representation, building technology, and more recently professional practice and computation have themselves become siloed courses of study within our institutions. Professional degree programs in building engineering and construction management have become further specialized and focused subsets of those categories. Even the most enterprising teacher has struggled to integrate effectively the areas of study that comprise professional educational curriculum, let alone sponsor interdisciplinary exchange across the broad platform of inquiry and information offered by institutions of higher learning. How might the analytical techniques of industrial ecology or silviculture be brought into the assessment of a student's design proposition in the architecture studio, along with the more conventional criteria of formal analysis, programmatic compliance organization, and technical feasibility? Could a first-year structures course address the endemic environmental impacts of a given structural material or consider alternate sources and supply chains or emerging means of simplifying current industrial processes? Might a course on construction detailing include carbon accounting as well as an overview of the thermodynamic forces that create climate and induce stress on buildings? The list of potential points of intersection and layers of overlap goes on. Could the integrated design studio transform from a space to practice the technical composition of a building into a supercharged platform for project-based inquiry and environmental assessment and integration?

For those of us who have the privilege and the responsibility of teaching in both the architectural design studio and the building technology classroom, we recognize the time constraints, academic biases, and organization challenges that serve as disincentive to such an overhaul of professional education. Instead of teaching only those solutions already enshrined in the current conventions of sustainable design, we need to overlay and underpin our curricula with the physical and biological sciences so as to illuminate the concepts and phenomena that encourage creative problem solving rather than promoting familiar solutions. A solid working understanding of the systems of material and energy formation and flow, of the cycles of atmospheric carbon exchange, of forest growth and mortality, and of material phase change are all fundamental to the effective decarbonization of building practice. The list of potential environmental consequences should suffuse our course catalogs. To the age-old building technology triad of "materials, means, and methods" we must add "*impacts*"—environmental but also social ones. While life cycle assessment should be a course; life cycle design should be the basis of our professional education. In so framing our teaching, we will encourage in our students a sense of responsibility while offering them a field of opportunity. From that, new approaches and innovations to design and construction will inevitably flow.

Inspiration and Influence
For thousands of years, architects, engineers, and master builders have sought to impress and inspire us with their work. Looking at a medieval chapel in Italy or a modern office tower in Shanghai, the canal network and walled gardens of Suzhou, or the circular aggregations of a Dogon village, a modest turf house in Iceland, or the colossal buildings of some totalitarian political regime, we experience

various feelings of awe, comfort, optimism, or depression. All of these emotions are communicated through architecture. Architecture, and the entirety of the built environment, have a unique potential to inspire human emotion, guide as well as facilitate human activity and heighten our perception of the world around us.

Why not direct that special power of architecture away from the goal of spectacle and into one of metabolic ecological integration, in which the built environment generates as much valuable material and energy as it consumes, in which resources are equitably distributed not just for the survival but for the comfort and joy of all of humanity and especially for those most vulnerable to the vicissitudes of stress—climatic, emotional, economic, physical. Can the transcendental power of architecture describe a path forward in the face of these stresses and encourage human participation in and contribution to the Earth's ecosystems? We are the architects of human habitat and therein lies our societal role and responsibility.

This is how we re-form the Anthropocene.

THE ANTHROPOCENE RE-FORMED

We are the orchestrators of the form and function of the built environment. Today, we operate within an economic paradigm in which the continuous growth of consumption has been the end goal. For over a century and a half of rapid commercial industrial expansion and an associated increase in global prosperity, the mentality of "take, make, and dump" has shaped our design thinking. Except where it carries economic penalty, we have assumed an infinite supply of natural resources and generally ignored the problem of the solid waste permeating the physical systems of our global habitat, effluents fouling our waters, and airborne pollutants trapping heat within our atmosphere.

An alternative approach replaces our linear, mechanistic model of global production and consumption with the *circular* and ecological concept of *geo-metabolism*. Working within this metabolic

system, we would aim to balance a cyclical exchange of industrial byproducts and residues through the recurring life cycles of buildings. Waste—instead of raw natural resources—would become the industrial feedstocks for manufacture of the durable components of our building assemblies—those made of metals, glass, and plastics—and then be successfully reused (or at least recycled) in a range of applications, including future buildings.

Natural capital like forests, waterways, wetlands, and soils would be restored and protected through careful planning and distribution of building and impermeable surfaces. Critical ecosystems protected and restored would be left in reserve as habitat and a provider of important ecosystem services; others, where appropriate, would be actively and sustainably engaged to generate a supply of bio-based building material and energy. Biogenic products—encompassing a wide range of cellulose fiber-based products, ranging from massive structural members to low-density insulating materials and finishes, would be cycled through a cascade of varying uses over repeated building life cycles until they're finally and safely returned to soils or burned as biomass energy.

Expanded in scope and scale, this fundamental principle of regenerative building extends to the formation of cities. The regenerative city is one that maintains itself metabolically and synergistically within a healthy regional eco-system. Its building economies operate in a convivial and balanced exchange of material, energy, and waste with the eco-system services its region supplies, all the while protecting the natural capital of various biomes—forests, soils, waters—along with the underlying landforms that contribute to those particular ecological systems.

Through all of it, as we aim to answer the demands of rapid urban growth, we would seek to restore the homeostatic equilibrium of a carbon cycle newly unburdened by excessive fossil CO_2 emissions. Could we consider carbon—if using economic terms—a protected asset, a commodity to be carefully traded? What would prevent us from transforming our cities into anthropogenic carbon sinks or—again in economic terms—carbon banks?

If the built environment is to be integrated into a homeostatic or self-sustaining planetary ecology, our species will be forced to rethink and retool our own systemic consumption of the material and technology that we call upon to produce and maintain it. As representatives and agents of a specific sector of human activity responsible for such a significant share of global environmental impact, it is essential that we overhaul our own approach to design, as both thought process and practice, and reach for more effective conceptual strategies to remake our work and the constructed and natural environments that arise from it.

We've gone to some length in this book to describe the daunting challenges of our planetary environmental crisis, and we've suggested tools and methods to begin to address our role in creating it. Just as we developed the technologies that got us into this predicament, perhaps we can apply that same ingenuity, albeit with more comprehensive and holistic understanding, to get ourselves out of it. Our goal, as individuals, as a discipline, and as a global community, must be the restoration of global balance and the amelioration of our Anthropocene disturbance.

Finally, we cannot remake our design practice and all of building in one fell swoop. We need to build incrementally (if quickly) with love and compassion as well as with intelligence and ingenuity. We need to be patient, caring, and understanding of ourselves, of others and of the environment. Despite the scale of the challenge, building a better world, like the design and construction of a good building, is just completing one everyday task after another.

Acknowledgments

Few building projects spring entirely from the mind and hand of a single individual. Nor can this trio of writers claim sole authorship of this book. The work of colleagues from across the fields of architecture, engineering, construction, scientific research, and education have catalyzed its conception and making. To all those who have contributed (either knowingly or through the inspiration that their own work has provided us), we offer our sincere thanks.

For several colleagues in particular, we reserve our deepest gratitude. Professor Pekka Heikkinen of Aalto University in Helsinki has been a partner throughout this occasionally arduous process, offering us support in many forms: sanctuary at and around Aalto University to work and escape the demands of everyday life, teaching, and practice; financial subsidy; wise guidance; and mostly, his selfless friendship. Director Anssi Lassila from the OOPEAA Office for Peripheral Architecture is both an admired colleague and a good friend, but here in particular, we have benefited from his and his firm's generous contribution of critical content, without which the book would have been much the poorer. We thank him for this gift and for his feedback.

Elizabeth Gray, founding partner at Gray Organschi Architecture, has graciously opened the firm's archives, placed members of her talented design team at the disposal of the authors, and otherwise welcomed and promoted the work this book has entailed. Without her generosity, intellectual support, and unfading patience and understanding, there would be no *Carbon: A Field Manual for Building Designers*.

In addition to these individuals and their institutions, we have been lucky to receive financial support from the Finnish Innovation Fund Sitra, and wish to thank especially Nani Pajunen for her excellent collaboration and steady support. We are also grateful to our copy editor Susan Dunsmore for her careful and painstaking review of the text. Our friend and colleague Philip Tidwell read a near final draft of the text and his comments were critical to our own understanding and subsequent refinement of what we hope the reader will draw from this book's pages.

Several gifted associates have contributed to the book's design and content. Our research associate Caroline Moinel at Aalto University and designers Katharina Heidkamp and Liisa Heinonen at the OOPEAA Office for Peripheral Architecture provided graphic guidance, archival acumen, and quantitative analysis that have inevitably graced these pages.

Design associates at Gray Organschi Architecture have played a critical role in the development and execution of the book's illustrations. The talents and hard work of Kelley Johnson, Armaan Shah, Aslan Taheri, Ben Grayson, Millie Yoshida, Mat Shaffer, and Noah Silvestry have lent force and clarity to the composition of each drawing. The legibility of the concepts that this book seeks to convey owes much to their keen eyes and capable hands.

Finally, we wish to thank the members of our immediate families, all of whom have patiently watched, waited, and tirelessly supported us as the final form of this book has emerged. It is their future, one shared with our fellow citizens around the planet, that has inspired us to put this work before you, our readers.

Glossary

Term	Definition in this book	See also
Biogenic carbon	Carbon in or from biomass. Biogenic carbon originates from the atmosphere.	
BREEAM (British Research Establishment Environmental Assessment Method)	An assessment method and rating system, developed by the British Research Establishment in the 1990s. BREEAM is available in several national or regional versions, and is widely used. BREEAM certification can be given for new buildings or refurbishment projects. There are five classes: Pass, Good, Very Good, Excellent, and Outstanding.	www. breeam .com
Building Information Model (BIM)	"Use of a shared digital representation of a built asset to facilitate design, construction and operation processes to form a reliable basis for decisions" (ISO 19650).	[1]
Carbon dioxide equivalent (CO_2e)	The total sum of greenhouse gases summed and translated into the global warming potential (GWP) of carbon dioxide (CO_2). Global warming is a result of several different GHGs. They all have different potential for warming the global climate. Because it would not be practical to have separate indicators for all GHGs, their GWP is usually converted into the GWP of CO_2 and reported as CO_2e.	[2]
Carbon footprint	The total sum of greenhouse gas emissions and removals in a product system expressed as carbon dioxide equivalents.	[4]
Carbon handprint	Climate benefits that are associated with a product or a service and that would not happen without it. A carbon handprint can be either relative or absolute. A *relative* handprint describes how much less emissions the studied object or project causes in comparison to a similar average one. An *absolute* handprint describes how much GHG removals are associated with the studied object or project.	[3]
Carbon sequestration	A process in which carbon is captured from the atmosphere into carbon storages. This can happen through biological, geological, physical, and technological processes. Carbon sequestration is sometimes referred to as "carbon dioxide removal" (CDR), especially in the case of anthropogenic sequestration processes.	[5]
Carbon sink	A reservoir that can absorb carbon from the atmosphere. Carbon sinks can be natural (e.g., forests, soils, aquatic ecosystems, or geological processes) or anthropogenic (e.g., artificial photosynthesis or direct capture of CO_2 from ambient air).	[6]

Term	Definition in this book	See also
Carbon storage	A deposit of carbon, which can be temporal or permanent. Carbon storages can be natural (e.g., trees, soil, or geological formations) or anthropogenic (e.g. CO_2-cured concrete).	[5]
Circular economy (CE)	There are several definitions of a circular economy. According to the European Commission, in a CE, "the value of products and materials is maintained for as long as possible; waste and resource use are minimized, and when a product reaches the end of its life, it is used again to create further value". The Ellen MacArthur Foundation defines it as "a framework for an economy that is restorative and regenerative by design" while expanding the definition also toward decoupling an economic activity from the use of resources and generation of waste.	[6, 7]
Cross-laminated timber (CLT)	A wooden panel made from layers of planks that are attached to each other typically with glue. CLT panels are used in construction for load-bearing or partition walls, floors, and roofs.	
Embodied emissions	The amount of GHGs of a building, associated with everything but the operational consumption of energy, water, and other substances. The embodied emissions arise from the production of construction products, construction works, transport, maintenance, repair works, demolition works, waste management, and final disposal.	
Emergy	The amount of any form of energy that is used in all direct and indirect transformations to make the studied object. Emergy can be understood as the total, holistic "energy memory" that has led to the current state of the studied object.	[8]
Energy recovery	Burning waste for energy. According to standard EN 15804, the efficacy of the recovery must be at least 65%, otherwise their incineration is not considered energy recovery.	[10]
Environmental Product Declaration (EPD)	A report that contains verified numeric information about the environmental impacts of a construction product. EPDs are mostly voluntary. They do not offer "ranking" for the environmental friendliness of the product, but offer exact, quantitative information instead. EPDs can be based on standard ISO 14025 or EN 15804.	[9,10]

Term	Definition in this book	See also
Exergy	The amount of the maximum useful work possible before a system would enter equilibrium with its surroundings. Exergy depends on the context.	[8]
Fossil carbon	Carbon in or from fossil reservoirs. Usually this refers to the ancient biological matter that has slowly been transformed into oil, coal, or gas in the Earth´s crust over millions of years.	
Global warming potential (GWP)	An index which is based on the potential of a GHG to warm the climate. Most commonly this potential is estimated over a 100-year period (GWP_{100}). The GWP of a product or project is a sum of the warming potential of all GHGs associated with the studied lifecycle.	
Greenhouse gas (GHG))	A gas that has a potential to warm the climate. There are both natural and anthropogenic sources for GHGs. GHGs absorb and emit radiation, which causes the greenhouse effect. Most common GHGs are water vapor (H_2O), carbon dioxide (CO_2), nitrous oxide (N_2O), methane (CH_3), and ozone (O_3). Different GHGs have different global warming potential.	
International Panel on Climate Change (IPCC)	An intergovernmental organization of leading experts of climate scientist. The IPCC was established in 1988 by the World Meteorological Organization (WMO) and the United Nations Environment Programme (UNEP). The IPCC publishes assessment reports (ARs) that describe the best scientific understanding of the state of the climate.	
LEED (Leadership in Energy and Environmental Design)	A green building rating system, developed by the U.S. Green Building Council and the leading international assessment scheme. LEED certification consists of a total of 110 points, which match with ranks Certified, Silver, Gold, and Platinum.	
Life cycle assessment (LCA)	A tool for the "compilation and evaluation of the inputs, outputs and potential environmental impacts of a product system throughout its life cycle." An LCA is a commonly used and internationally standardized approach. It has its origins and principles in systems theory.	[11]
Life Cycle Cost Analysis (LCCA)	A method for estimating the costs that are associated with the life cycle of the studied object or project. An LCCA usually follows the methodological principles of an LCA.	

Term	Definition in this book	See also
Material Flow Analysis (MFA)	A method for quantifying and reporting the mass or substance flows of the studied system. An MFA can be used for the inventory phase of an LCA. Because of its direct linkage to materials, an MFA has become an important analysis tool for circular economy.	
Non-renewable energy source	A source of energy that has (from a human viewpoint) a limited amount of energy. When energy is utilized for work, it is transformed into a lower degree of energy. In the case of non-renewable energy, however, the original amount of energy decreases. Carriers of non-renewable energy include fossil fuels, such as oil, coal, and natural gas.	
Operational emission	The total sum of GHGs that are associated with the operations of the studied buildings. These emissions arise typically from the use of electricity or other energy and water, and possible other substances (e.g., chemicals) that are essential to the operation of the building.	
Primary energy (PE)	Energy in a form in which it is present in nature, before being subject to processing. During and after the processing, there are normally losses of energy. Thus, PE is typically higher than the amount of energy that can be delivered into a system (e.g., the electricity grid).	
Recycling	A process in which waste is reprocessed into a new raw material. This involves several steps, during which the material ceases to be waste and gains characteristics similar to a virgin raw material.	
Renewable energy source	A source of energy that is renewable. It is typical for these sources that most of them do not decrease. Renewable energy usually refers to energy from wind, water, sun, or geothermal deposits, as well as the energy content of various biomasses.	
Reusing	Using an old building component again without processing it to the level of raw materials.	

References

1 CARBON?

1 D. Wallace-Wells, *The Uninhabitable Earth: A Story of the Future*, London: Penguin Environment, 2019.
2 ECORYS; Copenhagen Resource Institute, "Resource efficiency in the building sector," Rotterdam: European Commission, 2014.
3 Y. Malhi, "The concept of the Anthropocene," *Annual Reviews*, vol. 42, pp. 77–104, 2017.
4 J. Hansen, M. Sato, P. Hearthu, R. Ruedy, M. Kelley, V. Masson-Delmotte, G. Russel, G. Tselioudis, J. Cao, E. Rignot, I. Velicogna, B. Tormey, B. Donovan, E. Kandiano, and K. von Schuckmann, "Ice melt, sea level rise and superstorms: Evidence from paleoclimate data, climate modeling, and modern observations that 2°C global warming could be dangerous," *Atmospheric Chemistry and Physics*, vol. 16, pp. 3761–3812, 2016.
5 NOAA National Oceanic & Atmospheric Administration, "Trends in atmospheric carbon dioxide," 2018. Online. Available at: https://www.esrl.noaa.gov/gmd/ccgg/trends/full.html.
6 G. Foster, D. Royer, and D. Lunt, "Future climate forcing potentially without precedent in the last 420 million years," *Nature Communications*, vol. 8, no. 14845, 2017.
7 J. Hansen, P. Kharecha, M. Sato, V. Masson-Delmotte, F. Ackerman, D. Beerling, P. Hearty, O. Hoegh-Guldberg, S. Hsu, C. Parmesan, J. Rockström, E. Röhling, J. Sachs, P. Smith, K. Steffen, L. Van Susteren, K. von Schuckmann, and J. Zachos, "Assessing 'dangerous climate change': required reduction of carbon emissions to protect young people, future generations and nature," *PLoS ONE*, vol. 8, no. e81648, 2013.
8 W. Steffen, J. Rockström, K. Richardson, T. Lenton, C. Folke, D. Liverman, C. Summerhayes, A. Barnosky, S. Cornell, M. Crucifix, J. Donges, F. I. S. Lade, M. Scheffer, R. Winkelmann, and H. Schellnhuber, "Trajectories of the Earth system in the Anthropocene," *Proceedings of the National Academy of Sciences, August 6, 2018*.
9 J. Hansen, *Storms of My Grandchildren: The Truth About the Coming Climate Catastrophe and Our Last Chance to Save Humanity*, New York: Bloomsbury Publishing, 2009.
10 United Nations Environment Programme, "Emissions Gap Report," Nairobi: UNEP, 2019.
11 M. Allen, D. Frame, C. Huntingford, and C. Jones, "Warming caused by cumulative carbon emissions towards the trillionth tonne," *Nature*, vol. 458, no. 7242, pp. 1163–1166, 2009.
12 Intergovernmental Panel on Climate Change, "Global warming of 1.5°C: An IPCC special report on the impacts of global warming of 1.5°C above pre-industrial levels and related global greenhouse gas emission pathways, in the context of strengthening the global response to the threat of climate change," Geneva: IPCC, 2018.
13 Material Economics, "Circular economy: A powerful force for climate mitigation. transformative innovation for prosperous and low-carbon industry," Helsinki: Sitra, 2018.
14 CEN European Committee for Standardization, "EN 16449. Wood and wood-based products. calculation of the biogenic carbon content of wood and conversion to carbon dioxide," Brussels: CEN, 2014.
15 R. Crawford and A. Stephan, "The significance of embodied energy in certified passive houses," *International Journal of Civil, Environmental, Structural, Construction and Architectural Engineering*, vol. 7, no. 6, pp. 427–433, 2013.
16 M. Davies and G. Wynn (Eds.), "Better growth, better climate," Washington, DC: New Climate Economy and World Resources Institute, 2014.
17 The Global Commission on the Economy and Climate, "The sustainable infrastructure imperative: Financing for better growth and development. The 2016 New Climate Economy Report," Washington, DC: The New Climate Economy, 2016.
18 International Finance Corporation, "Green buildings: A finance and policy blueprint for emerging markets," Washington, DC: World Bank Group, 2019.
19 RIL, "State of buildings and property," Helsinki: Finnish Association of Civil Engineers RIL, 2019.

2 MEASURING CARBON FLOWS

1 W. McDonough and M. Braungart, *Cradle to Cradle: Remaking the Way We Make Things*, New York: North Point Press, 2002.
2 R. Srinavasan and K. Moe, *The Hierarchy of Energy in Architecture*, New York: Routledge, 2015.
3 R. Crawford and A. Stephan, "The significance of embodied energy in certified passive houses," *International Journal of Civil, Environmental, Structural, Construction and Architectural Engineering*, vol. 7, no. 6, pp. 427–433, 2013.
4 T. Ibn-Mohammed, R. Greenough, S. Taylor, L. Ozawa-Meida, and A. Acquaye, "Operational vs. embodied emissions in buildings: A review of current trends," *Energy and Buildings*, vol. 66, pp. 232–245, 2013.

5   N. Yokoo, T. Oka, K. Yokoyama, T. Sawachi, and M. Yamamoto, "Comparison of embodied energy/CO$_2$ of office buildings in China and Japan," *Journal of Civil Engineering and Architecture*, vol. 9, pp. 300–307, 2015.

6   F. Pomponi and A. Moncaster, "Embodied carbon mitigation and reduction in the built environment: What does the evidence say?," *Journal of Environmental Management*, vol. 2016, no. 181, pp. 687–700, 2016.

7   K. Moe, *Empire, State & Building*, New York: ACTAR, 2017.

8   A. Takano, F. Pittau, A. Hafner, S. Ott, M. Hughes, and E. de Angelis, "Greenhouse gas emissions from construction stage of wooden buildings," *International Wood Products Journal*, vol. 5, no. 4, pp. 217–223.

9   ISO (International Organization for Standardization), "ISO 14040. Environmental management. Life cycle assessment. Principles and framework," Geneva: ISO, 2006.

10   ISO (International Organization for Standardization_, "ISO 14044. Environmental management. Life cycle assessment. Requirements and guidelines," Geneva: ISO, 2006.

11   CEN European Committee for Standardization, "EN 15978. Sustainability of construction works: Assessment of environmental performance of buildings. Calculation method," Brussels: CEN, 2011.

12   J. Rockström, O. Gaffney, J. Rogelj, M. Meinshause, N. Nakicenovic, and H. Schellnhuber, "A roadmap for rapid decarbonization," *Science*, vol. 335, no. 6331, pp. 1269–1271, 2017.

13   CEN European Committee for Standardization, "EN 16757: Concrete and concrete elements," Brussels: CEN, 2017.

14   ISO (International Organization for Standardization), "ISO 14025:2006. Environmental labels and declarations: Type III environmental declarations. Principles and procedures," Geneva: ISO, 2006.

15   CEN European Committee for Standardization, "EN 15804:2012 + A2:2019. Sustainability of construction works. Environmental product declarations. Core rules for the product category of construction products," Brussels: CEN, 2019.

16   K. Lylykangas, A. Andersson, J. Kiuru, J. Nieminen, and J. Päätalo, "Rakenteellinen energiatehokkuus Structural energy efficiency," Helsinki: Ministry of the Environment, 2015.

17   S. Vares and J. Shemeikka, "LCA for local energy production and energy storage systems. LCA NORNET workshop Espoo 4th of October 2016," VTT Technical Research Center, 2016.

18   M. Kuittinen, "Method for whole life carbon assessment of buildings," Helsinki: Ministry of the Environment, 2019.

19   E. Possan, E. Felix, and W. Thomaz, "CO$_2$ uptake by carbonation of concrete during life cycle of building structures," *Journal of Building Pathology and Rehabilitation*, vol. 1, no. 7, 2016.

20   J. Edmonson, Z. Davies, S. McCormack, K. Gaston, and R. Leake, "Organic carbon hidden in urban ecosystems," *Scientific Reports*, vol. 2, no. 963, 2012.

21   M. Kuittinen, K. Adalgeirsdottir, and C. Moinel, "Carbon sequestration through urban ecosystem services: A case study from Finland," *Science of the Total Environment*, vol. 2016, no. 563–564, pp. 623–632, 2016.

22   United Nations, Department of Economic and Social Affairs, "Sustainable Development Knowledge Platform," Online. Available at: https://sustainable development.un.org/.

23   J. Rockström, W. Steffen, K. Noone, Å. Persson, S. Chapin, E. Lambin, T. Lenton, M. Scheffer, C. Folke, H. Schellnhuber, B. Nykvist, C. de Wit, T. Hughes, S. van der Leeuw, H. Rodhe, and S. Sörlin, "Planetary boundaries: Exploring the safe operating space for humanity," *Ecology and Society*, vol. 14, no. 2, 2009.

24   M. Najjar, K. Figueiredo, M. Palumbo, and A. Haddad, "Integration of BIM and LCA: Evaluating the environmental impacts of building materials at an early stage of designing a typical office building," *Journal of Building Engineering*, vol. 14, November, pp. 115–126, 2017.

25   T. Lidberg, M. Gustavsson, J. Myhren, F. Olofsson, and L. Trygg, "Comparing different building energy efficiency refurbishment packages performed within different district heating systems," *Energy Procedia*, vol. 105, no. 2017, pp. 1719–1724, 2017.

26   Y. Schwartz, R. Raslan, and D. Mumovic, "The life cycle carbon footprint of refurbished and new buildings: A systematic review of case studies," *Renewable and Sustainable Energy Reviews*, vol. 81, pp. 231–241, 2018.

27   A. Dodoo, L. Gustavsson, and R. Sathre, "Life cycle primary energy implication of retrofitting a wood-framed apartment building to passive house standard," *Resources, Conservation and Recycling*, vol. 54, no. 12, pp. 1152–1160, 2010.

28   A. Dodoo, L. Gustavsson, and U. Tettey, "Final energy savings and cost-effectiveness of deep energy renovation of a multi-storey residential building," *Energy*, vol. 135, no. 1873–6785, pp. 563–576, 2017.

3   CASE STUDIES IN DECARBONIZATION

1   CEN European Committee for Standardization, "EN 15978. Sustainability of construction works - Assessment of environmental performance of buildings: Calculation method," Brussels: CEN, 2011.

2   G. Hammond and C. Jones, "Inventory of Carbon and Energy (ICE), version 2.0," Bath: University of Bath, Sustainable Energy Research Team, 2011.

3   N. Dodd, M. Cordella, M. Traverso, and S. Donatello, "Level(s) – A common EU framework of core sustainability indicators for office and residential buildings. Part 3: How to make performance assessments using Level(s). Draft Beta v1.0," Seville: European Commission, Joint Research Centre, 2017.

4   M. Kuittinen, "Method for whole life carbon assessment of buildings," Helsinki: Ministry of the Environment, 2019.

5   A. Takano, A. Hafner, L. Linkosalmi, S. Ott, M. Hughes, and S. Winter, "Life cycle assessment of wood construction according to the normative standards," *European Journal of Wood and Wood Products*, vol. 2015, no. 73, pp. 299–312, 2015.

6   CEN European Committee for Standardization, "EN 16449. Wood and wood-based products. calculation of the biogenic carbon content of wood and conversion to carbon dioxide," Brussels: CEN, 2014.

7   CEN European Committee for Standardization, "EN 16485. Round and sawn timber. Environmental Product Declarations. Product category rules for wood and wood-based products for use in construction.," Brussels: CEN, 2014.

8   B. Lagerblad, "Carbon dioxide uptake during concrete life cycle: State of the art," Stockholm: Cement och Betong Institutet, 2005.

9   D. Zianis, P. Luukkonen, R. Mäkipää and M. Mencuccini, "Biomass and stem volume equations for tree species in Europe," Helsinki: The Finnish Society of Forest Science, 2005.

10   J. Edmonson, Z. Davies, S. McCormack, K. Gaston, and R. Leake, "Organic carbon hidden in urban ecosystems," *Scientific Reports*, vol. 2, no. 963, 2012.

11   M. Kuittinen, K. Adalgeirsdottir, and C. Moinel, "Carbon sequestration through urban ecosystem services: A case study from Finland," *Science of the Total Environment*, vol. 2016, no. 563–564, pp. 623–632, 2016.

12   World Bank, "CO_2 emissions (metric tons per capita)," Online. Available at: https://data.worldbank.org/indicator/EN.ATM.CO_2E.PC.

13   M. Giani, G. B. N. Dotelli, and L. Zampori, "Comparative life cycle assessment of asphalt pavements using reclaimed asphalt, warm mix technology and cold in-place recycling," *Resources, Conservation and Recycling*, vol. 104, no. A, pp. 224–238, 2015.

14   U.S. Department of Energy, "State & local energy data: Emissions for New Haven, Connecticut," Online. Available at: https://apps1.eere.energy.gov/sled/#/results/emissions?city=New%20Haven&abv=CT&section=electricity&zip=06515&currentState=Connecticut&lat=41.3266814&lng=-72.9637728000002.

15   Northeast Energy Efficiency Partnerships, "Connecticut Building Standard Guidelines - Compliance manual for high performance buildings," Lexington, MA: Northeast Energy Efficiency Partnerships, Inc., 2011.

16   European Council, "Directive 2010/31/EU of the European Parliament and of the Council of 19 May 2010 on the energy performance of buildings (recast)," Strasbourg: European Parliament, 2010.

4   DECARBONIZING DESIGN

1   T. Häkkinen, M. Kuittinen, A. Ruuska, and N. Jung, "Reducing embodied carbon during the design process of buildings," *Journal of Building Engineering*, vol. 4, pp. 1–13, 2015.

2   A. Ruuska and T. Häkkinen, "The significance of various factors for GHG emissions of buildings," *International Journal of Sustainable Engineering*, vol. 8, no. 4–5, pp. 317–330, 2014.

3   V. Vasenev and Y. Kuzyakov, "Urban soils as hot spots of anthropogenic carbon accumulation: Review of stocks, mechanisms and driving factors," *Land Degradation & Development*, vol. 29, no. 6, pp. 1607–1622, 2018.

4   J. Seppälä, T. Heinonen, T. Pukkala, A. Kilpeläinen, T. Mattila, T. Myllyviita, A. Asikainen, and H. Peltola, "Effect of increased wood harvesting and utilization on required greenhouse gas displacement factors of wood-based products and fuels," *Journal of Environmental Management*, vol. 247, no. 1, October, pp. 580–587, 2019.

5   M. Jones, T. Bhat, T. Huynh, E. Kandare, R. Yuen, C. Wang, and S. John, "Waste-derived low-cost mycelium composite construction materials with

improved fire safety," *Fire and Materials*, vol. 42, no. 17, pp. 816–825, 2018.

6 M. Pawlyn, *Biomimicry in Architecture*, London: RIBA Publishing, 2016.

7 Stewart Brand, *How Buildings Learn: What Happens After They're Built*, London: Viking Press, 1994.

5 RE-FORMING THE ANTHROPOCENE

1 Ellen MacArthur Foundation, *Towards the Circular Economy* Vol. 1 *An Economic and Business Rationale for an Accelerated Transition*, Cowes: Ellen MacArthur Foundation, 2012.

2 M. Baily, J. Manyika, and S. Gupta, "U.S. productivity growth: An optimistic perspective," *International Productivity Monitor*, 2013.

3 M. Röck, M. Mendes Saade, M. Balouktsi, F. Nygaard Rasmussen, H. Birgisdottir, R. Frischknecht, G. Habert, T. Lützkendorf, and A. Passer, "Embodied GHG emissions of buildings: The hidden challenge for effective climate change mitigation," *Applied Energy*, vol. 258, 15 January, p. 114107, 2019.

4 World Green Building Council, "World GBC net zero carbon buildings commitment," New York: World Green Building Council, 2019.

5 G. Churkina, A. Organschi, C. Reyer, A. Ruff, K. Vinke, Z. Lu, B. Reck, T. Graedel, and M. Schellnhuber, "Buildings as a global carbon sink," *Nature Sustainability*, vol. 2020, no. 3, pp. 269–276, 2020.

6 T. Pajula and S. P. H. Vatanen, "Carbon Handprint Guide," Espoo: VTT Technical Research Centre, 2018.

7 J. Rockström, O. Gaffney, J. Rogelj, M. Meinshausen, N. Nakicenovic, and H. Schellnhuber, "A roadmap for rapid decarbonization," *Climate Policy*, vol. 355, pp. 1269–1271, 2017.

8 Milieu Ltd, Ökopol; Risk and Policy Analysts and RVIM, "Study for the strategy for a non-toxic environment of the 7th Environment Action Programme," Brussels: European Commission - Directorate-General for Environment, 2017.

9 J. Arfvidsson, T. Toratti, and S. Mundt-Petersen, "Service life and moisture safety," in *Wood in Carbon Efficient Construction*, Brussels: CEI-Bois, pp. 99–106, 2013,

10 S. Lewis and M. Maslin, *The Human Planet: How We Created the Anthropocene*, London: Penguin Random House, 2018.

11 United Nations Population Division, "World Population Prospects 2019", New York: UN, 2019.

GLOSSARY

1 ISO (International Organization for Standardization), "ISO 19650: BII, Building Information Modelling." Geneva: International Organization for Standardization, 2017.

2 D. Stoker, G. Qin, S. Plattner, N. Allen, Bindoff, F. J. Bréon, U. Church, S. E. P. Cubash, P. Forster, N. Friedlingstein, J. Gillet, D. Gregory, E. Hartmann, B. Jansen, R. Kirtman, K. Knutti, P. Krishna Kumar, J. Lemke, V. Marotzke, and G. Masson-Delmotte, "Technical Summary," in *Climate Change 2013: The Physical Science Basis. Contribution of Working Group I to the Fifth Assessment Report of the Intergovernmental Panel on Climate Change*, Cambridge: Cambridge University Press, 2013.

3 M. Kuittinen and T. Häkkinen, "Reduced carbon footprint of buildings: New Finnish standards and assessments," *Buildings & Cities*, vol. 1, no. 1, pp. 182–197, 2020.

4 ISO (International Organization for Standardization), "ISO 14067: Greenhouse gases. Carbon footprint of products. Requirements and guidelines for quantification and communication," Geneva: International Organization for Standardization, 2018.

5 S. Rackley, *Carbon Capture and Storage*, Oxford: Elsevier, 2017.

6 European Commission, "Communication from the Commission to the European Parliament, the Council, the European Economic and Social Committee of the Regions on a monitoring framework for the circular economy," Strasbourg: European Commission, 2018.

7 Ellen MacArthur Foundation, "Towards the circular economy," Vol. 1 "An economic and business rationale for an accelerated transition," Cowes: Ellen MacArthur Foundation, 2012.

8 R. Srinavasan and K. Moe, *The Hierarchy of Energy in Architecture*, New York: Routledge, 2015.

9 ISO (International Organization for Standardization), "ISO 14025:2006. Environmental labels and declarations: Type III environmental declarations – Principles and procedures," Geneva: ISO, 2006.

10 CEN European Committee for Standardization, "EN 15804:2012 + A2:2019. Sustainability of construction works. Environmental product declarations. Core rules for the product category of construction products.," Brussels: CEN, 2019.

11 ISO (International Organization for Standardization), "ISO 14044. Environmental management. Life cycle assessment. Requirements and guidelines," Geneva: ISO, 2006.

Index